Literature Library Classics and Information Science

Joginder Pant

CYBER TECH PUBLICATIONS
4264/3, Ansari Road, Daryaganj, New Delhi-110002 (India)
Ph.: 011-23244078, 011-43559448 Fax: 011-23280028
E-Mail: cyberpublicationsdelhi@yahoo.com
Website: www.cybertechpublications.com

LITERATURE LIBRARY CLASSICS AND INFORMATION SCIENCE

Joginder Pant

First Edition 2010

Published by :

G.S. Rawat for **Cyber Tech Publications**
4264/3, Ansari Road, Daryaganj, New Delhi-110002 (India)
Ph.: 011-23244078, 011-43559448 Fax: 011-23280028
E-Mail: cyberpublicationsdelhi@yahoo.com
Website: www.cybertechpublications.com

Printed at: Asian Offset Printers, Delhi-53

Preface

What will the library of tomorrow be, and what should it be? Such questions may not be new in the history of libraries, but at the turn of the twenty-first century they are being raised with urgency and purpose. A rapidly changing information service environment, combined with a seriously challenging financial environment, are pushing information providers—in particular, libraries—to think in new ways about how they provide information services to their users.

In organizing this book I started from the premise that the current environment offers libraries the opportunity to re-think what they do, how they do it, and why. We invited speakers who have thought about these questions in their positions at research centers, public libraries, funding organizations, and in technology departments. Two of the speakers provide perspectives from abroad. All have much to offer as we consider new models for providing access. This book offers a unique opportunity for a cross-fertilization of ideas on the topic of emerging visions for access in the twenty-first century.

— *Author*

CONTENTS

1

Library Science and Reference Services

Library science is an interdisciplinary science incorporating the humanities, law and applied science to study topics related to libraries, the collection, organization, preservation and dissemination of information resources, and the political economy of information. Historically, library science has also included archival science. "The distinction between a library and an archive is relatively modern". This includes how information resources are organized to serve the needs of select user groups, how people interact with classification systems and technology, how information is acquired, evaluated and applied by people in and outside of libraries as well as cross-culturally, how people are trained and educated for careers in libraries, the ethics that guide library service and organization, the legal status of libraries and information resources, and the applied science of computer technology used in documentation and records management.

Academic courses in library science typically include Collection management, Information Systems and Technology, Cataloguing and classification, Preservation, Reference, Statistics and Management. Library science is constantly evolving, incorporating new topics like Database Management, Information Architecture and Knowledge Management, for example.

There is no generally agreed distinction between *library science*, *library and information science*, and *librarianship*. To a certain extent they can be considered interchangeable, perhaps adopted to increase the "science" aspect, or improve the popular image of librarians. The term library and information science (LIS) is sometimes used; most librarians consider it as only a terminological variation, intended to emphasize the scientific and technical foundations of the subject, and its relationship with information science. LIS should not be confused with information theory, the mathematical study of the concept of information, or information science, a field related to computer science and cognitive science. One operational view, implied by some textbooks, is that librarianship means the professional aspects of work as a librarian, such as certification, in-service training, and issues of gender equality.

HISTORY

Library and information science, it may be argued, began with the first effort to organize a collection of information and provide access to that information.

Early History

At Ugarit in Syria excavations have revealed a palace library, temple library, and two private libraries which date back to around 1200 BCE, containing diplomatic texts as well as poetry and other literary forms. In the 7th century, King Ashurbanipal of Assyria assembled what is considered "the first systematically collected library" at Nineveh; previous collections functioned more as passive archives. The legendary Library of Alexandria is perhaps the best known example of an early library, flourishing in the 3rd century BC and possibly inspired by Demetrius Phalereus.

Ancient Information Retrieval

One of the curators of the imperial library in the Han Dynasty is believed to have been the first to establish a library classification system and the first book notation system. At this time the library catalogue was written on scrolls of fine silk and stored in silk bags.

Jefferson's Method

Thomas Jefferson, whose library at Monticello consisted

of thousands of books, devised a classification system inspired by the Baconian method which grouped books more or less by subject rather than alphabetically, as it was previously done. Jefferson's collection became the nucleus of the first national collection of the United States when it was transferred to Congress after a fire destroyed the Congressional Library during the War of 1812. The Jefferson collection was the start of what we now know as the Library of Congress.

20th Century

The term "library science" first appeared in the early 1930's, in the title of S. R. Ranganathan's *The Five Laws of Library Science*, published in 1931, and in the title of Lee Pierce Butler's 1933 book, *An introduction to library science* (University of Chicago Press). Butler's new approach advocated research using quantitative methods and ideas in the social sciences with the aim of using librarianship to address society's information needs. This research agenda went against the more procedure-based approach of "library economy," which was mostly confined to practical problems in the administration of libraries. While Ranganathan's approach was philosophical it was tied more to the day-to-day business of running a library.

In more recent years, with the growth of digital technology, the field has been greatly influenced by information science concepts. Although a basic understanding is critical to both library research and practical work, the area of information science has remained largely distinct both in training and in research interests.

TRAINING IN LIBRARIANSHIP

Most professional library jobs require a professional post-baccalaureate degree in library science, or one of its equivalent terms, library and information science as a basic credential. In the United States and Canada the certification usually comes from a master's degree granted by an ALA-accredited institution, so even non-scholarly librarians have an originally academic background. In the United Kingdom, however, there have been moves to broaden the entry requirements to professional library posts, such that qualifications in, or experience of, a number of other disciplines have become more acceptable. For the main discussion of this topic, see Education for librarianship

SUBDISCIPLINES

Subdisciplines of library science include the study of:

- Human Information Behaviours (information-seeking, search strategies, and use)
- Knowledge Organization (which includes bibliographies, cataloguing, classification, indexing & abstracting, metadata, semantic & syntactic analysis (controlled vocabularies, etc.))
- Digital libraries
- Collection development
- Preservation
- Public reference and other services
- Scholarly communication (includes bibliometrics, informetrics, scientometrics, webmetrics)

TYPES OF LIBRARY SCIENCE PROFESSIONALS

- Librarian
- Archivist
- Cataloguer
- Computer, Data, and Information Systems professionals
- Curator
- Indexers
- Information architect
- Information broker
- Metadata Architects
- Metadata Managers
- Preservation Administrators and Conservators

LIBRARIANS IN DIFFERENT TYPES OF LIBRARIES

Public

The study of librarianship for public libraries covers issues such as cataloguing; collection development for a diverse community; information literacy; community standards; public services-focused librarianship; serving a diverse community of adults, children, and teens; intellectual freedom; censorship; and legal and budgeting issues.

School

The study of school librarianship covers library services for children in schools up until (including) university. In some regions, the local government may have stricter standards for the education and certification of school librarians (who are often considered a special case of teacher), than for other librarians, and the educational programme will include those local standards. School librarianship may also include issues of intellectual freedom; pedagogy; and how to build a cooperative curriculum with the teaching staff.

Academic

The study of academic librarianship covers library services for colleges and universities. Issues of special importance to the field may include copyright; technology, digital libraries, and digital repositories; academic freedom; open access to scholarly works; as well as specialized knowledge of subject areas important to the institution and the relevant reference works. Some academic librarians are considered faculty, and hold similar academic ranks as professors, while others are not. In either case, the minimal qualification is a Master's degree in Library Studies or Library Science, and, in some cases, a Master's degree in another field.

Archives

The study of archives covers the training of archivists, librarians specially trained to maintain and build archives of records intended for historical preservation. Special issues include physical preservation of materials and mass deacidification; specialist catalogues; solo work; access; and appraisal. Many archivists are also trained historians specializing in the period covered by the archive.

Special

Special librarians include almost any other form of

librarianship, including those who serve in medical libraries (and hospitals or medical schools), corporations, news agency libraries, or other special collections. The issues at these libraries will be specific to the industries they inhabit, but may include solo work; corporate financing; specialized collection development; and extensive self-promotion to potential patrons.

Preservation

Preservation librarians most often work in academic libraries. Their focus is on the management of preservation activities that seek to maintain access to content within books, manuscripts, archival materials, and other library resources. Examples of activities managed by preservation librarians include binding, conservation, digital and analog reformatting, digital preservation, and environmental monitoring.

THEORY AND PRACTICE

Many practicing librarians do not contribute to LIS scholarship but focus on daily operations of their own library systems. Other practicing librarians, particularly in academic libraries, do perform original scholarly LIS research and contribute to the academic end of the field.

On this basis, it has sometimes been proposed that LIS is distinct from librarianship, in a way analogous to the difference between medicine and doctoring. In this view, librarianship, the application of library science, would comprise the practical *services* rendered by librarians in their day-to-day attempts to meet the needs of library patrons.

Other uses of these terms do not make the distinction and treat them as synonyms.

Powell's widely used introductory textbook does not make a formal distinction, but its bibliography uses the word librarianship as the heading for articles about the library profession.

CURRENT ISSUES IN LIS

- Education for librarianship
- Information policy

- Information communication technologies (ICT's)
- Information Society
- Equity of Access
- Sustainability and ICT's
- Children's Internet Protection Act
- Censorship
- Information explosion
- Information literacy
- Government Information
- Decreased funding for established libraries
- Copyright
- Intellectual property rights
- Intellectual freedom
- Digital divide
- Open access
- Patriot Act
- Public lending right
- Slow fires
- Serials crisis
- Current digital/scanning technologies
- Remote access

GREAT LIBRARIES OF THE ANCIENT WORLD

- The libraries of Ugarit (in modern Syria), ca 1200 BC, include diplomatic archives, literary works and the earliest privately-owned libraries yet recovered.
- The library of King Ashurbanipal, 7th century BC, in Nineveh (near modern Mosul, Iraq)— Considered to be "the first systematically collected library", it was rediscovered in the 19th century. While the library had been destroyed, many fragments of the ancient cuneiform tables survived, and have been reconstructed. Large portions of the Epic of Gilgamesh were among the many finds.

- The Library of Alexandria, fl. 3rd century BC. The date of its destruction uncertain, but it supposedly housed one of the largest collections in the classical world.
- The Library of Pergamum at Pergamum (in what is now Turkey), also in the 3rd century BC, the Attalid kings formed the second best Hellenistic library after Alexandria, founded in emulation of the Ptolemies. When the Ptolemies stopped exporting papyrus, partly because of competitors and partly because of shortages, the Pergamenes invented a new substance to use in codices, called pergamum or parchment after the city. This was made of fine calfskin, a predecessor of vellum and paper.
- The Villa of the Papyri, in Herculaneum, Italy— The only library known to have survived from classical antiquity, this villa's large private collection may have once belonged to Julius Caesar's father-in-law, Lucius Calpurnius Piso in the 1st century BC. Buried by the eruption of Mount Vesuvius that destroyed the town in 79 AD, it was rediscovered in 1752, around 1800 carbonized scrolls were found in the villa's top story. Using modern techniques such as multi-spectral imaging, previously illegible or invisible sections on scrolls that have been unrolled are now being deciphered. It is possible that more scrolls remain to be found in the lower, unexcavated levels of the villa.
- Caesarea Maritima, a late 3rd century AD establishment located in present-day Israel, had a great early Christian library. Through Origen and the scholarly priest Pamphilus, the theological school of Caesarea won a reputation for having the most extensive ecclesiastical library of the time, containing more than 30,000 manuscripts: Gregory of Nazianzus, Basil the Great, Jerome and others came to study there.
- The great seats of learning in ancient India, namely Takshasila, Nalanda, Vikramshila, Kanchipuram and other universities, also maintained vast libraries of palm leaf manuscripts on various subjects, ranging from theology to astronomy.

- The House of Wisdom at the Academy of Gundishapur in Baghdad, established during the Sassanid Empire in the 3rd through 6th centuries AD; destroyed with the fall of the empire in 651.

DIGITAL LIBRARY

A digital library is a library in which collections are stored in digital formats (as opposed to print, microform, or other media) and accessible by computers. The digital content may be stored locally, or accessed remotely via computer networks.

The first use of the term *digital library* in print may have been in a 1988 report to the Corporation for National Research Initiatives The term *digital libraries* was first popularized by the NSF/DARPA/NASA Digital Libraries Initiative in 1994. The older names electronic library or virtual library are also occasionally used, though *electronic library* nowadays more often refers to portals, often provided by government agencies, as in the case of the Florida Electronic Library.

DIGITIZATION

Digitization is the process of representing an object, an image, or a signal (usually an analog signal) by a discrete set of its points or samples. The result is called "digital representation" or, more specifically, a "digital image", for the object, and "digital form", for the signal.

Analog signals are continuously variable, both in the number of possible values of the signal at a given time, as well as in the number of points in the signal in a given period of time. However, digital signals are discrete in both of those respects, and so a digitization can only ever be an approximation of the signal it represents. The digital representation does not necessarily lose information in this transformation since the analog signal usually contains both information and noise.

A digital signal may be represented by a sequence of integers. Digitization is performed by reading an analog signal A, and, at regular time intervals (sampling frequency), representing the value of A at that point by an integer. Each such reading is called a sample.

A series of integers can be transformed back into an analog signal that approximates the original analog signal. Such a transformation is called DA conversion. There are two factors determining how close such an approximation to an analog signal A digitization D can be, namely the sampling rate and the number of bits used to represent the integers.

In the past few years, procedures for digitizing books at high speed and comparatively low cost have improved considerably with the result that it is now possible to plan the digitization of millions of books per year for creating digital libraries.

TYPES OF DIGITAL LIBRARIES

The term *digital library* is diffuse enough to be applied to a wide range of collections and organizations, but, to be considered a digital library, an online collection of information must be managed by and made accessible to a community of users. Thus, some web sites can be considered digital libraries, but far from all. Many of the best known digital libraries are older than the web including Project Perseus, Project Gutenberg, and ibiblio. Nevertheless, as a result of the development of the internet and its search potential, digital libraries such as the European Library and the Library of Congress are now developing in a Web-based environment.

A distinction is often made between content that was created in a digital format, known as *born digital*, and information that has been converted from a physical medium, *e.g.*, paper, by digitizing. The term *hybrid library* is sometimes used for libraries that have both physical collections and digital collections. For example, American Memory is a digital library within the Library of Congress. Some important digital libraries also serve as long term archives, for example, the ePrint arXiv, and the Internet Archive.

COLLABORATIVE DIGITIZATION PROJECTS

There are many collaborative digitization projects throughout the United States and in Europe, Australia and Asia. Two of the earliest projects were the Collaborative Digitization Project in Colorado and NC ECHO-North Carolina

Exploring Cultural Heritage Online, based at the State Library of North Carolina. These projects helped to establish and publish best practices for digitization and work with regional partners to digitize cultural heritage materials. Additional criteria for best practice have more recently been established in the UK, Australia and the European Union.

ADVANTAGES

The advantages of digital libraries as a means of easily and rapidly accessing books, archives and images of various types are now widely recognized by commercial interests and public bodies alike. Traditional libraries are limited by storage space; digital libraries have the potential to store much more information, simply because digital information requires very little physical space to contain it. As such, the cost of maintaining a digital library is much lower than that of a traditional library. A traditional library must spend large sums of money paying for staff, book maintenance, rent, and additional books. Digital libraries do away with these fees.

Digital libraries can immediately adopt innovations in technology providing users with improvements in electronic and audio book technology as well as presenting new forms of communication such as wikis and blogs.

- No physical boundary. The user of a digital library need not to go to the library physically; people from all over the world can gain access to the same information, as long as an Internet connection is available.
- Round the clock availability. A major advantage of digital libraries is that people can gain access to the information at any time, night or day.
- Multiple accesses. The same resources can be used at the same time by a number of users.
- Structured approach. Digital libraries provide access to much richer content in a more structured manner, *i.e.* we can easily move from the catalogue to the particular book then to a particular chapter and so on.
- Information retrieval. The user is able to use any search term (word, phrase, title, name, subject) to search the

entire collection. Digital libraries can provide very user-friendly interfaces, giving clickable access to its resources.

- Preservation and conservation. An exact copy of the original can be made any number of times without any degradation in quality.
- Space. Whereas traditional libraries are limited by storage space, digital libraries have the potential to store much more information, simply because digital information requires very little physical space to contain them. When a library has no space for extension digitization is the only solution.
- Networking. A particular digital library can provide a link to any other resources of other digital libraries very easily; thus a seamlessly integrated resource sharing can be achieved.
- Cost. In theory, the cost of maintaining a digital library is lower than that of a traditional library. A traditional library must spend large sums of money paying for staff, book maintenance, rent, and additional books. Although digital libraries do away with these fees, it has since been found that digital libraries can be no less expensive in their own way to operate. Digital libraries can and do incur large costs for the conversion of print materials into digital format, for the technical skills of staff to maintain them, and for the costs of maintaining online access (*i.e.* servers, bandwidth costs, etc.). Also, the information in a digital library must often be "migrated" every few years to the latest digital media. This process can incur very large costs in hardware and skilled personnel.

PROBLEMS

Some people have criticized that digital libraries are hampered by copyright law, because works cannot be shared over different periods of time in the manner of a traditional library. The content is, in many cases, public domain or self-generated content only. Some digital libraries, such as Project Gutenberg, work to digitize out-of-copyright works and make them freely available to the public. An estimate of the number of distinct bocks still existent in library catalogues from 2000BC to 1960, has been made.

Other digital libraries (more specifically, digital *collections* such as [OverDrive]http://www.overdrive.com, which may be acquired by libraries) accommodate copyright concerns by licensing content and distributing it on a commercial basis, which allows for better management of the content's reproduction and the payment (if required) of royalties.

Access to digital libraries and their collections is dependent upon a stable information technology infrastructure (power, computers, communications links etc.). Hence, despite the egalitarian potential of the digital library, many of those who could most benefit from its global reach (for instance in the Third World) are not able to do so.

ACADEMIC REPOSITORIES

Many academic libraries are actively involved in building institutional repositories of the institution's books, papers, theses, and other works which can be digitized or were 'born digital'. Many of these repositories are made available to the general public with few restrictions, in accordance with the goals of open access. Institutional, truly free, and corporate repositories are often referred to as digital libraries.

DIGITAL ARCHIVES

Archives differ from libraries in several ways. Traditionally, archives were defined as:

1. Containing primary sources of information (typically letters and papers directly produced by an individual or organization) rather than the secondary sources found in a library (books, etc.);
2. Having their contents organized in groups rather than individual items. Whereas books in a library are catalogued individually, items in an archive are typically grouped by provenance (the individual or organization who created them) and original order (the order in which the materials were kept by the creator);

3. Having unique contents. Whereas a book may be found at many different libraries, depending on its rarity, the records in an archive are usually one-of-a-kind, and cannot be found or consulted at any other location except at the archive that holds them.

The technology used to create digital libraries has been even more revolutionary for archives since it breaks down the second and third of these general rules. The use of search engines, Optical Character Recognition and metadata allow digital copies of individual items (*i.e.* letters) to be catalogued, and the ability to remotely access digital copies has removed the necessity of physically going to a particular archive to find a particular set of records. The Oxford Text Archive is generally considered to be the oldest digital archive of academic primary source materials.

Project Gutenberg, Google Book Search, Windows Live Search Books, Internet Archive, Cornell University, The Library of Congress World Digital Library, The Digital Library at the University of Michigan, and CMU's Universal Library are considered leaders in the field of digital archive creation and management. There are hundreds of regionals such as the Wisconsin Historical Society. The Vatican maintains an extensive digital library inventory and associated technology. The entire works of Martin Luther are held at Emory University and are being digitized under an $8M Grant from Coca-Cola heirs, and the Packard Foundation maintains digitization facilities near the Acropolis in Athens, Greece, as examples.

SEARCHING

Most digital libraries provide a search interface which allows resources to be found. These resources are typically deep web (or invisible web) resources since they frequently cannot be located by search engine crawlers. Some digital libraries create special pages or sitemaps to allow search engines to find all their resources. Digital libraries frequently use the Open Archives Initiative Protocol for Metadata Harvesting (OAI-PMH) to expose their metadata to other digital libraries, and search engines like Google Scholar, Google, Yahoo! and Scirus can also use OAI-PMH to find these deep web resources.

There are two general strategies for searching a federation of digital libraries:

1. distributed searching, and
2. searching previously harvested metadata.

Distributed searching typically involves a client sending multiple search requests in parallel to a number of servers in the federation. The results are gathered, duplicates are eliminated or clustered, and the remaining items are sorted and presented back to the client. Protocols like Z39.50 are frequently used in distributed searching. A benefit to this approach is that the resource-intensive tasks of indexing and storage are left to the respective servers in the federation. A drawback to this approach is that the search mechanism is limited by the different indexing and ranking capabilities of each database, making it difficult to assemble a combined result consisting of the most relevant found items.

Searching over previously harvested metadata involves searching a locally stored index of information that has previously been collected from the libraries in the federation. When a search is performed, the search mechanism does not need to make connections with the digital libraries it is searching-it already has a local representation of the information. This approach requires the creation of an indexing and harvesting mechanism which operates regularly, connecting to all the digital libraries and querying the whole collection in order to discover new and updated resources. OAI-PMH is frequently used by digital libraries for allowing metadata to be harvested.

A benefit to this approach is that the search mechanism has full control over indexing and ranking algorithms, possibly allowing more consistent results. A drawback is that harvesting and indexing systems are more resource-intensive and therefore expensive.

FRAMEWORK

A digital library can be built around specific repository software. The best known examples of this are DSpace, Eprints, Fedora, dLibra, and Greenstone Digital Library Software.

THE FUTURE

Large scale digitization projects are underway at Google, the Million Book Project, MSN, and Yahoo!. With continued improvements in book handling and presentation technologies such as optical character recognition and ebooks, and development of alternative depositories and business models, digital libraries are rapidly growing in popularity as demonstrated by Google, Yahoo!, and MSN's efforts. Just as libraries have ventured into audio and video collections, so have digital libraries such as the Internet Archive.

EUROPEAN LIBRARY

The European Library is a service on the World Wide Web that offers access to the resources of the 47 national libraries of Europe. The resources, both digital and non-digital, include books, magazines, journals, audio recordings and other material. The European Library portal offers free searching, and delivers metadata records as well as digital objects: some free, others at cost. The global management of The European Library is based on a consortium of 23 subscribing national libraries, all in charge of maintaining and developing the portal services.

HISTORY

The European Library portal was created in cooperation with 9 national libraries and CENL (Conference of European National Librarians) under TEL (The European Library: Gateway to Europe's Knowledge) project. Initiated in 2001, the TEL project ended in 2004 and was funded under the Fifth Framework Programme of the European Commission. The national libraries involved in the project were those of Finland, Germany, Italy (Florence), Italy (Rome) Netherlands, Portugal, Slovenia, Switzerland and United Kingdom.

TheEuropeanLibrary.org portal was launched on March 17, 2005, hosting over 500,000 visitors in a little more than a year. There are currently 23 national libraries' searchable collections available from the portal and further 21 national libraries' collections accessible through the portal hyperlinks. National libraries of Austria, Croatia and Serbia joined in July 2005.

The national libraries of the 10 European Union new Member States joined as full participants of The European Library service under TELMEMOR (The European Library: Modular Extensions for Mediating Online Resources) (2005-2007). On January 1 2006 the national libraries of Estonia and Latvia as well as the Danish Royal Library became full members of the consortium. In July of 2006 the national libraries of the Czech & Slovak Republics and Hungary were able to display all their digital resources in the portal and Cyprus, Lithuania, Malta, Poland had all their digital content live in The European Library by the end of December 2006.

The European Library has taken a further step towards its enlargement with EDLproject. This adds the digital objects and items of the remaining 9 EU & EFTA national libraries within the EDL project launched in September 2006. The countries involved are either members of the European Union or the European Free Trade Association: Belgium, Greece, Iceland, Ireland, Liechtenstein, Luxembourg, Norway, Spain and Sweden.

Next to assisting participants in becoming full partners of The European Library, the project focuses on multi-linguality, undertakes the first steps towards a European Metadata Registry and is creating a roadmap for potential digitization efforts in the national libraries.

EDLproject has also been responsible for 2 successful workshops looking at the technical and political issues of bringing other cultural heritage digital repositories together as a European digital library. EDL project is financially supported by the European Commission under the eContentplus Programme and will run for 18 months.

PLANS

In the near future, The European Library aims to become the central gateway to all electronic resources for 47 European national libraries. On March 2, 2006 the European Commission issued a press release stating that The European Library shall provide infrastructure for the European Digital Library, a common service to access the collections of all major digital heritage holders (libraries, archives and museums) in Europe.

SEARCH TOOL

TheEuropeanLibrary.org portal is constantly adjusting to the new end-users needs and mirrors the growth in member national libraries. At first, the portal was in an experimental stage and only accessible through Internet Explorer 6.0 web browser. Since June 2005 visitors using Internet Explorer (PC users) but also Camino (MAC users), Netscape, Mozilla or Firefox can benefit from The European Library services. Other browsers like Opera, Safari and Galeon are not yet compatible with the architecture of The European Library portal (client-side XML parsing). TheEuropeanLibrary.org portal is maintained by The European Library Office located in the premises of the Dutch Royal Library in The Hague and is managed by Jill Cousins, Director of The European Library. Since March 2007 The European Library searchbox ('mini library') can be transported to other websites.

LIBRARY OF CONGRESS DIGITAL LIBRARY PROJECT

The Library of Congress National Digital Library Programme (NDLP) is assembling a digital library of reproductions of primary source materials to support the study of the history and culture of the United States. Begun in 1995 after a five-year pilot project, the programme began digitizing selected collections of Library of Congress archival materials that chronicle the nation's rich cultural heritage. In order to reproduce collections of books, pamphlets, motion pictures, manuscripts and sound recordings, the Library has created a wide array of digital entities: bitonal document images, grayscale and colour pictorial images, digital video and audio, and searchable e-texts. To provide access to the reproductions, the project developed a range of descriptive elements: bibliographic records, finding aids, and introductory texts and programmes, as well as indexing the full texts for certain types of content.

The reproductions were produced with a variety of tools: scanners, digital cameras, devices that digitize audio and video, and human labour for rekeying and encoding texts. American Memory employs national-standard and well established industry-standard formats for many digital reproductions, *e.g.*, texts encoded with Standard Generalized Markup Language

(SGML) and images stored in Tagged Image File Format (TIFF) files or compressed with the Joint Photographic Experts Group (JPEG) algorithm. In other cases, the lack of well established standards has led to the use of emerging formats, *e.g.*, RealAudio (for audio), QuickTime (for moving images), and MrSID (for maps). Technical information by types of material and by individual collections is also available at this site.

VISION

A physical library is more than a catalogue that points to volumes on shelves. A digital library is more than a database, and the future National Digital Library will be much more than a universal union catalogue. We envision the National Digital Library as a set of distributed repositories of managed content and a set of interfaces (some of which will resemble traditional catalogues) to that content. Some interfaces may offer comprehensive access to the entire resource, while others will be specialized by content, by intended audience, or by primary purpose. Some interfaces will be closely tied to a particular repository, while others will provide access to a selection of content from distributed repositories.

Access to the content in the National Digital Library will not be limited to searching a bibliographic database. Even in traditional libraries, users do not start every visit by searching the catalogue. Instead, library patrons browse current issues of favourite journals or lists of new acquisitions, use specialized indexes to journal literature, or consult bibliographies, references from scholarly publications, and lists of readings. The digital library must be usable in equivalent ways. School teachers who use the online collections at the Library of Congress have already communicated their eagerness to find shortcuts to the most valuable materials so that they can quickly illustrate classroom presentations or develop lesson plans.

From the user's point of view, the digital library has the potential, in ways not yet realized and not possible with traditional library resources, to be an extension to every desktop, classroom, and personal library. Patterns of use of the World Wide Web already demonstrate that teachers, scholars, and students will want to refer to items in the digital realm as active links from reading lists, articles, textbooks, and term papers. It is also intended that students will be able to work with these items in their own electronic environments, constructing presentations, reports, and online projects.

On September 27, 2006, the Library of Congress' Geography and Map Division announced the milestone of placing the 10,000th map on its Web site. They started digitizing maps in 1996.

DIGITAL LIBRARY USERS

In 1989, to help launch the American Memory pilot project, a consultant surveyed 101 members of the Association of Research Libraries and the 51 state library agencies. The survey disclosed a genuine appetite for on-line collections, especially in research libraries serving higher education. The American Memory pilot (1990-1995) identified multiple audiences for digital collections in a special survey, an end-user evaluation and in thousands of conversations, letters and encounters with visitors.

The most thorough audience appraisal carried out by the Library of Congress consisted of an end-user evaluation conducted in 1992-1993. Forty-four school, college and university, and state and public libraries were provided with a dozen American Memory collections on CD-ROMs and videodisks (these formats are no longer being supported). Participating library staff, teachers, students and the public were polled about which digitized materials they had used and how well the delivery systems worked. The evaluation indicated continued interest by institutions of higher education as well as public libraries. The surprising finding, however, was the strong showing of enthusiasm in schools, especially at the secondary level.

The evaluation team learned that recent reforms in education had created a need for primary-source historical materials such as those in the Library's incomparable collections. Teachers welcomed digitized collections to aid in the development of critical thinking skills; school librarians used the electronic resource to inculcate research skills. These findings have been validated in the educational outreach programme initiated by the Library of Congress in 1995 and initially funded by the W. K. Kellogg Foundation.

EDUCATIONAL OUTREACH

In 1995, in conjunction with the launch of the Library of Congress National Digital Library Programme, the Library brought together leading history and social studies K-12 teachers and librarians to consider how archival on-line resources could best be used in the nation's schools. The participants at this Educator's Forum validated earlier findings: that while the primary sources were in great demand, for teachers to be able to make effective use of them, they needed additional materials to frame the collections and the topics represented in the collections. To this end in 1996, the Library of Congress developed The Learning Page—a gateway to the digital collections, which provides contextual material, search help, sample lesson plans and activities, special presentations, and descriptions of the digital collections for K-12 school teachers and media specialists. New material is continuously added to this page.

In 1997, the Library initiated the American Memory Fellows Programme, which brought together 25 two-person teams of K-12 educators to explore the collections and to develop sample lesson plans, teaching activities, and Web sites that could be used in their local communities. Throughout the 1997-1998 school year, these educators will participate in an online forum as they test and evaluate their materials under development. The Library continued the American Memory Fellows Programme in the summer of 1998 with the goal of building champions for their collections in schools across the country.

DATA FORMAT MANAGEMENT

Data Format Management (DFM) is the application of a systematic approach to the selection and use of the data formats used to encode information for storage on a computer.

In practical terms Data Format Management is the analysis of data formats and their associated technical, legal or economic attributes which can either enhance or detract from the ability of a digital asset or a given information systems to meet specified objectives. Data Format Management is necessary as the amount of information and number of people creating it grows. This is especially the case as the information with which users are working is difficult to generate, store, costly to acquire, or to be shared.

Data Format Management as an analytic tool or approach is data format neutral.

Historically individuals, organization and businesses have been categorized by their type of computer or their operating system. Today, however, it is primarily productivity software, such as spreadsheet or word processor programmes, and the way these programmes store information that also defines an entity. For instance, when browsing the web it is not important which kind of computer is responsible for hosting a site, only that the information it publishes is in a format that is readable by the viewing browser. In this instance the data format of the published information has more to do with defining compatibilities than the underlying hardware or operating system.

DIGITAL PRESERVATION

Some of the information in this article or section has not been verified and might not be reliable. It should be checked for inaccuracies and modified as needed, citing sources.

Digital preservation refers to the management of digital information over time. Preservation of digital information is widely considered to require more constant and ongoing attention than preservation of other media. This constant input of effort, time, and money to handle rapid technological and organisational advance is considered the main stumbling block for preserving digital information. Indeed, while we are still able to read our written heritage from several thousand years ago, the digital information created merely a decade ago is in serious danger of being lost.

Digital preservation can therefore be seen as the set of processes and activities that ensure the continued access to information and all kinds of records, scientific and cultural heritage existing in digital formats.In the language of digital imaging and electronic resources, preservation is no longer just the product of a programme but an ongoing process. In this regard the way digital information is stored is important in ensuring their longevity.

Digital preservation is defined as: long-term, error-free storage of digital information, with means for retrieval and interpretation, for all the time span that the information is required for. "Retrieval" means obtaining needed digital files from the long-term, error-free digital storage, without possibility of corrupting the continued error-free storage of the digital files. "Interpretation" means that the retrieved digital files, files that, for example, are of texts, charts, images or sounds, are decoded and transformed into usable representations. This is often interpreted as "rendering", *i.e.* making it available for a human to access. However, in many cases it will mean able to be processed by computational means.

STRATEGIES

There are several strategies which individuals and organizations may use to combat the loss of digital information.

Refreshing

Refreshing is the copying of data onto newer media or systems. For example, transferring census data from an old tape to a new one or transferring an MP3 from a hard drive to CD. This strategy may need to be combined with migration when the software or hardware required to read the data is no longer available or is unable to understand the format of the data. Refreshing will likely always be necessary due to the deterioration of physical media.

Migration

Migration is the transferring of data to newer system environments (Garrett et al., 1996). This may include conversion of resources from one format to another (*e.g.*, conversion of Microsoft Word to PDF or OpenDocument), from one operating system to another (*e.g.*, Solaris to Linux) or from one programming language to another (*e.g.*, C to Java) so the resource remains fully accessible and functional. Resources that are migrated run the risk of losing some type of functionality since newer formats may be incapable of capturing all the functionality of the original format, or the converter itself may be unable to interpret all the nuances of the original format. The latter is often a concern with proprietary data formats.

Replication

Creating duplicate copies of data on one or more systems is called *replication*. Data that exists as a single copy in only one location is highly vulnerable to software or hardware failure, intentional or accidental alteration, and environmental catastrophes like fire, flooding, etc. Digital data is more likely to survive if it is replicated in several locations. Replicated data may introduce difficulties in refreshing, migration, versioning, and access control since the data is located in multiple places.

Emulation

Emulation is the replicating of functionality of an obsolete system (Rothenberg, 1998). For example, emulating an Atari 2600 on a Windows system or emulating WordPerfect 1.0 on a Macintosh. Emulators may be built for applications, operating systems, or hardware platforms. Emulation has been a popular strategy for retaining the functionality of old video game systems. The feasibility of emulation as a catch-all solution has been debated in the academic community (Granger, 2000).

Raymond A. Lorie has suggested a Universal Virtual Computer (UVC) could be used to run any software in the future on a yet unknown platform (Lorie, 2001). The UVC strategy uses a combination of emulation and migration. The UVC strategy has not yet been widely adopted by the digital preservation community.

Trustworthy Digital Objects

Digital objects that can speak to their own authenticity are called *trustworthy digital objects* (TDOs). TDOs were proposed by Henry M. Gladney to enable digital objects to maintain a record of their change history so future users can know with certainty that the contents of the object are authentic (Gladney, 2004). Other preservation strategies like replication and migration are necessary for the long-term preservation of TDOs.

NATIONAL DIGITAL INFORMATION INFRASTRUCTURE AND PRESERVATION PROGRAMME

The National Digital Information Infrastructure and Preservation Programme is a national strategic programme being led by the Library of Congress to preserve digital content. The programme was mandated in 2000 by the U.S. Congress, and the Library is forming a national network of committed partners with defined roles and responsibilities that are dedicated to preserving specific types of digital content that is at risk of loss if it is not now preserved.

OVERVIEW

The preservation of digital content has become a major challenge for society, especially for libraries and archives whose mission is to preserve the intellectual and cultural heritage of the nation. Thus, in 1998 the Library of Congress began to develop a digital strategy with a group of senior managers who were charged with assessing the roles and responsibilities of the Library in the digital age. This oversight group was headed by the Associate Librarian for Strategic Initiatives, the Associate Librarian for Library Services and the Register of Copyrights. This group held several planning meetings to assess the current state of digital archiving and preservation.

Mission

Develop a national strategy to collect, archive and preserve the burgeoning amounts of digital content, especially materials that are created only in digital formats, for current and future generations.

RECOMMENDATIONS OF NATIONAL ACADEMY OF SCIENCES (NAS)

At the same time, Librarian of Congress James H. Billington commissioned the National Research Council Computer Science and Telecommunications Board of the National Academy of Sciences (NAS) to evaluate the Library's readiness to meet the challenges of the rapidly evolving digital world. The NAS report, LC 21: A Digital Strategy for the Library of Congress, recommended that the Library, working with other federal and nonfederal institutions, take the lead in a national, cooperative effort to archive and preserve digital information.

FUNDING

In December 2000, Congress appropriated $100 million (rescinded to $99.8 million) for a national digital-strategy effort, to be led by the Library of Congress. The Library was chosen not only because of its mission to "sustain and preserve a universal collection of knowledge and creativity for future generations," but also because of its role as one of the leading providers of high-quality content on the Internet.

BACKGROUND OF DIGITAL EFFORTS

The Library of Congress has been a pioneer in the field of digital information. Even before there was a World Wide Web, the Library was digitizing and making selected items from its collections available in electronic form. The programme was called American Memory, and it began as a pilot in 1990. American Memory was originally a CD-ROM project, in which discs were distributed to 44 schools and libraries across the country to determine whether there was any interest in being able to access important materials relating to American history from the Library's collections. By the time the pilot concluded in 1994, there was ample evidence that many people wanted these materials and they wanted more of them.

When the public Web became widely available in 1994, the materials that were distributed on CD-ROM could now be accessed much more widely with this emerging distribution tool. American Memory debuted on the Web on Oct. 13, 1994. American Memory helped fulfil the goal of Dr. Billington, who came to the Library in 1987 with the objective of making the riches of the Library accessible to all Americans, not just those who could come to Washington. As of 2007, more than 11 million items from the collections of the Library and other repositories are available from American Memory, and the Library's Web site is one of the most popular in the federal government.

The Library continues to digitize its collections for distribution on the Web and it has since developed several other Web sites, including Thomas, a congressional database; America's Library, a site for kids and families; the Wise Guide, a monthly magazine; Exhibitions, which offers online versions of major Library exhibitions; and Global Gateway, which features the international collections of the Library and its partners. The sites are all accessible at www.loc.gov.

CONGRESSIONAL LEGISLATION

The U.S. Congress has asked the Library of Congress to lead a collaborative project, called the National Digital Information Infrastructure and Preservation Programme. In December 2000, Congress passed special legislation (Public Law 106-554) in recognition of the importance of preserving digital content for future generations, appropriating $100 million to the Library of Congress to lead this effort. (A government-wide rescission of.22 percent in late December 2000 reduced this special appropriation to $99.8 million.)

This effort falls within the Library's mission, which is "to make its resources available and useful to Congress and the American people and to sustain and preserve a universal collection of knowledge and creativity for future generations." This mission extends to materials in electronic formats as well. In addition, the Library is the home of the U.S. Copyright Office and is thus already engaged in issues relating to copyright in a digital environment.

ORGANIZATIONS PARTICIPATING

The National Digital Information Infrastructure and Preservation Programme is a cooperative effort. The Library is working closely with partners to assess considerations for shared responsibilities. Federal legislation calls for the Library to work jointly with the Secretary of Commerce, the director of the White House Office of Science and Technology Policy, and the National Archives and Records Administration.

The legislation also directs the Library to seek the participation of "other federal, research and private libraries and institutions with expertise in the collection and maintenance of archives of digital materials," including the National Library of Medicine, the National Agricultural Library, the Research

Libraries Group, the Online Computer Library Centre and the Council on Library and Information Resources. The Library is also working with the nonfederal sector. The overall strategy is being executed in cooperation with the library, creative, publishing, technology and copyright communities. In early 2001 the Library established a National Digital Strategy Advisory Board to help guide it through the planning process. This board is made up of experts from the technology, publishing, Internet, library and intellectual-property communities as well as government.

The Library has also established a working group to look at ways that current copyright law can address how libraries and archives handle digital materials when preserving them and making them available to users.

NATIONAL SIGNIFICANCE

The availability of electronic information is today taken for granted. With the rapid growth of the Internet and the World Wide Web, millions of people have grown accustomed to using these tools as resources to acquire information—from a Ph.D. candidate conducting research for a dissertation to a teacher who might not be able to take a class on a field trip to see historical artifacts to a lifelong learner.

Digital has become the principal medium to create, distribute and store content, from text to motion pictures to recorded sound. Digital content now embodies much of the nation's intellectual, social and cultural history. Because digital materials can be so easily altered, corrupted or even lost, these materials must be saved now if they are to remain available to today's and tomorrow's generations.

The Digital Preservation Programme is providing a national focus on important policy, standards and technical components necessary to preserve digital content. Investments in modelling and testing various options and technical solutions will take place over several years, resulting in recommendations to the U.S. Congress about the most viable and sustainable options for long-term preservation. The National Digital Information Infrastructure and Preservation Programme is a public service project of major importance to the nation as well as the world.

CALIFORNIA DIGITAL LIBRARY

The California Digital Library, or CDL, is the University of California's 11th University Library. The CDL assists the ten University of California libraries in sharing their resources and holdings more effectively, in part through negotiating and acquiring consortial licenses on behalf of the entire University of California libraries system. It also produces an open-access digital repository for scholarship produced at the University of California, known as the eScholarship Repository, the Online Archive of California, Calisphere, Counting California, and the union catalogue of the UC libraries, Melvyl.

NATIONAL SCIENCE FOUNDATION

The National Science Foundation (NSF) is a United States government agency that supports fundamental research and education in all the non-medical fields of science and engineering. Its medical counterpart is the National Institutes of Health. With an annual budget of about $5.91 billion (fiscal year 2007), NSF funds approximately 20 percent of all federally supported basic research conducted by the United States' colleges and universities. In some fields, such as mathematics, computer science, economics and the social sciences, NSF is the major source of federal backing.

The NSF's director, its deputy director, and the 24 members of the National Science Board (NSB) are appointed by the President of the United States, and confirmed by the United States Senate. The director and deputy director are responsible for administration, planning, budgeting and day-to-day operations of the foundation, while the NSB meets six times a year to establish its overall policies. The current NSF director is Dr. Arden L. Bement, Jr., and the current deputy director is Dr. Kathie L. Olsen.

GRANTS AND THE MERIT REVIEW PROCESS

Although many other federal research agencies operate their own laboratories—notable examples being the National Aeronautics and Space Administration (NASA) and the National Institutes of Health (NIH)—NSF does not. Instead, it seeks to fulfil its mission chiefly by issuing competitive, limited-term grants in response to specific proposals from the research community. (NSF also makes some contracts.) Some proposals are solicited, and some are not; NSF funds both kinds.

NSF receives about 40,000 such proposals each year, and funds about 10,000 of them. Those funded are typically the projects that are ranked highest in a merit review process. These reviews are carried out by panels of independent scientists, engineers and educators who are experts in the relevant fields of study, and who are selected by NSF with particular attention to avoiding conflicts of interest. (For example, the reviewers cannot work at NSF itself, nor for the institution that employs the proposing researchers.) All proposal evaluations are confidential.

Most NSF grants go to individuals or small groups of investigators who carry out research at their home campuses. Other grants provide funding for mid-scale research centres, instruments and facilities that serve researchers from many institutions. Still others fund national-scale facilities that are shared by the research community as a whole. Examples of national facilities include NSF's national observatories, with their giant optical and radio telescopes; its Antarctic research sites; its high-end computer facilities and ultra-high-speed network connections; the ships and submersibles used for ocean research; and its gravitational wave observatories.

In addition to researchers and research facilities, NSF grants also support science, engineering and mathematics education from pre-K through graduate school. Undergraduates can receive funding through REU summer programmes. Graduate students are supported through IGERT (Integrative Graduate Education Research Traineeships) and AGEP (Alliance for Graduate Education and the Professoriate) programmes and through the Graduate Research Fellowships, NSF-GRF.

SCOPE AND ORGANIZATION

NSF's workforce numbers about 1700, nearly all working at its Arlington, Virginia headquarters. That includes about 1200 career employees, 150 scientists from research institutions on temporary duty, 200 contract workers, and the staff of the

National Science Board office and the Office of the Inspector General, which examines the foundation's work and reports to the NSB and Congress.

Research Directorates

NSF organizes its research and education support through seven directorates, each encompassing several disciplines:

- Biological Sciences (molecular, cellular, and organismal biology, environmental science)
- Computer and Information Science and Engineering (fundamental computer science, computer and networking systems, and artificial intelligence)
- Engineering (bioengineering, environmental systems, civil and mechanical systems, chemical and transport systems, electrical and communications systems, and design and manufacturing)
- Geosciences (geological, atmospheric and ocean sciences)
- Mathematical and Physical Sciences (mathematics, astronomy, physics, chemistry and materials science)
- Social, Behavioural and Economic Sciences (neuroscience, psychology, sociology, anthropology, linguistics and economics)
- Education and Human Resources (science, technology, engineering and mathematics education at every level, pre-K to grey)

Other Research Offices

NSF also supports research through several offices within the Office of the Director:

- Office of Cyberinfrastructure
- Office of Polar Programmes
- Office of Integrative Activities
- Office of International Science and Engineering

Crosscutting Programmes

In addition to the research it funds in specific disciplines, NSF has launched a number of crosscutting projects that coordinate the efforts of experts in many disciplines. Examples include initiatives in:

- Nanotechnology
- The science of learning
- Digital libraries
- The ecology of infectious diseases

In many cases, these projects involve collaborations with other U.S. federal agencies.

HISTORY AND MISSION

Some historians of science have argued that the result was an unsatisfactory compromise between too many clashing visions of the purpose and scope of the federal government. NSF was certainly not *the* primary government agency for the funding of basic science, as its supporters had originally envisioned in the aftermath of World War II. By 1950, support for major areas of research had already become dominated by specialized agencies such as the National Institutes of Health (medical research) and the U.S. Atomic Energy Commission (nuclear and particle physics). That pattern would continue after 1957, when U.S. anxiety over the launch of Sputnik led to the creation of the National Aeronautics and Space Administration (space science) and the Defense Advanced Research Projects Agency (defense-related research).

Nonetheless, NSF's scope has expanded over the years to include many areas that were not in its initial portfolio, including the social and behavioural sciences, engineering, and science and mathematics education. Today, as described in its 2003–2008 strategic plan, NSF is the only U. S. federal agency with a mandate to support *all* the non-medical fields of research.

In the process, moreover, the foundation has come to enjoy strong bipartisan support from Congress. Especially after the technology boom of the 1980s, both sides of the aisle have generally embraced the notion that government-funded basic research is essential for the nation's economic health and global competitiveness, as well as for the national defense. That support has manifested itself in an expanding budget—from $1 billion in 1983 to just over $5.91 billion by FY 2007. (fiscal year 2007).

Timeline

Pre-World War II: Academic research in science and engineering is not considered a federal responsibility; almost all support comes from private contributions and charitable foundations.

World War II: There is a growing awareness that America's military capability owes a great deal to the nation's strength in science and engineering. Congress considers several proposals to provide federal support for research in these fields.

1945: Vannevar Bush, head of the government's wartime Office of Scientific Research and Development, issues a report to President Harry S. Truman, entitled *Science—The Endless Frontier*. The report lays out a strong case for having the federal government fund scientific research, arguing that the nation would reap rich dividends in the form of better health care, a more vigorous economy, and a stronger national defense. The report also proposes creating a new federal agency, the "National Research Foundation," to administer this effort.

1945–1950: Although there is broad agreement in Washington with the principle of federal support for science, there is far less agreement on exactly how that effort should be organized and managed. Thrashing out a consensus requires five years of negotiation and compromise.

1950: On May 10, President Truman signs Public Law 507, creating the National Science Foundation. The act provides for a National Science Board of twenty-four part-time members and a director as chief executive officer, all appointed by the president.

1951: In early March, Truman nominates Alan T. Waterman, the chief scientist at the Office of Naval Research, to become the first Director of the fledgling agency. With the Korean War underway, money is tight: the agency's initial budget is just $151,000.

1952: After moving its administrative offices twice, NSF begins its first full year of operations with an appropriation from Congress of just $3.5 million, a figure far less the almost $33.5 million requested. Twenty-eight research grants are awarded.

1957 : On October 5, the Soviet Union orbits Sputnik 1, the first ever man-made satellite. The successful rocket launch forces a national self-appraisal that questions American education, scientific, technical and industrial strength. For 1959, Congress increases the NSF appropriation to $134 million, nearly $100 million higher than the year before. By 1968, the NSF budget will stand at nearly $500 million.

1958 : NSF selects Kitt Peak, near Tucson, Arizona, as the site of the first national observatory, a research centre that would make state-of-the-art telescopes available to every astronomer in the nation. (Prior to this time, there was no equal access; major research telescopes were privately funded, and were available only to the astronomers who taught at the universities that ran them.) Today, that idea has expanded to encompass the National Optical Astronomy Observatory, the National Radio Astronomy Observatory, the National Solar Observatory, the Gemini Observatory and the Arecibo Observatory, all of which are funded in whole or in part by NSF. Along the way, moreover, NSF's astronomy programme has forged a close working relationship with that of NASA, which was also founded in 1958: just as NASA has responsibility for the U. S. effort in space-based astronomy, NSF provides virtually all the U. S. federal support for ground-based astronomy.

1959 : The United States and other nations operating in Antarctica conclude a treaty that reserves the continent for peaceful and scientific research. Shortly thereafter, a presidential directive based on the treaty gives NSF the responsibility for virtually all U.S. operations and research on the continent; the U.S. Antarctic Programme continues to this day.

1960 : Emphasis on international scientific and technological competition further accelerates NSF growth. The Foundation starts the Institutional Support Programme, a capital funding programme designed to build a research infrastructure among American universities; it will be the single largest beneficiary of NSF budget growth in the 1960s. NSF's appropriation is $152.7 million; 2,000 grants are made.

1968 : The Deep Sea Drilling Project begins. Over the years, the project reveals much new evidence about the theories of continental drift, sea floor spreading and the general usefulness of the ocean basins. The programme also becomes a model of international cooperation as several foreign countries join the operation.

1972 : NSF takes over management of twelve interdisciplinary materials research laboratories from the Defense Department's Advanced Research Projects Agency (DARPA). These university-based laboratories had taken a more integrated approach than did most academic departments at the time, encouraging physicists, chemists, engineers, and metallurgists to cross departmental boundaries and use systems approaches to attack complex problems of materials synthesis or processing. NSF begins to expand these laboratories into a nationwide network of Materials Research Science and Engineering Centres.

1977 : The first "Internet" is developed. This interconnection of unrelated networks is run by DARPA. Over the next decade, increasing NSF involvement leads to a three-tiered system of internetworks managed by a mix of universities, nonprofit organizations and government agencies. By the mid-1980s, primary financial support for the growing project is assumed by the NSF.

1983 : The agency budget tops $1 billion for the first time. Major increases in the nation's research budget are proposed as the country recognizes the importance of research in science and technology, as well as education. A separate appropriation is established for the U.S. Antarctic Programme. NSF receives more than 27,000 proposals and funds more than 12,000 of them.

1985 : In November NSF delivers ozone sensors, along with balloons and helium, to researchers at the South Pole so they can measure stratospheric ozone loss. The action is taken in response to findings made in May of that year, indicating a steep drop in ozone over a period of several years. The Internet project, now known as NSFNET, continues.

1990 : NSF's appropriation passes $2 billion for the first time.

1990s : NSF funds the development of several curricula based on the NCTM standards, devised by the National Council of Teachers of Mathematics. These standards are widely adopted by school districts during the subsequent decade. However, in what newspapers such as the Wall Street Journal later call the "math wars", organizations such as Mathematically Correct complain that some elementary texts based on the standards, including Mathland, have almost entirely abandoned any instruction of traditional arithmetic in favour of cutting, colouring, pasting, and writing. During that debate, NSF is both lauded and criticized for favouring the standards.

1991: In March, the NSFNET acceptable use policy is altered to allow commercial traffic. By 1995, with the private, commercial market thriving, NSF decommissions the NSFNET, allowing for public use of the Internet.

1993: Students and staff working at the NSF-supported National Centre for Supercomputing Applications (NCSA) at the University of Illinois, Urbana-Champaign, develop Mosaic, the first freely available browser to allow World Wide Web pages that include both graphics and text. Within 18 months, NCSA Mosaic becomes the Web browser of choice for more than a million users, and sets off an exponential growth in the number of Web users.

1994: NSF, together with NASA and DARPA, launches the Digital Library Initiative. One of the first six grants goes to Stanford University, where two graduate students, Larry Page and Sergey Brin, begin to develop a search engine that uses the links between Web pages as a ranking method. They will later commercialize their search engine under the name Google.

1996: NSF-funded research establishes beyond doubt that the chemistry of the atmosphere above Antarctica is grossly abnormal and that levels of key chlorine compounds are greatly elevated. During two months of intense work, NSF researchers learn most of what we know today about the ozone hole.

1998: Two independent teams of NSF-supported astronomers discover that the expansion of the universe is actually speeding up, as if some previously unknown force, now known as dark energy, is driving the galaxies apart at an ever increasing rate.

2000 : NSF joins with other federal agencies in the National Nanotechnology Initiative, dedicated to the understanding and control of matter at the atomic and molecular scale. Today, NSF's roughly $300 million annual investment in nanotechnology research is still one of the largest in the 23-agency initiative.

2001 : NSF's appropriation passes $4 billion.

The NSF's Survey of Public Attitudes Toward and Understanding of Science and Technology reveals that the public has a positive attitude toward science but a poor understanding of it.

2004–5 : NSF sends "rapid response" research teams to investigate the aftermath of the Indian Ocean Tsunami and Hurricane Katrina. An NSF-funded engineering team helps uncover why the levees failed in New Orleans.

2005 : NSF's budget stands at just over $5.6 billion.

2006 : NSF's budget stands at $5.91 billion for the 2007 fiscal year that began on October 1, 2006 and runs through September 30, 2007.

2007 : NSF requests $6.43 billion dollars for FY 2008. (NSF Budgets).

PUBLIC ATTITUDES AND UNDERSTANDING

NSF surveys of public attitudes and knowledge have consistently shown that the public has a positive view of science but has little scientific understanding. The greatest deficit remains the public's understanding of the scientific method.

2

Emergence of Digital Reference Library Services

Introduction

The digital library is an electronic or virtual library where information is selected, acquired, processed, organised, stored and retrieved in digital form. The developed countries have already digitized their libraries. The developing countries are in the process of digitization of their libraries. The users of digital libraries are the universal users who should have facility to access to all created and acquired digital sources of information in the form of electronic text, image, map, sound, video and multimedia. Thus the digital libraries are attributed to electronic databases and capable of handling large data and servicing users effectively in resource sharing environment.

DIGITAL LIBRARY INFRASTRUCTURE

A digital library has certain technological requirements such as:

i. Locally developed database

ii. Local library system with adequate personal computers having LAN and CD-ROM Drives.

iii. Electronic mail service

iv. Network connection to have access to other data bases

v. Various functions to coordinate, manage the entry and retrieve data.

vi. Multimedia Kit

vii. Well trained manpower

viii. Computer Hardware with Audio-Visuals, Video Conferencing Kit, Pentium Web Server, Laser Printer, Scanner, Barcode Scanner, Barcode Printer, Digital graphic printer and UPS.

ix. Software and its accessories.

The super structure of digital library rests on some important factors like: (i)the human need for information especially that is timely and relevant and (ii) accumulation of information, and all the supporting infrastructure that includes research community, professional associations, libraries and publishers, advances in methods and technology leading to developments in net working, information science, information storage and retireval, hyper-media, human-computer interaction, artificial intelligence and other areas of computer science that make digital libraries a possible proposition.

DIGITAL LIBRARY SERVICES

Always library services are followed by library works. But now the advancement in information technology has brought changes in the concept of traditional library work as well as service. The recent trend and change in the information related field especially in collection, storing, processing and dissemination of information have resulted in to the evolution of digital libraries. Now most of the reference books like encyclopaedias, dictionaries, directories, hand books, etc. are published in electronic form. Similarly about 50% of the existing secondary resources like abstracting and indexing services are available in electronic form for example, Chemical Abstracts Service, Index Medicus, Engineering Index.

At present most of the digital libraries have been highlighted mainly on providing access to diverse digital information resources. The provision of personalized reference and information services is considered as one of the important characteristics of the library and information profession. However reference services include (i) Either finding the required information on behalf of users, or assisting users in finding information themselves; (ii) Instruction in the use of library resources and services, and (iii) user guidance in which users are guided in selecting the most appropriate information sources and services. In this changing scenario, reference works of modern libraries are influenced by a set of related technical and economic factors, especially the increasing use of technology and techniques.

To cite some examples, the recent developments in the INTERNET and in Web Technologies have brought significant changes in the concept of traditional reference services and a number of web-based "expert services", that are now offered by many non-library organisation. Information services are provided to the users on demand as well as anticipating the user needs including various forms of current awareness and selective dissemination of information services. Such services are provided to the users to keep them abreast of the latest developments in their field of interest through on-line search services in digital information environment, even by the non-library organisations like Dialogue.

Personalized Services

Most of the researches on digital library development have focused on access to and retrieval of digital information but they have overlooked the personalized service aspects, as primary goal of library information services. However the technology and information resources, on their own, can not make up an effective digital library. On priority basis the personalized services in a digital library environment would help the users to find information resources available in a digitally chaotic world. In a Delphy study it was revealed that (I) the primary roles library professionals play in digital libraries include organization of macro and micro-documents (Cataloguing and indexing), selection and acquisition and acting as gateways to the provision of information services, and (ii) the best reasons of developing a digital library include: increasing access to information serving and users needs and bringing organization to the unstructured universe of electronically available information. However there is a demand for end-user instruction on the use of digital libraries and the digital library professionals who are subject specialists should help users to formulate disciplinary search strategies and provide assistance in developing new digital information resources.

Web-based Reference and Information Services

Several reference and information services are now available on the web and many of these services are provided by non-library organization. Also a web site that provides a categorized listing of libraries that offer real-time reference services using specific software, live interactive communication tools, call centre management software, bulletin board services and other INTERNET technologies. Of course, most of these services are designed for registered users of some specific libraries in-digital information environment. HodgKin has made an aggregation approach to reference and information services.

According to which more than one reference sources is made accessible digitally and also it is more practicable in terms of visibility and profitability than a single reference source. Further (I) it's reference service becomes much better known to professional users and thus easier to find, by providing access to several reference works, (ii) by tackling a number of reference works at a time, the publishers can achieve economics of scale in production and development (iii) the user's search session is likely to be much more powerful and fruitful.

According to Chowudhury and Chowudhury online reference and information services can be broadly categorized into three groups: (I) those from publishers, database search services and specialized institutions (ii) those provided by libraries and /or experts through the INTERNET and (iii) where the users need to conduct a search and find information through the web. Also they have listed several online information services that belong to the first category comprising various current awareness, and SDI services, for example:

a) Contents pages services from commercial publishers, such as Elsevier's Contents Direct Service and IDEAL Alert from Academic Press.
b) Information on new books available for free from publishers and vendors, such as Wiley Book, Notification Service from Wiley, and Amazon.com.

c) SDI services from online search services providers, such as Dialogue (Dialogue Alerts)

d) Current contents and ISI Alerting Services from ISI and so on.

However some of these services, particularly the contents page services from publishers of journals, are free, while for others, such as Dialogue Alerts, or Current Contents from ISI, users need to register and pay for the services. There are also some web-based reference services where users need to conduct a search in order to answer their reference query. For example, the Internet Public Library (www.pl.org.), Britannica (www.britanica.com), the Electric Library (http/ask.library.com/refdesk.asp) and the Internet Library for librarians (www.company.com/inforetriever/). Most of these web-based reference services are available free of charge but some charge a small amount as fee. For example, the Electric Library charges an annual subscription fee.

Search Engine Services

Sherman made a comparision among three web-based reference services like (a) Ask Jeeves, (b) the Electric Library, and (c) Information please and observed that:

(a) Ask Jeeves (www.askjeeves.co.uk) basically a search engine, is useful for complex questions and is a good choice for searchers who lack Boolean or other searching skills, because of its strong natural language parser and question-and-answer template structure. The users can ask a question on a given topic and it comes up with a list of questions on the same or similar topics; the users can select any of those predefined questions and then it provides further answers. It processes each query syntactically (to analyse the grammer) and semantically (to determine meaning) and then its answer processing engine provides the question template response (list *Parida* of questions the users see after they ask a question). When the users clicks on a response, the answer-processing engine retrieves the answer template that contains links to the answer locations. Thus Ask Jeeves can help users to select a query from a predefined set of queries on a given topic. So it is considered as a useful model for reference and information services in digital libraries.

(b) The Electric Library is an excellent choice for a serious researcher in need of timely content from a wide array of otherwise unavailable sources. It provides access to various on line reference sources and allows users to either select a specific source or conduct a search on a range, or all, of the sources.

(c) Information please is a suitable tool for students and other researchers, as an authoritative source of facts and pointers for further investigation.

Moreover Chowdhury and Chowdhury have suggested some other useful search engine services like (I) Web help.com (www.about.com) that claims to offer real time search assistance with a real live expert-any time, day or night, (ii) About.com (www.about.com) is a service that shows a number of pre-defined categories related to a search topic given by the user. For example, a simple search on 'e-commerce' not only produces a list of sites, but also provides a set of topics related to e-commerce, such as e-commerce-definition, e-commerce security, the advantages and disadvantages of e-commerce, e-commerce statistics and so on.

Digital Reference Services for General Public

Today web-based digital reference services are being provided by a network of public libraries. The users make their query on an enquiry page and it is automatically routed to one of the participating libraries which records it as an e-mail message to the user containing necessary and available information. For example, the British Library, London provides special reference services for business, scientific, technical, medical, patent and environmental information which range from answering simple queries up to complex questions involving on line data base searches. Of course some of these services are free if users put simple queries, but for complex queries users need to pay at the prescribed rate which covers the costs of staff time, on-line searching and value added tax (VAT). The British Library provides STM (Science, Technology and Medicine)

Search Service for which users need to pay (www.bl.uk/services/current/stm-search.html). Similarly New York Public Library (Digital Library), American Library of Congress, Alexandria Digital Library, Berkeley Digital Library, Bibliotheque Nationale de France, Victoria State Library, Vatican Library, etc. are some other libraries which provide digital reference services for users.

Digital Reference Services of Academic Libraries

Web based reference services are also now being provided by academic libraries, Recently a study report on web-based reference services reflects the current practices of digital library services in seventy academic libraries of USA. The study shows that university libraries allow their patrons to put reference questions in a variety ways: 99% offer e-mail reference, 96% offer reference services by appointment while 29% of the libraries offer real-time virtual reference. These libraries use customer relationship management (CRM) software packages for providing web-based reference services in the virtual reference environment.

Cooperative Digital Library Services

The rising cost of digital reference sources and its proper processing by the trained manpower and also the initial infrastructural investment for introducing new services in libraries have influenced different *Emergence of Digital Library Services* organisations to choose a cooperative model of digital reference services. As a result some cooperative projects have been launched for providing web-based reference services to the users who can ask for such services from a remote location at any time. The Library of Congress, USA has launched the collaborative digital reference service with a mission to provide the users, anywhere anytime through an international digital network of libraries. This network has three main components consisting of (I) Member Profiles (ii) Request Manager-Software for entering, routing and answering reference queries; and (iii) knowledge Base-a searchable database of questions and answer sets. In this network a participating library sends a question to the system on behalf of a user and the system looks in to the knowledge base for a match.

Then a reply is sent to the relevant library through e-mail. Incase the question and its corresponding answer is not found in the knowledge base, then it is passed on to the Request Manager where using the profiles of participating libraries and their information resources collection, expertise etc., relevant query is passed on to an appropriate library. This library receives the query, finds an answer and sends back reply to the results store and answer to the knowledge base. Thus the Knowledge Base and Request Manager become able to provide reference service in digital environment. However, the Library of Congress and OCLC have developed a cooperative "Question Point" the advanced generation of collaborative Digital Reference Service (CDTS) in June 2002 which integrates local as well as global electronic reference networks.

Present Scenario

All the six IITs (Indian Institute of Technology) created as centres of excellence for higher training, research and development in science, engineering and technology, have automated their libraries and now they have access to more than one thousand electronic journals. The Central Library IIT, Delhi has switched over to the Silver Platter's Electronics Reference Library (ERL) technology for providing access to bibliographic databases subscribed on CD-ROM.

The technology facilitates simultaneous and integrated access to ERL complaint reference databases to multiple users across the LAN / WAN Via TCP / IP. This library offers network-based CD-ROM search services from the CD-ROM databases subscribed in the central library. Most of its databases have now been transferred to ERL technology and its CD-NET system has been installed for searching of CD-ROM databases on the campus intranet. This Library has started subscribing to the web-based full-text electronic journals with availability of high speed INTERNET connection and about 1330 electronic journals are accessible full text.

In most of the higher learning and research institutes in India such as the Regional Engineering Colleges (RECs), Tata Institute of Fundamental Research (TFIR), Indian Institute of Science (IIS), Indian Statistical Institute (ISI), Indian

Agricultural Research Institute (IARI), Institute of Veterinary Research of India (IVRI), All India Institute of Medical Science (AIMS), Indian Institute of Management (IIMs), Institute of Physics, Institute of Life Science, Shaha Institute Nuclear Physics, The Medical College Libraries etc., have automated their library systems. Some of them are in the process of digitization of rare and valuable documents. Digital library services in India are in developing stage. At present most of the university libraries have taken steps to provide web-based reference and information services in digital environment in addition to their traditional library services. These services include:

- Access to library catalogues and union catalogues.
- Access to bibliographic databases
- Access to subject gate ways in specific disciplines
- Providing links to web sites
- Accessing and procuring e-reference sources
- Subscribing to e-journals
- Reference services provided by librarians and experts on the web *Parida*
- Document delivery services
- On-line current awareness services
- Digitization of library resources, considering their intellectual value.

The University Grants Commission (UGC) of India has launched the major initiative for setting up nation wide communication network for Indian universities called UGC-Infonet. Each university was to establish a LAN in its campus linking all the teaching departments including library. ERNET of India and INFLIBNET Centre, Ahmedabad are conducting a series of training programmes for technical staff of each participating university library for managing and maintaining the network at their premises. The INFLIBNET Centre will administer and monitor the E-Journal programme and will have independent electronic access to all the publications to help with the process. The INFLIBNET Centre has carried out training programmes in various places to spread awareness and to develop expertise in the University community in the use of E-Resoures under the networked environment. The INFLIBNET Centre has developed and also recently released library automation software package new version for university libraries (SOUL) for building up digital library services. Soul is Windows based user friendly software, based on client server architecture with multi-user and multi language facilities which supports internationally known standards such as CCF, AACR-II andMARC-21, etc. Thus INFLIBNET centre is patronizing for digitization of college and university libraries and encouraging e-subscription and e-learning in Indian Universities and colleges.

The DELNET (Delhi Library Network) created as a metropolitan network in 1988, has changed its name to Developing Library New Work (DELNET) in 2000. The main objectives of DELNET are to promote resource sharing among its member libraries, develop a network of member libraries, collect store and disseminate information, offer computerized information services in digital environment.The DELNET presently avails the high speed satellite communication facilities of NIC spread across the country and its 620 member libraries can access about 35 lakh bibliographic records in machine readable form.

Also it maintains an online union catalogue of books available in its member libraries in CCF format. Its union catalogue is continuously updated. DELNET has been networking the libraries of about 400 affiliated institutes of AICTE, New Delhi. DELNET presents two management software packages *i.e.* DELMARC and DELPLUS.

Conclusion

The digital library movement in India is rapidly increasing and the traditional libraries are now on their way to digitization in a phased manner. Of course, the financial constraint of different institutions and government departments, creates problem to acquire necessary IT equipment and infrastructure. In India UGC and INFLIBNET Centre have taken steps to develop a consortium where college, university and research libraries can join for subscription to on-line journals. Similarly procurement of e-reference sources on CDs can be made and on-line current awareness service of the content pages of the journals subscribed may be provided on the Intranet.

However in a developing country like India where resources are limited, funds are inadequate, the library professionals have to take careful and judicious decisions in selecting library materials for digitization. Also the library and information professionals have to keep on watch for newer technological developments and noticeable changes in the use of many information platforms such as Internet, multimedia and digital library. Thus the library personnel should develop their professional proficiency and communication skill in order to meet the challenges emerging out of digital library services.

DEMANDING EQUALITY IN LIBRARY SERVICES

A comprehensive country wide survey of persons with disability revealed that approx: over 90 million people are suffering from one or the other kind of disability. It can be said that about 12 million are blind, 28.5 are partially visually impaired, 12 million people have speech and hearing defects, 6 million are orthopaedically handicapped, 24 million are mentally retarded, 7.5 million are mentally ill and 1.1 are cured of leprosy.

The National Sample Survey Organisation (NSSO-1991) revealed that 1.9% of the country's total population were affected with physical and sensory disabilities and surveys conducted by various research organisations indicate that about 3% are mentally disabled. Disabled people in India have been subjected to direct and indirect discrimination for centuries. There is little doubt that it is discrimination not disability that disables people. They deserve a comprehensive legislation to tackle the blatant discrimination against them.

With human rights organisations voicing their concerns both nationally and internationally and also acting as their guardians, an increasing number of countries are vigorously preparing policies favourable to the disabled people. In India the recent guidelines framed by the Govt. called "THE PERSONS WITH DISABILITIES (Equal opportunities, protection of rights and full participation) ACT 1995 ensures that the appropriate Govts and local authorities implement the Act which says:

a. ensure that every child with a disability has access to free education in an appropriate environment till he attains the age of 18 years

b. endeavour to promote the integration of students with disabilities in the normal school.

c. promote setting up special schools in Govt. and private sector for those in need of special education in such a manner that children with disabilities living in any part of the country have access to such schools.

d. endeavour to equip the special schools for children with disabilities with vocational training facilities.

Although the new Act will help to develop positive action programmes, there are no positive guidelines for helping the disabled to have access to an effective library and information services programme. If the law offers them equal opportunities they must also ensure that people serving the disabled such as the Govts and NGO's find new ways of serving the disabled. Here, Libraries and Library workers can play their part to hasten the process of full and total integration of the disabled in the society in a big way.

Needs of the Disabled

Individuals with disability have varying degrees of need. Their needs are just like those who are not disabled. They often strive hard for a high quality of life as other normal individuals. Unfortunately many a times people fail to understand that disability in simple terms is nothing but a natural part of the human experience. Often they are shrouded by misconceptions such as, that the disabled are forced to lead a poor quality of life. But the fact is, a person with disability with all limitations can carry out normal activities of living if they have an easy access to community based long term services such as an attendant care, accesses to buildings, public transportation, side walks etc.

Even the severely disabled, when provided with quality health care services and the necessary equipments are able to carry on the tasks similar to those done by the non-disabled. One cannot but feel disturbed that inspite of having the capacity they have to continue remaining disabled because of lack of a strong community based support system. A disabled who is in the prime of his youth, demands an equal opportunity and must therefore be offered a range of assistance such as examination support, specialised equipments, library assistance, note taking in class, reader sign interpreters and parking provisions etc. Only when they have a strong support such as the ones mentioned above they can hope to lead normal lives.

Types of Disability

In order to assist the disabled in leading an active and purposeful life it is important to identify and understand the various types of disability that can be assisted. They can broadly be classified as Physical and Mental disabilities.

I. Physical Disabilities:

a. *Spinal Chord Injury:* It is an injury or damage done to the spinal chord due to an accident or a fall, which may result in partial or complete paralysis. The most common condition that occurs when there is a spinal injury is Paraplegia-meaning, paralysis of legs affecting both movements and sensation. Another condition is Quadriplegia-a degree of paralysis in all four extremities such as arms and legs.

b. *Amputated Limbs:* Amputees are those persons who have one or more missing limbs as a result of accidents caused by vehicles, machinery or any other deformity caused during birth. Such persons can be partially mobile.

c. *Blindness/ Visual impairment:* There are several kinds of visual impairment of which the most common is blindness which can occur due to various reasons such as malnutrition during childhood, illness, or due to accidents. Persons with visual disability have a wide range of abilities as well as limitations. They may be able to read large print and may even move about without any mobility equipments in most situations or sometimes they may be able to perceive light and darkness and perhaps even colours.

d. *Hearing Impairment:* Individuals may be affected by hearing impairment at all ages, the extent of which could be mild or severe depending upon the age of onset, degree and type of loss. Each individuals adjustment to hearing loss is different from one another. Some can be assisted with hearing aids while others are not affected by it. Persons who are deaf due to hearing loss after the age of 20, tend to have fair understanding, near normal speech and hearing but may require instructions to gain useful speech reading.

II. Mental Disabilities

a. *Learning disability:* It is a disorder which affects the basic psychological processes of understanding or using written or spoken language. It can damage the ability to speak, read, write, listen, spell or do mathematical calculations. Conditions such as brain injury, minimal brain dysfunction, dyslexia, and developmental aphasia are examples of learning disabilities.

b. *Mental Illnesses:* These encompass Schizophrenia, anxiety disorders and depressive disorders. Schizophrenia is a highly complex disorder which is caused due to a series of chemical changes in the brain. It usually occurs between the age groups of 15-25 years and is characterised by fragmented thoughts followed by an inability to process information. The condition affects the individuals family, professional and social life making him incapable of functioning normally. Surprizingly their intelligence is not affected and many of them are capable of leading partially normal life if they follow their regular pattern of medication and rehabilitation programmes such as those offered by half-way-homes.

c. *Mental Retardation:* It is distinguished from mental illness because of its presence before birth. A condition characterised by abnormal brain development in the womb not corresponding with normal physical growth. Their learning ability, reasoning power and judgement all develop at a slower pace. Accidents, poisoning, or illness after birth can be a cause for mental retardation. Many of the mentally retarded people are able to participate in activities with non-disabled people given an appropriate adaptation and support. Others may require a long term structured programme. With adequate training and education such persons can be more self reliant citizens. They can be found holding non-skilled or semi skilled jobs and can be made to effectively integrated into the social structure.

Creating a Model Library Programme for the Disabled

In order to create an efficient and effective library programme for the disabled, Libraries need managers who are upto date and are aware of the latest developments that are likely to have profound effect on their services. It is their collective responsibility to promote quality services by gaining a good insight into the problems faced by the disabled. Library staff must recognise that some disabled persons have no control over their behaviour and must be competent enough to handle difficult situations.

They must be prepared to give individual attention so as to understand their strongest communication mode. Therefore the following aspects are essential to develop a model library programme for them by way of: a) Training of Library staff, b)Developing User Assistance Schemes, c) Offering Special Services

a) *Training of Library Staff:* Professional library services depends largely on the continuous upgrading of staff through training on a regular basis. It could be fortnightly, monthly, or seasonal training. Special training requirements can be determined by the Library management and training Officers depending upon the skills and training needs of the individuals. Once the need has been assessed the method of training can be planned. Here is a simple and effective training plan that can be implemented:

Objective: To familiarize with important aspects of disability and disabled users in a Library environment.

Structure: A five day course of lectures, discussions and practical work. The practical training could be held in small groups giving each group an opportunity to work with all types of disabled users.

Materials: A resource package of the training manual.

Contents:

- Concepts on disability: (visits to hospitals, centres for the blind and other kinds of handicapped persons).
- Developing communication and counselling skills.
- Professional library services, single line of command, concentration of effort, time bound work, field orientation and linkage with research.
- Case studies.

Review: In training and work review sessions staff of all levels can report and discuss their successes from which lessons may be drawn.

b) *Developing User Assistance Schemes:* Once the Library worker gets trained they will feel that it is their collective responsibility to provide quality services by gaining a good insight into the problems faced by the disabled and thereby he/ she will be competent enough to create an efficient and effective user assistance scheme such as:

- Providing the disabled users with reading lists and catalogues, high demand materials and lecture tapes that are held in open reservation.
- Delivering books and other documents from library shelves.
- Photocopying of Library materials and enlarging for the partially blind.

- Paging books from stacks and shelf areas.
- Extending loan periods or modifying other lending rules on an individual basis.
- Accepting telephone requests and providing reference service.
- Conducting orientation tours and information skills sessions.
- Providing audio visual equipments.
- Assisting in the use of computer aided learning equipments such as CD-ROMS, optical disks etc.
- Providing access to library facilities by ensuring that directional signs are labelled at appropriate locations with large, simple and clear messages.

c) *Offering Special Services:* Different types of disability require different types of specialised services. The same theory holds good for library services as well and hence the trained library personnel will taken into consideration the following points to fulfil the objectives:

- Library services for the blind must enable them to have access to equipments such as Braille printers, Braille embosser and tape duplicators, Kuzweil reader (a text-to speed reading machine with synthesised speech output), closed circuit TVs for magnifying regular text, PCs with CD ROMS, Powermacs with CD ROMS, large print tape writers, special track tape recorders, computers that are having adaptable equipments such as voice eyes.
- Services for speech and hearing impaired users must include TTD communications (a device also known as TTY-text type telephone) for those needing library questions answered on telephone. Librarians must also familiarise themselves with American sign language which is considered to be the common language of the deaf community.
- For the physically challenged the library facility must be barrier free to wheel chairs and other mobility devices and ensuring that all devices

including door handles are designed for easy manipulation.

- Persons suffering from mental disability can be served by helping to locate and retrieve materials. Because reading is a common problem for them they may enquire assistance in identifying the materials of both the print and electronic types of documents. They also need help in turning catalogue cards or keying in commands on the computer. People suffering from mental illness such as Schizophrenia must be motivated to read books on self-development and may require constant counselling to use library resources to overcome their depression. This is termed as "Bibliotherapy", that is, using books for therapy.

Conclusion

Libraries and library workers can thus play a significant role in bringing hope to the otherwise dismal situations of the disabled world. Adequate financial support must be sought in order to sustain the above mentioned library services and subsequently expand them to suit the latest technological advancement.

There is a need to explore new sources of funding taking into account the reality that the networking of Indian libraries can save funds by way of avoiding duplication of services and also help in providing an efficient inter library loan service thus reducing the time of the reader considerably. Like normal individuals the disabled also need information and other services to help them raise above their disability.

Library and information centres in educational institutions must be encouraged to raise funds by marketing their services. In the process they must try to integrate not only persons with disability with normal users but also integrate the electronic media with their collections and develop local networks. Libraries and Librarians will thus bridge the gap of disability and ability by creating a networked society where in, every individual will be connected without any discrimination.

LIBRARY REFERENCE DESK

Explanation

Just as the employees of retail stores know where everything is shelved in their store, librarians are experts in the arrangement of items in their library, and the information in them, as well as how information is organized outside the library. Library users are encouraged not to be shy about asking a reference librarian for help. Even though some librarians may appear busy working on a project, their primary duty when they are at the desk is to help library users find what they are looking for.

Purpose and Usage

Library users can consult the staff at the reference desk for help in finding information. Using a structured reference interview, the librarian works with the library user to clarify their information need and determine what information sources will fill it. The ultimate help provided may consist of reading material in the form of a book or journal article, instruction in the use of specific searchable information resources such as the library's online catalogue or subscription bibliographic/fulltext databases, or simply factual information drawn from the library's print or online reference collection. Typically, a reference desk can be consulted either in person, by telephone, through email or online chat, although a library user may be asked to come to the library in person for help with more involved research questions. A staffed and knowledgeable reference desk is frequently regarded an essential part of a library.

The services that are provided at a reference desk may vary depending on the type of library, its purpose, its resources, and its staff.

Resources

Resources that are often kept at a library reference desk may include:

- A small collection of reference books (called *ready reference*) that are most often used, so that the librarians can reach them quickly, especially when they are on the phone, and so that the books will be returned in time for someone else to use later the same day. The library's full reference collection is usually nearby as well.

- Newspaper clipping files and other rare or restricted items that must be returned to the reference desk.
- A file box of index cards with the answers to frequently asked questions, and/or drawers with folders of pamphlets and photocopies of pages that, from previous experience, were difficult to find. These enable librarians to find such information quickly without leaving the desk—even faster than they could look it up in a reference book or using the Internet.
- Books and other items that are being held for library users who asked the librarian by phone to set them aside for them to pick up later the same day, or within the next few days.
- Books from the circulating collection that have been set aside for students working on a special assignment, and are temporarily designated to be used only within the library until the project is due.
- Printed lists of items in the library that are not in the catalogue, such as school yearbooks, old telephone directories, college course catalogues, and local history sources.

Services

Services that are often available at a library reference desk may include:

- A sign up sheet for reserving time to use computers that have Internet access, or word processing software.
- If a desired book has been checked out, one can place the book 'on hold', which prevents the person who has checked it out from renewing it, and the person who placed the 'hold' is notified when the book has been returned. (Some libraries provide this service at the circulation desk.)
- Interlibrary loan of books and other material from other branch libraries in the same library system, or from a

cooperating library anywhere in the world. (Some libraries provide this service at the circulation desk.)

- The opportunity to recommend that the library purchase something for its collection that it doesn't have, which may be needed or of interest to other library users.

The librarian who sits at the reference desk can usually do the following by virtue of their professional training and experience:

- The librarian can look up a brief, factual answer to a specific question.
- The librarian can use the catalogue to find out whether the library owns an item with a particular title or author, or that contains a short story, chapter, song, or poem with a particular title, or to compile a list of books by a particular author or on a particular subject.
- The librarian can briefly teach the user how to use the catalogue and how to use its advanced features, or recommend the proper subject words or terms that are used in the catalogue for the topic the user has in mind.
- The librarian can often take the library user directly to the shelves with books on a certain topic without using the catalogue.
- The librarian is familiar with the contents of hundreds of reference books, and can recommend books that might contain the answer to a particular question.
- The librarian can teach the library user to use online databases such as magazine and newspaper articles, and recommend words and search strategies for the topic the user has in mind.
- The librarian can recommend reliable web sites, give advice on searching the Internet for information, and evaluate the reliability of the information on web sites.
- If the library doesn't have information on a given topic, or if the library user wants more information, the librarian can refer the library user to another library or to an organization that can be contacted by phone or mail.

Staff Qualifications

In the United States, the library staff member that sits at a reference desk is generally required to have a Masters in Library Science. However, if there is a lack of qualified applicants, particularly in rural areas of the country, a person with an Associate Degree, a Certificate in Library Technology, or a Bachelors Degree in Library Science may be performing these duties if they have made up the difference with practical experience while working in a library.

In many academic libraries, student assistants are used as the primary contact, sometimes at an "information desk."

Electronic Reference Services

With the development of the Web, digital reference services are beginning to take over some of the roles of the traditional reference desk in a library. There is disagreement over whether or not this development is desirable or inevitable.

Digital Reference Services

Digital reference is a service by which library reference service is conducted online, and the reference transaction is a computer-mediated communication.

The word "reference" in this context refers to the task of providing assistance to library users in finding information, answering questions, and otherwise fulfilling users' information needs. Reference work often but not always involves using reference works, such as dictionaries, encyclopedias, etc. This form of reference work expands reference services from the physical reference desk to a "virtual" reference desk where the patron could be writing from home, work or a variety of other locations.

History

The earliest digital reference services were launched in the mid-1980s, primarily by academic and medical libraries, and provided by e-mail. These early-adopter libraries launched digital reference services for two main reasons: to extend the hours that questions could be submitted to the reference desk, and to explore the potential of campus-wide networks, which at that time was a new technology. With the advent of the graphical World Wide Web, libraries quickly adopted webforms for question submission. Since then, the percentage of questions submitted to services via webforms has outstripped the percentage submitted via email.

In the early-to mid-1990s, digital reference services began to appear that were not affiliated with any library. These digital reference services are often referred to as "AskA" services. Examples of AskA services are the Internet Public Library, Ask Dr. Math, and Ask Joan of Art.

FORMS OF DIGITAL REFERENCE

Webforms

Webforms are created for digital reference services in order to help the patron be more productive in asking their question. This document helps the librarian locate exactly what the patron is asking for. Creation of webforms requires design consideration. Because webforms substitute for the reference interview, receiving as much information as possible from the patron is a key function.

Aspects commonly found within webforms:

- A return email address to send the answer to the question
- The question being asked
- What sources have been consulted by the patron
- How the patron is planning to use the information
- Location of the patron (are they a library patron?)
- A name to personalize the interaction
- A date by which the information is needed
- The type of sources being requested (print or electronic)

Chat Using Commercial Applications

Several applications exist for providing chat-based reference. Some of these applications are: Virtual Reference Toolkit, 24/7 Reference, QuestionPoint, Tutor.com, AspiringKidz.com, Vienova.com and VRLplus. These applications bear a resemblance to commercial help desk applications. These applications possess functionality such as: instant messaging, co-browsing, webpage-and document-pushing, customization of pre-scripted messages, storage of chat transcripts, and statistical reporting.

Chat Using Instant Messaging

Instant messaging (IM) services are used by some libraries as a low-cost means of offering chat-based reference, since most IM services are free. Utilizing IM for reference services allows a patron to contact the library from any location via the internet. This service is like the traditional reference interview because it is a live interaction between the patron and the librarian. On the other side the reference interview is different because the conversation does not float away but instead is in print on the screen for the librarian to review if needed to better understand the patron. IM reference services may be for the use of in-house patrons as well as patrons unable to go to the library. If library computers support IM chat programmes, patrons may IM from within the library to avoid losing their use of a computer or avoid making embarrassing questions public.

Tips for successful IM reference services:

- Create a profile to convey information about the library and increase online presence.
- Accept imperfection in conversations without spending time to go back and make corrections. Most wcrds are recognizable through context.
- Become familiar with and use accepted IM abbreviations such as LOL (Laugh Out Loud).
- Don't panic. While speed is important it is more important to not feel rushed.

3

Reference Library

A reference library does not lend books and other items; instead, they must be read at the library itself. Typically such libraries are used for research purposes, for example at a university. Some items at reference libraries may be historical and even unique.

Examples of reference libraries include the British Library in London and the Bodleian Library at Oxford University.

RESEARCH LIBRARY

A research library is a library which contains an in-depth collection of material on one or several subjects. A research library will generally include primary sources as well as secondary sources. Large university libraries are considered research libraries, and often contain many specialized branch research libraries.

Research libraries can be either reference libraries, which do not lend their holdings, or lending libraries, which do lend all or some of their holdings. Some extremely large or traditional research libraries are entirely reference in this sense, lending none of their material; most academic research libraries, at least in the U.S., now lend books, but not periodicals or other material.

VIRTUAL REFERENCE

Virtual reference services are the remote delivery of reference source materials that are provided to users who are not inside the library. They are used by people seeking to utilize resources who are unable (or unwilling) to visit a library. Providing remote based services for patrons has been a steady practice of libraries over the years. For example, a number of reference questions have been answered via phone, fax email and voice conferencing. However, with the widespread use and adaptation of Web culture, it has been the library institutions' goal to incorporate and utilize remote based programmes for the user's advantage.

Features

Each virtual service that is offered by libraries is unique. However each programme that is used has six distinct features.

Knowledge Base

A knowledge base can be described as a chunk of information that users can access independently. An example of this is can a serialized listing of Frequently Asked Questions (FAQ) that a user can read and use at his or her leisure.

Online Chat

Instant messaging has become a very popular Web based feature. Instant messaging is a real time conversation that utilizes typed text instead of language. Users may feel a sense of satisfaction with the use of this tool because of their personalized interaction with staff.

Email

The use of email in responding to reference questions in libraries has been in use for years. Also, in some cases with Instant Messaging feature, a question may be asked that cannot be resolved in online chat. In this instance the staff member may document the inquiring patron's email address and will the user a response.

Co-browsing

Co-browsing involves the ability to interact and control a user's web browser. This function enables the librarian to actually "see" what the patron has on his or her computer screen. And this two way viewing system may aid the staff member in resolving the patron's issue.

Pre-constructed Message

In Virtual Reference Systems some forms of communication such as basic instructions for the use of databases, standard greetings and farewells are automated.

Statistical Reporting

This feature is important in order for the library staff to effectively learn how the systems is used, to see patterns of use and the evaluate the overall effectiveness of the system.

PROVIDERS

The audience for the book includes library science students and librarians new to academic reference positions, which this reviewer agrees are the primary targets. Several of the contributions were designed to be humorous. Some of these short pieces work well, and others are not as successful. Humor is difficult to carry off and runs the risk of offending audiences. Such comments as "on all that the library has to offer: its knowledge resources, calm demeanor, and mature charm," (p. 39) and "we get to help people and that feels good" (p. 154) can impress readers as trite. The humorous chapters make the audience for this book library and information science students and librarians new to academic reference services rather than those well established in the field.

The chapters cover traditional areas of reference as well as the important digital and virtual components of modern reference. More specifically, the case studies include descriptions of virtual tutorials for information literacy training, reference triage, marketing services and programmes, and relational and digital reference. Other topics vary from strategic planning and assessment of outcomes, the role of information literacy, trends toward more teaching and less face-to-face interaction, and costing and modelling of services for planning. The essays cover topics related to diversity, culture, special (problem) users, changing and evolving trends in librarianship and reference, and the role and experience of being an academic reference librarian. The case studies and essays represent a range of content from ideas to practical descriptions of successful and unsuccessful programmes— sometimes more can be learned from what does not work in other settings than what does work. The authors are all experienced reference librarians from a wide range of public and private academic libraries in the United States.

Very useful information and data are embedded in various sections. For example, the chapter by Guerrero on "What They Don't Teach You in Library School" has an excellent vision statement and the goals are measurable, realistic, and helpful (p. 66–7). Guerrero also includes a satisfaction survey that could be adapted to other institutions. Dent includes a useful open-book library quiz for college students (p. 14–8). Library school faculty will find the exercises with each section useful.

One of the most useful aspects of this book is the description of the methods used to evaluate various programmes and services. The evaluation component of any project or programme is the most difficult to do, most often neglected or done poorly, and, in the era of evidence-based librarianship, probably the most important. Learning evaluation skills is difficult and the provision of methods that have worked (or not worked) with data and analyses is a valuable contribution to the research foundation of the profession. Good research builds on previous strong research. This book provides a strong foundation for academic librarians to do their own research in the area of reference services and training.

Introduction to Reference Services in Academic Libraries is not the first or only text on the subject. The broad range of case studies and the essays, combined with the exercises and research example, make it an ideal textbook for library and information science students and those early in their career as academic reference librarians. It also belongs in the professional collection of most large academic libraries. This book is the first in a series of textbooks on academic reference services and makes this reviewer look forward to more volumes.

Introduction

This guide represents an extensive revision of the third edition, compiled for the Texas State Library and Archives Commission in 1999. The first edition was published in 1986, the second in 1993. All earlier editions were distributed to libraries throughout Texas and to many library agencies outside the state. The purpose remains the same as that of the first three editions: to assist libraries in providing quality reference service and in the selection, acquisition, and use of a core-reference collection. The third edition was the first to include CD-ROMs and Internet sites. This edition places even greater emphasis on electronic sources, listing worthwhile databases available either through the Internet, the Texas State Library's TexShare programme, or on CD-ROMs, along with those for print materials.

A "core-reference collection" is identified here as a small number of print sources that will meet the basic needs of libraries of all sizes. Although electronic materials have had a tremendous impact on reference services, print sources remain essential in providing quality service to the public. The electronic sources, however, can often serve as updates or supplements to print materials or can be utilized in place of print for less popular topics.

Large libraries with a higher level of funding available to them will supplement this core list with additional materials selected to meet the needs of their patrons. Because of limited funding, however, small libraries must choose only the most essential reference works. About one-fourth of Texas public libraries serve a population of less than 5,000. For these small libraries, local support combined with allocations from other sources such as one of the 10 regional library systems probably amounts to between $6,000 and $7,000 annually for collection development. If 10% to 15% of that amount is spent on reference tools (the percentage suggested), only an average of between $600 and $700 is available each year for developing the reference collection. This guide is designed specifically to help these small libraries determine which reference books are most likely to meet their basic needs.

For many subject areas, especially those that are not in heavy use, libraries may decide that the Internet will meet their need for information on the topic and that purchasing a source is unnecessary. That is, of course, a decision governed by local demands. Despite the availability of Internet sources, in some instances print materials are still recommended. Maps, for instance, are available in abundance on the Internet, but libraries still need a good atlas and maps of local areas—plats, city, county, state, etc. A number of dictionaries are available online, but most users prefer to relay on print editions.

USING THE GUIDE

Section I: The Reference Process

This section is divided into two parts: "Reference Services" and "Using Reference Books." "Reference Services" consists of essays in which various aspects of service are discussed—the service per se, reference questions, the reference interview, finding the answer, service guidelines, and types of reference sources. "Using Reference Books" contains discussions and exercises in using four basic types of reference works—almanacs, encyclopedias, dictionaries, and quotation sources. The aim of the exercises is to improve search skills and to demonstrate the special value of these types of reference works.

Section II: Priority Ranking of Sources

This section of the guide is designed to help small libraries in the selection and acquisition processes. Some works should be bought on a regular basis—annually, biennially, or every two to five years (Groups A1-A4). Other titles are divided into five groups (Groups B1-B5) in order of estimated reference value in libraries generally. The titles in Group B1 are recommended as first purchases, followed by those in each of the remaining groups, Group B2 before Group B3, etc. It is important that the selector take these rankings as suggestions, not as a rigid selection plan.

Section III: Sources

Reference materials in this section are of two types, print sources and electronic sources. Print works included have met the usual selection criteria: authority, accuracy, currency, and convenience of arrangement. With these criteria in mind, cost has remained an important factor in recommending sources. Most reference books listed are priced at less than $45, with many costing less than $15. Since print sources are sometimes more convenient to use than Internet sites, libraries may opt to purchase as many print works as their budgets allow. In cases where a reference book is available in both trade (hardback) edition and in paperback, price information for both editions is provided. If a reference source is not likely to have heavy use, the less expensive paperback edition is recommended as a first choice. All works listed were in print at the time of compilation.

Electronic sources that have been incorporated into the listings—the Internet, TexShare databases available through the Texas State Library & Archives Commission, and CD-ROMs—have been carefully screened for quality and reliability. For a few topics, only Web sites are given for the area. Examples include: abbreviations, parenting, anatomy, and nutrition. For these topics there were either no acceptable print materials or the materials were too expensive to recommend. All Internet addresses were accurate as of July 31, 2003.

The arrangement of recommended sources is in 17 sections beginning with "General Works." Sources are then arranged in sections either by type (biography) or by subject area (literature). The previous edition included "Politics and Law" in one section, while this edition divides the two areas. Comments concerning the subject area and many topics are included throughout this section of the guide.

The number of print and electronic sources includes 202 entries. Of the total number of entries, 122 are for book sources plus 36 additional books cited in annotations or notes, compared to 134 entries and 48 additional sources cited in notes in the previous edition. Entries include 87 electronic sources plus 40 cited in annotations or chapter introductions. Forty-seven of the books cited are new to this edition; in some instances they represent better sources than those included in the last edition, while in other instances they replace out-of-print works. Seventy-five entries are repeat listings from the previous guide with updating for editions and costs. In the previous guide, electronic sites were included either in the annotation or in shaded boxes. In this edition, the majority are listed in numbered, annotated entries along with books, while others are included in annotations for books. Information for cited print sources includes bibliographic information and approximate cost utilizing a code. ISBN's are not included. Frequent changes by the publisher are the reasons for these omissions. Costs tend to fluctuate and library discounts vary. ISBN's are often changed with a new printing when only minor updates are made. In both instances, information becomes quickly dated. Exact cost and ISBNs can be obtained from the Books in Print database available through TexShare. The price code is listed below and appears at the bottom of each page in Section III. The coded price appears in parentheses in the bibliographic entry for print sources; a number alone refers to the trade (hardback) edition. A coded price followed by the abbreviation "pa" refers to the paperback edition.

DIGITAL INFORMATION SERVICES

The exponential growth of information in the World Wide Web and the number of users searching for information on the web sites is increasing day by day. To cope with the situation digital libraries have emerged with the tasks of massive digitization, storage, access, digital knowledge mining, digital reference services, electronic information services, search coordination, and manage the archive and its access. A Digital Library is a machine readable representation of materials which might be found in a library, together with conventional information sources, intended to help users find specific information.

A Digital Library service is an assemblage of digital computing, storage, and communications machinery together with the software needed to reproduce, emulate, and extend the services. A full service digital library must accomplish all essential services of traditional libraries and also exploit digital storage, searching, and communication (Gladney, Henry M et.al.1994). So, digital libraries are viewed as a boon for the present and future generations. The present article focuses on the service aspects of digital libraries.

Objective: The paper overviews the advantages of digital libraries and describes various types of services available to offer by digital libraries. Evaluates the present Indian University library system and suggests means for introduction of the digital libraries in the higher education knowledge centres.

Role of Digital Library in New Millennium Information Environment: Any document that is not collected and preserved is likely to be lost, as it is unavailable both now and future. Digitization is a viable solution to make it eternal; to maintain the digital collections and provide access digital libraries became essential in the contemporary information society.

The convergence of computer, telecommunication, information, and multimedia helped in the development of digital library. Digital library is more flexible than conventional library as it is portable, largely accessible, integrated with national and international sources of information. The purpose of digital library is stated by Ravi, Chandra and Sharma (2000) as:

- To expedite the systematic development of procedures to collect, store and organize the information in digital form.
- To encourage cooperative efforts to save and share the investments in research sources, computing and communication network
- To promote efficient delivery of information economically round the world.
- To strengthen the communication and collaboration between creator and user of the information.
- To provide the leadership for the successor for dissemination of knowledge in the area of research.
- To solve the space problem of the library as the library is a growing organism
- To preserve the library reading material for a longer duration
- To solve the resource crunch in the library budget being spent for the purchase of books and journals.

Digital library has an open architecture built on a collection of distributed information repositories where the information is stored in multiple formats which contains both metadata and data. It provides seamless access to the heterogeneous information sources and provides interoperability. It has user-friendly easy-to-use interfaces and query facilities and serves users better. The potential advantages of a digital library over a paper library are-faster addition to the data collection with better quality control, improved search functionality and faster access to information found, but also more freedom and reduced bureaucracy for individual users.

Sharma and Arora (2005) mentioned some of the main advantages of digital library as:

- It makes the library collection for global use
- It saves the time of the users
- It solves the space problem
- It reduces the staff strength
- It facilitates the function of the library
- It precludes the problems of theft, defacing, tearing of pages and binding of library documents, which are universal
- It increases the life of the documents
- It provides the latest and accurate information.

Information Services and Digital Libraries: The convergence of computer, telecommunication, information, and multimedia helped in the development of digital library services. The importance of personalized services grew with the introduction of new technologies and services in libraries. The style of multimedia browsing combined with distributed search is the main theme of Internet information services today (Schatz, 1997). Digital libraries have the ability to provide a previously unattainable level of service (Chen, 2000).

A digital library must accomplish all the essential services of traditional libraries and also exploit the well-known advantages of digital storage, searching and communication. Emphasizing the need for personalized services in digital libraries, Lombardi (2000) mentioned that 'helping clients find resources in a digitally chaotic world is the first priority'. The richest online information is not beneficial to end-users unless they know what resources are available and how to extract the required information from the appropriate resources (Ming, Ding Choo, 2000).

Digital Library should provide physical and intellectual access to a highly distributed, heterogeneous collection of information resources. Access should be independent of time and distance and should be flexible and personalized to the individual. Digital libraries guide user's search toward the best available resources and avoid the problem of overburdening the users with too much information. Services provided by customer oriented digital libraries may include proactive services such as selective dissemination of information (SDI) (Salto, 1968) or may provide real-time routing of information to customers. In a customer oriented Digital Library the collection profile may be constructed by combining the user profiles for all users, which the Digital Library is intended to serve.

In a digital environment university libraries have a new role to fill. While the format of information resources may change, the way of accessing information too may vary and the style of serving the user may be different but still the vision and mission of university library will be same. To fulfil the mission of the library it has to provide the age old reference services, retrieval and dissemination of information and at the same time it has to stretch its services to information search services, to organize the information resources for easy access, to filter qualitative information from the vast ocean of World Wide Web, to facilitate translation services to resolve both linguistic and format incompatibilities and also to take up publishing service in which libraries also aggregate information, add value to information products, and create new information. However, the ability of the library to arrange for access from *outside* the library to materials stored electronically, such that users with suitable equipment and skills can use these resources by themselves, constitutes a much more substantial extension of library service.

University Digital Libraries and Information Services–A Review: In today's global economy successful societies will be those that can develop, disseminate and apply knowledge and adapt flexibility to ever more rapidly changing circumstances. Higher Education has to be at the centre of these changes. Now, in higher educational institutions libraries are transforming rapidly to meet the demands of the e-age. In

India at present there exist 201 State Universities, 102 Deemed Universities and 20 Central Universities.

In a university library, digital information resources include full-text articles, databases, theses and dissertations, e-journals, e-books, multimedia databases, etc. Other information resources, *e.g.* university course calendars, university statutes, course registration information, thesis and dissertation guidelines, style guides, etc., are also needed by users of an academic community. As these information resources are spread across different servers and in different home pages, academic users find it difficult to obtain the needed information for their work in a desired format at the right time.

The university libraries have to provide links to various information resources according to users' needs, by establishing digital information kiosks or centres. Indian university libraries have long way to go to achieve this dream of digital library services. Digital information services is must in Indian universities as the number of faculty who undertake research works are many in number and also they guide research scholars in their research activities. The number of scholars enrolled in the universities to do research too is increasing and their information needs varies in the new technological environment. At present with the support of UGC most of the Indian university libraries are automated. And majority of them are providing OPAC to its users. In this 21 st century the main question is about digitization.

Some of the libraries are having electronic documents and e-journals. Most of the university libraries are having internet connection and they are providing these facilities to their users in different nomenclature like cyber lab, cyber net, internet browsing centre, e-learning centre etc. By going for digital library services the university library can provide speedy access to qualitative information resources. At present more than 50 Indian university libraries subscribing e-journals through UGC Infonet. Among the Indian university libraries, Indira Gandhi Memorial Library of Hyderabad University and Delhi University Library leading ahead in digital resources and digital library services. Delhi University Library System having more than 30 libraries in its fold, accomplishing task of reaching a wider academic community. It has advanced web activity with the subscription of large number of electronic databases being made available through campus network to teachers, students and research scholars. It has a good collection of electronic resources on classic literature. It also provides finding aids and gateways, Internet search tools, e-resources on public domain, World Bank documents and reports etc. It also introduced electronic referencing where by reference service is done through e-mail service. Indira Gandhi Memorial Library has digitized its books collection, which are not under copy right act. It also provides services such as full text, Bibliographical search databases, theses databases etc.

In a networked environment, access to information does not mean ownership but here the library has negotiated the means by which users gain access to information resources. The development in electronic access to scholarly journals is a key example of the shift from ownership to access.

While electronic access to journals appears to be a godsend to patrons and researchers, cutting out countless hours of tedious bibliographic detective work, the behind-the-scenes decisions and negotiations conducted by librarians to provide the service are fraught with numerous complex issues. Electronic serials must be evaluated against the relative importance of content. For example, scientific journals may lack full equations, graphics, and charts. Journals within the social sciences and humanities may lack book reviews and advertisements. These content issues must be weighted against issues of speed and ease of access (Miller, Peters, Pappano, & Manuel, 1999). A further issue to be considered is the ability to access earlier issues of an electronic subscription. Indian university libraries are providing facilities but it is high time for them to provide quality based customer services.

Suggestions: The university libraries in India, in spite of limitations, can move forward by introducing value added digital information services. The following services may be considered for adoption by university libraries, which are already in offering by many university libraries abroad. Today's libraries aim to provide not only access to and delivery of information but have increasingly incorporated proactive services aimed at assisting in the interpretation and application of information to fulfil user information requirements. Indian university libraries should rise up to meet the present information needs of their users by going for digitization and providing various services which a digital library alone can provide to its clientele.

More flexible methods of document delivery are one of the key attractions of the digital library. A concept of just-in-time information delivery, rather than just-in-case (Baker, 2004) where library patrons can identify required material from a workstation, order it, and wait for its delivery back to the workstation. Such a model can save a library the cost of exorbitant serials subscriptions as well as the associated costs of housing back runs of printed serials. The figure given below clearly depicts some of the services which a university digital library can provide to its clientele.

Search: University digital libraries can help the users to search for information. Search services help users to select relevant information from one or more collections. As an intermediary service, users with particular:

Repackaging needs are linked to appropriate resources adding value via the speed and flexibility of the retrieval end the compression of information through the improvement of the information's signal to noise ratio. Digital library's search services provide fast access to dynamic information as well as multiple static collections for a wider range of users. The success of a search service relies on the implementation of a powerful retrieval engine and a flexible user interface. The search service should allow users to do "across database"' searching without having to modify a query. The approach requires constantly hunting for, connecting to, and integrating a variety of resources which, as a function of time, are constantly updated, relocated, created, and scattered across the breadth of cyberspace. Search service coverage needs to extend beyond text to multiple meta formats, including images, sound and video.

There is a need for uniform search interface and users should be supported in the decision about which database to start with and when to stop. This could lead to the creation of search services of search services or tertiary search services to guide users and dynamically group related resources based on requirements, background and other characteristics. Currently this service is supported by specialized search services which will likely increase in number over time.

Classification: Classification can be defined as the act of creating a logical organization of terms or classes (Needham, 1971). Typically libraries develop classification schemes that do this by grouping like objects and creating labels for the groupings. This process usually also involves defining the relationships of the resultant groups (broader, narrower, and related groups). The resultant structure is also referred to as a classification. Classification activities are clearly intermediary activities. They create links between information needs and information sources and add value to the information source by grouping related sources, providing labels for classes of resources, and often by creating a structure indicating relationships between classes.

Classification usually occurs prior to the processing of an information need and is frequently prerequisite to search or filtering. For example, subject searching relies on pre-assigned subject headings. Classification is often used to facilitate broadening or refining retrieval scope during searching or filtering (Brewer, Alan et. al.1996). Classification is a powerful intermediation service useful for discriminating information resources at both broad and specific levels. Digital Libraries will require both broad categorization to identify relevant libraries and specific categorization to select specific resources within libraries. In fact, it is likely that many levels of representation will be needed to support across collection and within-collection information seeking (Marchionini, 1971). In addition digital storage enables the development of machine-based classifications increasing the efficiency of classification activities, but also allowing the development of classifications that extend beyond the typicality that is the hallmark of traditional library classifications.

Information Filtration: There is good evidence that some workers in many information settings serve as unofficial information consultants to their colleagues. Historically individuals serving this role for other individuals and organizations have acted as information gatekeepers (Lewin,

1947). Filtering provides an improvement in the signal to noise ratio through the reduction of channel noise. This is accomplished by removing content which is not needed or undesired. A user will seek a service which improves productivity or enhances the value of information delivered. A Digital Library must support filtering from its inception to select messages and documents for incorporation into its collection. In traditional libraries this activity, referred to as collection development is the process of information acquisition controlled by judgments regarding acquiring information resources for incorporation into a collection. This activity clearly transfers to the

Digital Library. Filtration is also essential to the traditional collection management activities of weeding and preservation. These activities can carry over to University Digital Libraries.

Translation: The Internet is multilingual in several senses. It is concerned with multiple languages and a multitude of digital representations for text and multimedia objects which exhibit a lack of standardization. Incompatibilities in language and format occur in human-to-human, human-to-computer and computer-to-computer communication. Translation intermediary services should help resolve both linguistic and format incompatibilities. Translation services add value to information transfer by transforming a document into another language, or another format thus making it understandable to the user. An example of both language translation and data conversion services on the Internet is the AAArt Web Design Company (htqx//catalogue.cotn/aaart/) that offers the design and management of World Wide Web pages, including digitizing of text graphics, audio and video materials. They provide text translation into HTML format, and also language translation. Another translation service in a Digital Library is data capture which is facilitated through conversion of analog signals to digital messages.

For example, conversion from analog to digital representations is required to capture (digitize) real life objects from physical libraries for storage in a Digital Library. These physical objects can be texts, graphics, audio or video and such translations from analog to digital involve a potential loss of meaning including changes in perception and loss of context. These effects of digitizing information need further investigation (Numberg, Furu Richard Leggett, Marshall, Shipman III, Frank, 1995). Indian universities play a major role in generation and dissemination of knowledge by conducting research work. By providing translation services university digital library can support the research activities of its parental institution.

E-Publishing: E-Publishing is a form of intermediation that links the creators of information products with users. Libraries are often associated with the terminal aspects of the publishing process (*e.g.*, purchasing and circulating books) but libraries also aggregate information, add value to information products, and create new information. Digital Libraries will surely be even more active in all aspects of publishing and will provide many new forms of intermediation to link information seekers with the information resources. University digital library can do this service by publishing peer reviewed articles from staff and students and research scholars in the library web site.

Information Literacy: University digital libraries can provide online information literacy to its users. In a changed environment it is very important to educate the user how to recognize when information is needed and have the ability to locate, evaluate, and use effectively the needed information. Timeliness is an important variable in many information seeking activities. Archivists and librarians consider information from a life-cycle perspective-some information is timeless (fiction, biography, etc.) and some are highly temporal (*e.g.*, news, events calendars, etc.) University libraries should have their own web sites and it must be kept up-to-date by weeding and augmenting regularly. For example, instructional materials maintained in a Digital Library must be updated.

Two developments are necessary to better link users to timely materials. First, a framework for "freshness dating" that becomes part of the standard meta record for information objects must be created and implemented. This framework should specify multiple temporal thresholds for different types of information objects and be accepted as part of the collection development and acquisition policy of Digital Libraries. Second, software tools must be invented that automate as much of the time stamping as possible and that alert staff and users when information must be updated or removed. Together, these developments define intermediary services that address the temporal aspects of publishing. Another traditional library activity that will surely expand in University Digital Libraries is the collection and creation of reviews or annotations for information resources. University digital libraries can also provide online career guidance to its users.

Conclusion

Humans are skilled at reading a few thousand words and extracting complex concepts. Faced with a billion pages (roughly the size of the web), they are helpless. Computers can index every word in a billion pages and search the indexes for simple patterns almost instantaneously (Arms, William Y.2000). In the new millennium one has to understand the present need of the user and try to find solution or right information to meet the user need. Recently many are depending on web-based references to provide information services to their clients. At present there is a need for user training or information literacy programmes to educate the user in conducting complex subject searches, e-mail communications, online chat, videoconferencing etc. Digital libraries can provide qualitative information services faster than the traditional libraries and save the time of the user. In higher educational institutions the libraries should face the challenge of redesigning library services.

DEVELOPMENT OF CONSER CATALOGUING POLICIES

The CONSER (Cooperative Online Serials) Programme has recently developed and published its policies and practices for cataloguing remote access computer file serials. Module 31 of the *CONSER Cataloguing Manual* (*CCM*), "Remote Access Computer File Serials," was drafted by Melissa Beck of UCLA and covers cataloguing policies for remote access computer file serials. The module opens with a full discussion of the kinds of online resources CONSER considers to be remote access computer file serials. Also included in the module are policies for periodicals in multiple file formats, the recording of location and access information, and other significant bibliographic information. These policies were developed over many months in consultation with a number of other projects, institutions, offices, and individuals active in the field of networked information and remote access computer file serials.

Module 31 defines a "remote access computer file serial" as follows:

> *A remote access computer file serial is a work issued in designated parts for an indefinite period of time* (i.e., *that meets the definition of a serial); and in a machine-readable format, accessed "via input/output devices connected electronically to a computer"* (AACR2). *This is in contrast to a direct access computer file serial which is issued in a physical carrier, for example CD-ROMs or floppy disks.*

The most frequently encountered type of remote access serial is an electronic journal or newsletter available through a computer network, such as the Internet.

Module 31 also states that CONSER does not consider the following to be serial publications: list server discussion lists (including digests), catalogues, databases, Gopher and World-Wide Web servers, and other online services.

(The remainder of this paper will use the term "electronic serial" to mean "remote access computer file serial" unless the more specific term is needed for clarity.)

The effort to develop cataloguing tools for networked resources and electronic serials spans many years and involves numerous players in different areas of the library community. This has been an ongoing process involving individuals closely attuned to the major developments in the publishing community. Over the years, CONSER has followed the numerous advances in the standards for cataloguing electronic serials. With the integration of USMARC bibliographic formats, now in process, serials cataloguers will soon be in position to utilize all the computer file bibliographic record elements. CONSER has taken a major step in developing policies for these new elements with the publication of Module 31 of the *CCM*. We will first present a broad overview of a number of related efforts and developments in the publishing and library communities, and then discuss the development of Module 31 of the *CCM* and the major issues it addresses.

Electronic Serials on the Internet

In the late 1980s, the electronic serials available on the Internet were primarily distributed as ASCII files via discussion lists (direct e-mail or Telnet were sometimes used instead). A variation on this approach was to distribute a table of contents file instead of the entire issue. After reading the table of contents file, the user would access the issue (or separate articles) using e-mail or FTP. Over time, other file formats, such as Adobe Acrobat, PostScript, and WordPerfect were used to supplement or replace ASCII files. This overcame some of the limitations of ASCII files, such as their lack of fonts or graphics.

In the early 1990s, a greater range of Internet technologies were used to distribute or access electronic serials, including Archie, Gopher, USENET newsgroups, and WAIS. Gopher archives were especially important, because they allowed users to easily browse and retrieve current and back issues of electronic serials. WAIS and other searching tools allowed publishers to create searchable databases of their electronic journals.

After the 1993 release of NCSA's Mosaic World-Wide Web browser, overall use of the Web increased dramatically. A variety of other Web browsers, such as Netscape, have subsequently been developed. Widespread use of Web browsers, with their easy-to-use graphical user interfaces, have transformed information distribution on the Internet. Using the Web, publishers can easily distribute hypertext documents with multimedia components to a global audience, and they have been actively experimenting with Web versions of new or existing electronic serials.

Basic Cataloguing Questions with Electronic Serials: This rapid development in the organization and presentation of electronic serials has raised a variety of basic cataloguing questions. Internet services, such as discussion lists and World-Wide Web servers, have challenged serials librarians to reconsider aspects of the traditional definition of seriality, especially with regard to citable issues and their designations.

The display of bibliographic information has also become more complex with electronic serials. Often, this information is dispersed over several files, giving cataloguers multiple sources for description that can contain different presentations of bibliographic information. The availability of multiple document formats has generated questions about computer file editions and the number of catalogue records needed to represent them. Many institutions have also been hesitant to include catalogue records for Internet resources because of uncertainty about how to record location and holdings information.

Cataloguing Standards for Computer Files

Since the 1980s, problems associated with cataloguing electronic serials have received attention at numerous ALA Computer Files Discussion Group meetings. Discussions covered the application of the *Anglo-American Cataloguing Rules*, 2nd ed. (*AACR2*), "Computer Files" and the *International Standard Bibliographic Description for Computer Files* (*ISBD (CF)*). Among the issues discussed included an integrated USMARC format that could contain serial and computer file elements in one record; guidelines for implementing *AACR2*, and problems associated with electronic access and holdings information. In June 1991, the ALA Machine Readable Bibliographic Information Committee (MARBI) discussed a number of data elements needed to accommodate the description and access of a broad array of networked resources.

The group focused on data resources (*e.g.*, electronic text and data files) as the kind of electronic resources that are more amenable to bibliographic description using *AACR2*, and the USMARC bibliographic format. Work was begun to identify specific record elements that could be used to expand the USMARC format to accommodate these resources. This work was later reflected in *MARBI Proposal* 93-4, which made recommendations for the following elements and fields: 008/26 (type of computer file), 256 (computer file characteristics), 516 (type of computer file or data note), and 856 (electronic location and access).

Changes to the 008/26 fixed-field element that were approved by MARBI include the addition of four "type of file" codes to enhance fixed-field retrieval of various types of computer files. Recommendations for the 256 field included an expansion of descriptors beyond the three terms now provided for use by *AACR2*: "computer data," "computer programmes," or "computer data and programmes." This change was aimed at allowing cataloguers to choose user-oriented descriptions of computer files from an open list of descriptors which might include such terms as "electronic newsletter" or "electronic book."

The proposal also recommended making field 516 obsolete since "nature and scope" data is generally provided in a 500 field, and an open list of descriptors available for use in the 256 would provide "type of file" information in a more complete fashion.

The 516 field recommendation was not approved. Nor was the 256 field recommendation, because expansion of the file characteristics field is governed by *AACR2*, and it requires a change in cataloguing rules. The 256 field recommendation was taken up by the ALA Committee for Cataloguing: Description and Access (CC:DA) for consideration under a separate proposal.

The following recommendations for changes to the 856 field were approved by MARBI. The proposal advocated that data elements in the 856 field be parsed for portability between systems and formats, with the expectation that systems would provide machine links to the actual publications. It also took into consideration the Internet Engineering Task Force's work on the Universal Resource Locator (URL) and the Universal Resource Name (URN). The URL was later incorporated for use in the 856 field. The MARBI proposal also cited the need for guidelines on the use of *AACR2* and USMARC, and it noted the phenomenal rise in the number of electronic serials being published.

The Network Development and MARC Standards Office at the Library of Congress has made available updated guidelines on the use of the 856 field. These guidelines cover its numerous subfields and different indicator values that identify the various modes of access. They now include an expansion of the modes of access that can be identified in the field and new coding for dial access.

On another front, the ISBD (CF) Review Group recently issued a draft of the second edition of the standard that proposes several changes to better handle files available on the Internet. Among the changes is an expanded list of terms for use in the file characteristics area of the record (USMARC field 256). The April 1995 Summary Report of the ISBD (CF) Review Group proposed that "the whole treatment of the designation of file [be] thoroughly reworked and developed, with area 3 (file characteristics area) emerging as the one most thoroughly changed in revised CF."

The second edition draft supports continuing use of "computer data" and "computer programmes," but includes several lists of additional descriptive terms (*e.g.*, computer journal, computer newsletter, and computer interactive multimedia). One advantage in using this area of the record instead of a note field is the more prominent position of the information which follows the title and edition statements in the record. Development of the field in the *ISBD (CF)* could increase the likelihood of an expansion of the field in the rules.

OCLC and Internet Resources

OCLC's two Internet projects have been instrumental in focusing librarians' attention on the means and methods for describing electronic serials.

OCLC's first project, which was conducted in 1992, tested existing cataloguing tools and focused on the application of *AACR2* and USMARC. As part of this cataloguing experiment, use of a coded USMARC location and access field for electronic resources was tested. Field 852 from the *USMARC Format for Holdings Data* was used to record network location information in parsed subfields. The project resulted in *MARBI Proposal 93-4*, which included a number of recommendations (as outlined above), along with the addition of the 856 field for electronic location and access.

OCLC's 1993 report on the first project, *Assessing Information on the Internet*, gives a comprehensive analysis of the provision of bibliographic information for a wide range of internet resources, including electronic serials. A more recent OCLC Internet Cataloguing Project, begun in 1995, has also been a driving force in the increase in the number of catalogue records created for Internet serials and in the development of consistent guidelines for creating these records. An invitation was sent out for OCLC participants to create records for Internet resources following local collection development policies. In their cataloguing guidelines for the project, OCLC refers to CONSER documentation for cataloguing remote access serials, including the *CONSER Editing Guide* (*CEG*) and Module 31 of the *CCM*.

Early CONSER Efforts to Catalogue Electronic Serials

With the integration of USMARC bibliographic formats on the horizon in the early 1980s, CONSER developed "interim" guidelines to catalogue electronic serials in the serials format. (CONSER cataloguers have been restricted to using the serials format because of the record distribution process for the CONSER database.) The guidelines were considered to be "interim" until format integration was complete. The serials format has only recently supported certain computer file fields, with coded information for computer files aspects to become available only after format integration is implemented early in 1996.

By the late 1980s and early 1990s, CONSER members began to fulfil their institutions' policies and commitments regarding electronic serials. The National Serials Data Programme (NSDP) and the University of Michigan have led the effort in CONSER. NSDP began to receive requests for the International Standard Serial Number (ISSN) and created minimal-level records in the serials format using *AACR2*, the *Library of Congress Rule Interpretations* (*LCRI*), and the *ISDS Manual*. NSDP also began to share its experience with other ISSN centres throughout the world. There was active discussion within the ISSN Network whether to assign separate ISSN to electronic versions of print serials. Several centres began to receive ISSN requests for electronic serials and experimented in creating catalogue records for them.

By the early 1990s, the University of Michigan also began to contribute records for electronic serials, and it later became involved with creating records for electronic serials archived by a project within the CICNet network. CICNet is an Internet access service connecting institutions in a seven-state region in the Midwest, organized by the Committee on Institutional Cooperation (CIC). The CIC Electronic Journals Collection (CIC-EJC), part of the CICNet electronic journal archives, is an authoritative source for electronic research and academic serial publications. The electronic serials available on this archive will be fully catalogued by CICNet members with the bibliographic records contributed to the OCLC Online Union Catalogue. CIC-EJC provides a managed approach to gathering and archiving electronic serials on its Gopher and Web servers. Cataloguing of the serials archived at the site is now being done with the cooperation of six institutions: University of Michigan, Indiana University, University of Illinois at Chicago, University of Wisconsin, University of Minnesota, and Ohio State University. Operating as associate CONSER members under the CIC project, these institutions plan to initially contribute at least 122 full-level records.

Development of *CCM* Module 31

The growing number of loosely related projects indicated a real need for consistency and guidance in applying *AACR2* and using USMARC coding for this new format of material. In 1994, CONSER initiated the drafting of Module 31 as an opportunity to explore some of the unresolved cataloguing issues surrounding electronic serials and to help formulate policies for fields newly available to the serials format. Melissa Beck drafted the module in late 1994. In discussing her work at the November 1994 CONSER Operations Meeting, she raised the following issues:

- Is the current serials definition, outlined in *AACR2* and *LCRI*, adequate for Internet resources?
- When is a document "published" in the network environment?
- How many records should be created for serials issued in multiple document formats?
- There are problems with identifying and citing the chief source and determining if a serial designation is present.
- Guidance is needed in coding the new 856 field.

- Should a new subject heading subdivision be developed for remote access computer files?
- How can we best maintain catalogue records for these dynamic materials?

To address these concerns and others, CONSER members used a number of forums to gather insight from a wide range of library and Internet communities.

As an example, the issue of multiple document formats was also raised in CONSER meetings at ALA Midwinter in 1995. The CONSER Electronic Resources Task Force, which was established in the summer of 1994, distributed a January 1995 interim report that discussed the issue and recommended that CONSER develop proposals on this matter. The "multiple formats" issue for cataloguers often centres on whether more than one edition is involved when the content of different versions is essentially the same. However, some publications do offer substantial differences in the content of different electronic versions. *Postmodern Culture* includes articles, identified as "hypermedia," that contain image, sound, or other non-text files in the HTML version that cannot be included in the ASCII version. The HTML version also includes hypertext links for moving to various locations within the publication or to related documents.

To specifically gain insight into the "multiple formats" question, an informal group of CONSER members posted queries to a number of cataloguing-and serials-related discussion lists. An initial query was followed by a message that contained catalogue record examples showing different treatments for serials in multiple document formats. Included in the message were single records for titles published in multiple formats and available via several access methods. Notes were included in the records to describe file formats and access methods. The message also included a two-record approach for the same titles showing ASCII and PostScript formats described on one record and the HTML format on another.

CONSER also sought feedback and advice on issues identified in early drafts of the module from several offices at the Library of Congress including: the Cataloguing Policy and

Support Office, the Network Development and MARC Standards Office, the Machine Readable Collections Reading Room, and the Computer Files Team of the Special Materials Cataloguing Division. After many months of meetings, online discussions, and reviewing drafts of Module 31, sufficient input and information was available for deciding on how to handle multiple document formats, location and access information, and other significant bibliographic information. What follows are the major issues and how they are addressed in Module 31.

What is a Remote Access Computer File Serial?: An issue that arose early in the development of Module 31 involved the kinds of online resources that are considered to be "remote access computer file serials." Definitions for "serials" and "remote access computer files" provided in the cataloguing rules hardly resolve the issue as to whether some of the new types of electronic resources may be treated as serial publications (*e.g.*, discussion lists). *LCRI* includes a section that addresses "special types of publications" considered to be serials in certain circumstances (*e.g.*, conferences and loose-leaf publications), without any mention of computer files or electronic serials. Module 31 takes a conservative approach by generally including as serials only publications that retain a print-like approach to designating individual issues. A potential shortcoming with this policy is that fewer new kinds of resources may be represented in the CONSER database. Ongoing efforts by a CONSER Electronic Resources Task Force, in consultation with the CONSER Operations Committee, will address the issue of whether a more inclusive serials definition is appropriate.

Networked Resources as Published Documents: Another basic bibliographic consideration involves the question as to whether networked resources are published documents. Guidelines for the first OCLC Internet Resources project brought this issue into focus a few years ago. Current documentation for the ongoing project follows a practical approach that considers all publications offered for access via the Internet as published documents. CONSER endorses this approach as a pragmatic solution that avoids the treatment of online resources as manuscripts. The publication area of the record is then provided, including place of publication and name of publisher, if available. The review draft of the second edition of the *ISBD (CF)* also follows this approach: "In the context of applying the *ISBD (CF)*, all remote access computer files are considered to be published." Users may be led to believe that an item is a completed work when its authors are continuing to revise its contents without clear indications of the revisions.

Multiple File Formats: The number of records needed to describe electronic serials in multiple file formats was one of the most significant issues to resolve. Neither *AACR2* nor the *LCRI* adequately address the question, but a clear policy is necessary for CONSER cataloguers using a common database. While input from meetings and online discussions did not show uniform agreement, there was significant support for using one record for electronic serials published in multiple formats, regardless of the type of formats involved or the extent of the differences between the versions. While some consider this approach at variance with the established practice in *AACR2* and *LCRI* for other formats, at present it seems to be the most practical approach for cataloguers. An alternative was presented by these authors that proposed treatment of publications that offer significantly different versions to be treated as two editions. The proposal recommended two records if one version is in ASCII format and another includes both non-textual files (*e.g.*, sound or graphic files) and nonlinear navigation (*i.e.*, hypertext linking).

The single-record approach was endorsed for several reasons, including cataloguing efficiency and a more useful catalogue. Many believe that it will be easier for the cataloguer to create a single record and that less record maintenance will be required. Another advantage with the single-record approach is that catalogue users will have fewer records to review when searching for online resources. Potential disadvantages include more complex records, less detailed information in the records, and greater difficulty in identifying the specific version made available at a particular site. Nevertheless, most have applauded CONSER for its pragmatic approach to this issue.

Multiple Sources of Bibliographic Information: Multiple sources of information about the publication is another complication for the cataloguer. Cataloguing rules instruct the serials cataloguer to describe in the body of the record the first issue or earliest issue available. The "chief source of information" for cataloguing computer files is the "title screen." This is described in *AACR2* as "a display of data that includes the title proper and usually, though not necessarily, the statement of responsibility and the data relating to publication." Module 31 offers detailed instructions for unconventional situations involving multiple sources of information, including how to record information from README files, table of contents files, file headers, and other electronic sources.

Computer File Characteristics Information: File characteristics information was another significant issue to resolve. There was little support from CONSER participants for the use of field 256 when the field was first evaluated for phase one of format integration. The field was not considered useful by CONSER cataloguers because of the limited terms available for the field. Use of a note field to describe computer file formats or record a more general description of the form or genre was considered a better approach.

CONSER currently uses field 516 (type of computer file or data note) to record computer file characteristics information, including format, genre, or general type of file information (*e.g.*, text and graphic files). The cataloguer can record in a single note field all the necessary information relating to computer file characteristics, and use the machine-generated display constant "type of file:" if desired. Module 31 illustrates different usage of the "type of file" note, including notes for numeric files and files available in the ASCII, Acrobat, and PostScript, and RichText formats.

The main disadvantage with this approach to file characteristics information is that it is not consistent with standard monographic cataloguing practices that rely on the use of field 256. Monographic cataloguers use field 538 (system details note) for more detailed information about file characteristics. The information, when included in field 516 or 538, is buried in the notes area of the record which is less frequently read by catalogue users. CONSER practice now places "type of file" information in a separate field (516) from "access and location" information (fields 538 and 856). The full record for *Emerging Infectious Diseases* (*EID*) as displayed in the OCLC Online Union Catalogue on 2/5/96, to see how the different fields are used to describe multiple file formats available via multiple Internet access methods (note the use of the 516, 538, and 856 fields). (Fixed-field information in the record will be converted by OCLC upon implementation of format integration.)

Location and Access Information: Describing electronic access information is another challenge for the cataloguer due to the different areas of the record involved, including the new electronic location and access field (856). *AACR2* requires cataloguers to "always specify the mode of access" for electronic serials in a note.

The CONSER "mode of access" note now includes more general information to limit redundancy with the 856 field, which contains the detailed information needed to locate and access documents. Serials cataloguers now use the note field 538 (system details information) for the more general information as the field is newly available through format integration. (CONSER records created before 1995 included electronic access information in a general note field.)

Development of CONSER practice for the 856 field will likely be an ongoing process until meaningful displays are developed for online catalogues and a certain degree of stability is found with the resources.

The field was designed to accommodate multiple methods of access and different file formats, but the structure of electronic serials can be complex, involving several subdirectories and numerous files. (Many scholarly electronic journals have individual article files to enhance article access.) CONSER is following the standard practice of separate 856 fields for each mode of access, if known, but is not generally adding separate fields for each format. This is mainly due to the organization of serial publications which doesn't always allow for a distinct path to each format. *Emerging Infectious Diseases*, for example, has separate subdirectories for each issue that include additional subdirectories for the available formats, which, in turn, contain individual article files.

Continuing CONSER Efforts

CONSER is continuing its efforts to further develop cataloguing practice for electronic serials and has recently issued new documentation on the core record and fixed-field elements for electronic serials. Two CONSER task forces—Electronic Resources and Format Integration—have been working on these issues.

The Electronic Resources Task Force has been working to develop recommendations for resolving many of the issues presented in this article including the: definition of "remote access computer file serials," treatment of multiple versions of electronic serials, examination of the utility of the 856 field, and others.

The Format Integration Task Force assisted in the development of the core record for electronic serials and in the documentation of new computer file fixed-field elements in the *CONSER Editing Guide*. Update 3 of the *CONSER Editing Guide*, issued spring 1996, reflects the complete implementation of format integration and includes the following: CONSER core record for electronic serials, description of CONSER practice in applying 006 and 008 fixed-field elements for computer files, and the 007 field for computer file physical characteristics.

The second and final phase of format integration is scheduled to take place in early 1996, and it involves the integration of the fixed-field portion of the bibliographic record. Under current plans, a CONSER electronic serial record will include computer file 007 and 008 fields with a serial 006 field. (OCLC will convert fixed-field information in CONSER records for electronic serials by adding 008 computer file elements and converting 008 serial elements into an 006 field.) This arrangement will effectively include in a single record all the serial and computer file elements, along with physical description fixed-field coding for computer file characteristics (field 007).

The addition of computer file fixed-field elements to the CONSER record may well impact on other areas of the record. Also, the likely development of the file characteristics area of the record may see the addition of field 256 to the CONSER record. Developments in the application of the 856 field will likely lead to more consistent cataloguing practices in recording location and access information.

Electronic serials have been on the CONSER agenda for several years now and will likely continue to be a pressing issue. CONSER will continue to rely on discussion lists for feedback from the cataloguing community to assist in the continuing development of cataloguing policies as well as participation in ALA, NASIG, and CONSER meetings. The continuing evolution of electronic serials will likely compel CONSER to maintain its focus in this area for some time to come.

4

Developing Library and Information Services for Distance Education

Librarians need to understand the mechanics and concepts of DE to provide effective distance library service.

When establishing Distance Librarianship (DL), traditional library standards and procedure can be applied as a guide. Providing post-secondary level DL service is the most challenging, as the information and consultation needs of students and faculty cannot be satisfied just with pre-packaged reading and information.

INTRODUCTION

Distance education (DE) has revolutionised and democratised the delivery and accessibility of education, and has also changed how critical support services, such as library and information service, are provided.

This guide examines distance librarianship (DL) from two perspectives:

- How library services contribute to distance education
- Ways librarians can deliver effective distance library service, and the issues affecting delivery.

Distance Education and Distance Librarianship

Libraries and librarians are as important to distance learning as they are to face-to-face education. Librarians need to understand the mechanics and concepts of DE to provide effective distance library service. In DE, learning takes place at the location of the student and not at the institution of instruction. Traditionally, distance learners were rural-based, middle aged and female. Today's distance learner is located anywhere, of any age and gender.

There are many terms used for DE, including asynchronous learning, external studies and individualised learning. Regardless of the terminology used, remoteness between learner, tutor and institution of instruction is constant.

There are two main DE modes:

- Learning totally at a distance from the institution of instruction, peers and course tutors (total distance)
- Learning at a distance with some form of institution/ peer/tutor contact (mixed mode).

DE covers the following learning needs:

- First chance learning, *e.g.* Schools of the Air, Australia www.assoa.nt.edu.au
- Second attempt at basic/secondary education, *e.g.* the National Extension College, U.K. www.nec.ac.uk
- Tertiary level education, *e.g.* the Indira Gandhi National Open University, India IGNOU, www.ignou.ac.in
- Obtaining professional qualifications, *e.g.* for Aviation Medicine at the University of Otago, New Zealand www.otago.ac.nz
- Life-long learning and continuing education, *e.g.* Intercultural Studies at Technikon SA, South Africa www.tsa.ac.za.

In DE, librarians:

- Ensure that library and information services conform with accreditation requirements
- Develop and maintain quality DE information resources, such as reading lists for students and course developers (educators, team leaders, media production personnel)
- Help distance learners acquire library skills, critical thinking, study and information literacy skills
- Advise distance educators on new and appropriate course materials

- Support the research and scholarship activities of DE faculty
- Identify other institutions that can assist with delivering distance library services to students.

Librarians must be included on DE course teams to ensure that:

- Timely distance library services and professional advice are available to students and faculty
- Library collections effectively support student and faculty information needs.

ESTABLISHING AND MANAGING DISTANCE LIBRARIANSHIP

Library and information service for DE is often an extension of the institution's existing traditional library service. When establishing DL procedure, traditional library standards and procedure can be applied as a guide. Examples of institutions with DL services are in the References section.

DL is used to provide most traditional library services such as consultation, reference and bibliographic searches, and course reading material. Generally, providing post-secondary level DL service is the most challenging, as the information and consultation needs of students and faculty cannot be satisfied just with pre-packaged reading and information.

The basic library and information services distance learners need are:

- Access to information resources, such as texts, supplementary reading and reference services
- Learning how to find the information they need from the information that is available
- Developing ways to apply the information gleaned and to make sound, information-based decisions.

Some guidelines for establishing DL:

- Produce a mission statement that defines clear goals and guiding principles for providing library services tailored to the institution's DE programming

- Assess the library and information service needs of the institution's DE programme, in consultation with DE course teams, faculty and possibly a student survey
- Determine the best media and delivery methods for DL services, such as audio or video tape, print or online material, to be distributed through traditional mail, courier, e-mail or for download from a Web site
- Determine additional costs for the DL component, such as new or additional materials, equipment and staff, and any staff training that may be needed
- Establish the level of funding available for DL from the institution, and explore ways to minimise and share costs through funding grants, collaboration with other institutions, or by forming corporate partnerships
- Establish a review and continuing education process, to ensure that DE student and faculty needs continue to be met
- Initiate a public relations programme to promote awareness of DL services, targeted to students and faculty.

GUIDELINES/STANDARDS FOR DISTANCE LIBRARY SERVICES

Institutional guidelines or standards for DL service, such as mission statements, help librarians:

- Meet international, professionally accepted and established standards
- Maintain consistent services between institutions
- Gauge the relative standard of their existing services.

Institutional DL guidelines should:

- Guarantee distance learners access to quality library services
- Aim to provide complete user satisfaction
- Pledge supportive, effective and cost-efficient service
- Ensure periodic review of the guidelines, so that they continue to meet changing student and faculty needs

- Include librarians in any decision-making or review process.

The guidelines and mission statements must reflect the institution's specific DE programme and services, so will vary by institution, country and region. Some helpful publications on establishing guidelines are in the References section.

A sample DL service statement is the 1997 Student Library Service Charter of The Open Polytechnic of New Zealand TOPNZ, www.openpolytechnic.ac.nz, that promises TOPNZ will:

- Lend material recommended in courses
- Undertake subject searches to support assessment requirements
- Provide bibliographies
- Provide other learning support such as study skills information.

TOPNZ also outlines in the Charter the modes it will use to communicate with its students, provide referrals, deliver services and provide fair access to library materials.

FACTORS IN ORGANISING DL SERVICE

Cost: The overall cost of providing library services at a distance depends on the range and type of services and resources provided, and on whether print, audio, video or electronic formats are used. If the budget for DL is limited, it is important to bear in mind that the print version of a publication generally costs less to purchase than its electronic version. It is also usually less expensive to secure the copyright for print material, than for material in an electronic format or for Web use. Libraries can cover costs by charging service fees to users, or by getting the institution to subsidise the purchase, access and delivery costs of DE materials.

Facilities: In-house library use by distance learners is minimal, so not much additional space is needed at on-campus library locations or at remote library sites for reading tables or conference rooms. Conversely, stack and storage facilities for distance library material should be generous as multiple copies are needed of each publication or resource for wide distribution, and to compensate for the time lag when transferring materials between distance learners and the library location.

Personnel: Many institutions starting DL service begin with one dedicated staff member and add personnel as quality, administrative or service demands rise. Increase the number of staff if you have large DE student enrolment, a wide range of courses and an educational level of post-secondary or higher. If the institution has to hire additional librarians for the DL service, the new staff must be trained in the equipment or technology used, if needed.

The duties of a DL services librarian can include:

- Staffing out-of-hours services
- Staffing remote library points
- Fielding inquiries, mailing and receiving materials
- Administering intellectual property clearances
- Offering input to DE course teams.

Public Relations: A DL service needs an ongoing, aggressive public relations (PR) programme to awaken and educate students, administrators, educators and others to the benefits of DL and to any new services or issues. PR activities can either be a direct library initiative or part of the institution's broader information and advertising package.

Effective PR methods include:

- Posting DL services information on the institution's website
- Short general flyers on DL services
- Circulars about timely, specific issues in DL
- Sending personalised information mail-outs to target groups of students or faculty
- Conducting personal visits to remote library sites
- Networking with faculty.

ISSUES IN PROVIDING DISTANCE LIBRARY SERVICES

The most important DL service considerations are:

- Timeliness of service

- Maintaining a high level and quality of access to DL materials
- Where possible, personal contact with students and faculty.

Distance, time-differences and inadequate communications often make it harder in DL to satisfy an information query or service, as ongoing client contact over a longer period is often necessary before the need is satisfied.

Access to Materials and Document Delivery

In addition to distance and time-difference barriers, national censorship and religious beliefs in receiving countries affect document and information delivery. In some countries, all e-mail and Internet sites are monitored before individuals can access or download them, or access may be blocked altogether. Electronic information sources (e-mail, e-books, databases, virtual libraries, Web pages) are heavily used in developed countries, but are not readily available or in widespread use in many developing countries.

DL services must be sensitive to these realities and establish non-electronic ways to field enquiries and to deliver services. For example, mail, fax or phone can be used for enquiries. Print copies or audio and videotapes of materials can be sent through regular mail or by courier.

Borrowing and service arrangements can also be made with libraries in other locations. Simon Fraser University Library www.lib.sfu.ca in British Columbia, Canada provides library services for distance learners of several other institutions. Librarians must identify libraries with collections and services appropriate to their students' needs before finding out if the libraries are interested in collaboration. A pilot assessment period with student feedback can help determine if the proposed service is accessible to them, and appropriate to their needs. Fees for these "loaned services" can be either charged to the student user, or paid through an arrangement between the contracting institution and the library providing the service.

Pre-packaged information services from commercial vendors such as Questia, XanEdu and ebrary can also be used for DL, through subscription or pay-per-use. For example, the Questia e-library www.questia.com claims to have over 70,000 book and journal titles covering multiple topics and subject areas, and it also offers reference services. The library should assess and inform students of any overlap in services provided by the commercial vendor and the DE institution, to avoid students having to pay for services already covered by their tuition fees.

Consultation Services

Consultation can be conducted through e-mail, toll-free telephone services, pre-packaged mail-out information or scheduled remote site visits. Institutions that have a toll-free telephone service should if possible also use it for library consultation. The frequency and duration of remote library site visits depend on the institution's DL budget, as well as how far the sites are from the parent institution. Institutions with large numbers of overseas students may not have the funds for site visits, whereas those with students within a reasonable distance can schedule frequent visits.

Reference Services

In the DE environment, students can use forms to make research queries, either in print or electronically. In the form, "trigger" or "prompt" questions replace face-to-face assistance in helping the student to properly complete a request. Institutions that already have dedicated library telephone services can use them for DL reference inquiries. Some institutions with Web-based services purchase online versions of major reference works to provide students with a convenient access point, such as Athabasca University's Digital Reference Centre http://library.athabascau.ca/drc

Bibliographic Searches

In some cases, and where enough staff is available, librarians execute full searches for distance learners. Another way is to provide a student manual on conducting bibliographic searches which explains search methods, such as moving from general to specific questions, and lists basic texts, journals and reference sources in various disciplines. More detailed "help" manuals can also be developed on a discipline-by-discipline basis.

Bibliographic Instruction (BI) and Information Literacy (IL) Instruction

Librarians must help learners access, evaluate and use information effectively and efficiently. For delivering BI and IL instruction at a distance, librarians take on a more active teaching, rather than facilitative, role. Centra eMeeting www.centranow.com is an electronic communication utility that has been used successfully to deliver BI at a distance. Deakin University, Australia's Smart Searcher Tutorial service www.deakin.edu.au/library/findout/learn uses interactive, web-based IL tutorial software from UNILINC Ltd. www.unilinc.edu.au. Alternative BI and IL delivery methods include radio, which has been used at the University of South Africa (UNISA, www.unisa.ac.za/library), and computer and video conferencing, which have been used by the Central Queensland University, Australia www.library.cqu.edu.au.

COPYRIGHT IN DISTANCE LIBRARIANSHIP

As libraries need to distribute multiple copies of the same information to distance learners, librarians must be very familiar with all of the current copyright issues affecting distance library provision, and need to be aware of local and international laws governing intellectual property. For example, present international agreements on broadcasting require an institution to obtain broadcast rights for any video and related formats used in DE. Libraries providing distance services should have a "rights clearance librarian" or "copyright librarian" to acquire on the library's behalf the legal right to make multiple copies of an information source. Usually these rights are given for a prescribed period, for an agreed fee. When a license expires, the officer is responsible for either renewing the license, or for removing and disposing of the relevant documents/duplicates.

TECHNOLOGY USE IN DISTANCE LIBRARIES

The rapid spread of ICT, recent reductions in technology costs and connection services due to economies of scale, and a rise in personal ownership of ICTs are making ICT use for DL seem more attractive. Many libraries in developed countries already use ICT as their main method of delivering information services and resources, through online chat rooms, e-mail services, listservs, fee-based or free online databases and reference services, teleconferencing and toll-free numbers. Nevertheless, an estimated 95% of the world's population does not have ready and immediate access to ICT. Often, the cost of the technology is prohibitive. If an institution relies primarily on ICT to deliver DL services, a potentially large number of learners, many of them from developing countries, will be unable to participate or benefit fully. Grants are available to help bridge the technology divide, such as a project by the Bill & Melinda Gates Foundation www.gatesfoundation.org to place computers in libraries in developing countries. However, perhaps a more long term, sustainable way to begin and maintain a start in ICT is to partner with other education institutions or an Internet Service Provider (ISP) on infrastructure costs. In the latter relationship, the ISP often offers reduced information technology (IT) connection rates for students at the partner educational institution. ICT may be used effectively for DL if:

- The institution is committed to providing a high level of library services to distance learners
- The initial and ongoing cost of hardware, software and connectivity charges are within the institution's financial means
- End users (students and faculty) have access to the ICT at their location.

Using Telecentres in Support of Distance Education, one of COL's Knowledge Series titles published in 2001 www.col.org/knowledge, provides some useful information on the role of technology in distance learning and of how telecentres can be used to deliver distance library services.

DISTANCE LIBRARY SERVICES IN DEVELOPING COUNTRIES

Historically, libraries in developing countries have been under-resourced, under-staffed and remote from the distance learner. Generally these libraries were unable to provide the range of services and materials needed, especially to support post-secondary education, and did not have hours of operation that were convenient for the distance learner. These factors remain significant challenges in the developing world, and for the institutions that provide DL services in such locations.

The following methods will help overcome some of these challenges:

- Rotating book boxes and other temporary "libraries" between predetermined locations, such as community centres
- Collaborative and reciprocal borrowing arrangements between local and regional institutions and public libraries, such as partnerships with British Council Libraries
- Developing pre-packaged primary, secondary and tertiary library resources for circulation
- Establishing "distance library corners" in other libraries, *e.g.* "IGNOU library corners" throughout India
- Establishing sub-regional groupings of libraries to support distance learning
- Establishing information delivery partnerships with a broad range of institutions
- Using mobile libraries, including buses, book-boats and donkey libraries
- Using commercial delivery services, such as courier services.

CONTINUING EDUCATION FOR DISTANCE LIBRARIANSHIP

Librarians need continuing education to keep current with developments in DE and DL. While there are no formal DL courses, many stand-alone conferences, seminars and workshops have a DL component. Distance librarians should attend DE conferences as well as library conferences, to network with distance educators, keep up to date on trends, developments and issues in DE, and to sensitise distance educators to the benefits of DE library support services. There is also professional literature on DL, and online librarianship and DE-oriented sites. More information is available from the References section.

Summary

Distance educators and administrators must appreciate the critical role that libraries play in providing support services for DE, and institutions must provide financial backing for staff, facilities and resources. Librarians, in turn, need to stay in touch with the changing needs of DE students and faculty. As Mark G. R. McManus puts it, "libraries must be active, political and effective builders of learning knowledge structures" if they are to provide effective, quality library and information services for DE.

LIBRARY 2.0 THEORY: WEB 2.0 AND ITS IMPLICATIONS FOR LIBRARIES

While the term is widely defined and interpreted, "Web 2.0" was reportedly first conceptualized and made popular by Tim O'Reilly and Dale Dougherty of O'Reilly Media in 2004 to describe the trends and business models that survived the technology sector market crash of the 1990s (O'Reilly, 2005). The companies, services and technologies that survived, they argued, all had certain characteristics in common; they were collaborative in nature, interactive, dynamic, and the line between the creation and consumption of content in these environments was blurred (users created the content in these sites as much as they consumed it). The term is now widely used and interpreted, but Web 2.0, essentially, is not a web of textual publication, but a web of multi-sensory communication. It is a matrix of dialogues, not a collection of monologues. It is a user-centred Web in ways it has not been thus far.

This characterization of the current state of the Web is at times contended, and though the clear delineation between the first and second Webs is here admitted to be rather arbitrary, it still must be recognized that the Web is indeed evolving into a more interactive, multimedia driven technological space, and this understanding of the term is used in this paper. As O'Reilly (2005) observes in what is often cited as the seminal work on

Web 2.0, personal web-pages are evolving into blogs, encyclopedias into Wikipedia, text-based tutorials into streaming media applications, taxonomies into "folksonomies," and question-answer/email customer support infrastructures into instant messaging (IM) services.

The implications of this revolution in the Web are enormous. Librarians are only beginning to acknowledge and write about it, primarily in the "biblioblogosphere" (weblogs written by librarians). Journals and other more traditional literatures have yet to fully address the concept, but the application of Web 2.0 thinking and technologies to library services and collections has been widely framed as "Library 2.0" (Miller 2005a; 2005b; 2006a; 2006b; Notess, 2006).

Most writers on Library 2.0 would agree that much of what libraries adopted in the first Web revolution are static. For example, online public access catalogues (OPACs) require users to search for information, and though many are beginning to incorporate Web 2.0 techniques by gathering data regarding a user (checked-out items, preferred searches, search alerts), they do not respond with recommendations, as does Amazon.com, a more dynamic, Web 2.0 service. Similarly, the first generation of online library instruction was provided via text-based tutorials that are static and do not respond to users' needs nor allow users to interact with one another. These, however, have begun evolving into more interactive, media-rich tutorials, using animation programming and more sophisticated database quizzes. Libraries are already moving into Web 2.0, but the move has only just begun.

Library 2.0

According to Miller (2005a), "Library 2.0" is a term coined by Michael Casey on his LibrayCrunch blog. Though his writings on Library 2.0 are groundbreaking and in many ways authoritative, Casey (2006a) defines the term very broadly, arguing it applies beyond technological innovation and service. In addition to Casey, other blogging librarians have begun conceptually exploring what Library 2.0 might mean, and because of this disparate discussion with very wide parameters, there is some controversy over the definition and relative importance of the term. The nature of this controversy Lawson (2006), Peek (2005), and Tebbutt (2006) explore and begin to adequately rectify, and Crawford (2006) provides a very thorough account of the ambiguity and confusion surrounding the term, partially suggesting that there is nothing inherently novel about the idea.

This paper attempts to resolve some of this controversy by suggesting a definition and theory for Library 2.0, as well as providing examples of its substantial implications for librarianship. A more exact definition and theory for Library 2.0 is necessary to focus discussion and experimentation within the community, and will be valuable in the implementation of new web-based services in the next several years (it is at this point important to note, as Breeding (2006) does, that many libraries are still struggling to adopt simple, static web-based services; interestingly, there are Web 2.0 services, such as the Public Library Interface Kit, or "Plinkit", that could assist in this struggle).

This paper defines "Library 2.0" as "the application of interactive, collaborative, and multimedia web-based technologies to web-based library services and collections," and suggests this definition be adopted by the library science community. Limiting the definition to web-based services, and not library services more generally, avoids potential confusion and sufficiently allows the term to be researched, further theorized, and renders it more useful in professional discourse. The application of Library 2.0 theory to aspects of librarianship reaching beyond Web 2.0 technology is welcome, of course, but should very likely be framed by a different vocabulary.

Indeed, Casey (2006a) recognizes the recurrence of similar ideas throughout library history, and Hale (1991) provides a landmark discussion of this user-centred philosophy external to web-services. There is simply no need to use the term "Library 2.0" in these environments. It is a much more useful theory if it is focused on web-services, much as Abrams (2005) has defined it.

A theory for Library 2.0 could be understood to have these four essential elements:

- It is user-centred. Users participate in the creation of the content and services they view within the library's web-presence, OPAC, etc. The consumption and creation of content is dynamic, and thus the roles of librarian and user are not always clear.
- It provides a multimedia experience. Both the collections and services of Library 2.0 contain video and audio components. While this is not often cited as a function of Library 2.0, it is here suggested that it should be.
- It is socially rich. The library's web-presence includes users' presences. There are both synchronous (*e.g.* IM) and asynchronous (*e.g.* wikis) ways for users to communicate with one another and with librarians.
- It is communally innovative. This is perhaps the single most important aspect of Library 2.0. It rests on the foundation of libraries as a community service, but understands that as communities change, libraries must not only change with them, they must allow users to change the library. It seeks to continually change its services, to find new ways to allow communities, not just individuals to seek, find, and utilize information.

Library 2.0 is a user-centred virtual community. It is a socially rich, often egalitarian electronic space. While Librarian 2.0 might act as a facilitator and provide support, he or she is not necessarily primarily responsible for the creation of the content. Users interact with and create resources with one another and with librarians. In some ways, it is a virtual reality for libraries, a Web manifestation of the library as place. A library's presence on the Web in Library 2.0 includes the presence of that library's constituency and utilizes the same applications and technologies as its community, a concept Habib (2006) recognizes in a very useful model for Library 2.0 in regards to academic libraries.

While these conceptual tenets of Library 2.0 might be rather dependable, envisioning the technological specifics of the next generation of electronic library services is at once both fraught with inevitable error and absolutely necessary. The details of how the applications so common to Web 2.0 will continue to evolve, and how libraries might utilize and leverage them for their patrons, are inherently hidden—they are wholly about innovation.

But the conceptual underpinning of a library's web-presence and how it must evolve into a multimedia presence that allows users to be present as well, both with the library or librarian and with one another, are clearly in need of development. The following prognostications are, then, more speculative than predictive. They are meant to conceptually explore and provide context to the relationship between the evolving Web and the evolving library, as outlined above, as a means to facilitate innovation and experimentation in library electronic services, and this list is by no means comprehensive.

Synchronous Messaging

This technology has already been embraced quite rapidly by the library community. More widely known as instant messaging (IM), it allows real-time text communication between individuals. Libraries have begun employing it to provide "chat reference" services, where patrons can synchronously communicate with librarians much as they would in a face-to-face reference context.

Many might consider IM a Web 1.0 technology, as its inception predates the technology market crash and it often requires the downloading of software, whereas most 2.0 applications are wholly web-based. It is here considered 2.0 as it is consistent with the tenets of Library 2.0: it allows a user presence within the library web-presence; it allows collaboration between patrons and librarians; and it allows a more dynamic experience than the fundamentally static, created-then-consume nature of 1.0 services. It is also considered 2.0 as it is becoming a more web-based application, and the software used by chat reference services is usually much more robust that the simplistic IM applications that are so popular (they often allow co-browsing, file-sharing, screen-capturing, and data sharing and mining of previous transcripts).

The future of these technologies in the library arena is interesting. By providing this interactive Web service, libraries have positioned themselves to adopt its successors quickly and expertly. Already the text-based nature of IM applications is changing into a more multimedia experience, where audio and video messaging is becoming more common.

Even as they provide more multi-sensory experiences, they will become ubiquitous, available throughout the library's web-presence. Already libraries are placing links to their chat reference services within resources themselves, such as at the article level in subscription databases. Much as a patron in a physical library is almost by definition never far from a librarian, chat reference becoming more pervasive could provide a similar circumstance in the world of the Web. The time is perhaps not far away when chat reference can take place within the framework of the library network, providing a more seamless experience.

Further, it is conceivable that should a user allow such a service, these chat reference services can be prompted when certain user seeking behaviours are detected.

For instance, as a user browses through certain resources, repeating steps and moving cyclically through a classification scheme or series of resources, a synchronous messaging service could be prompted to offer assistance. The physical counterpart to this is of course a patron wandering in book stacks, and a librarian, sensing their aimlessness, offering help. Library 2.0 will know when users are lost, and will offer immediate, real-time assistance.

Libraries may do well to continue adopting this technology as it evolves, as it allows reference services in an online media to closely approximate the more traditional services of the physical library.

The time will almost certainly soon come when Web reference is nearly indistinguishable from face-to-face reference; librarians and patrons will see and hear each other, and will share screens and files. In addition, the transcripts these sessions already provide will serve library science in ways that face-to-face reference never did. For the first time in the history of libraries, there will be a continuously collected transcription of the reference transaction, always awaiting evaluation, analysis, cataloguing, and retrieval for future reference.

Streaming Media

The streaming of video and audio media is another application that many might consider Web 1.0, as it also predates Web 2.0 thinking and was widely employed before many of the following technologies had even been invented. But for reasons similar to synchronous messaging, it is here considered 2.0. Certainly, for libraries to begin maximizing streaming media's usefulness for their patrons, 2.0 thinking will be necessary.

As mentioned, library instruction delivered online has begun incorporating more interactive, media-rich facets. The static, text-based explanation coupled with a handout to be downloaded is being supplanted by more experiential tutorials. The Association of College and Research Libraries' Instruction Section provides a database of tutorials, many of which are Web 2.0 in their nature, called Peer Reviewed Instructional Materials Online (PRIMO).

Many of these tutorials use Flash programming, screen-cast software, or streaming audio or video, and couple the media presentation with interactive quizzing; users respond to questions and the system responds in kind. These tutorials are perhaps the first of library services to migrate into more the more socially rich Web 2.0. Most, if not all, however, do not generally provide a means by which users can interact with one another, nor directly with librarians. This fact marks a possible potential for the continued development of these tutorials. These could take the form of multimedia chat rooms or wikis, and users will interact with one another and the learning object at hand, much as they would in a classroom or instruction lab.

Another implication of streaming media for libraries is more along the lines of collections instead of services. As media is created, libraries will inevitably be the institutions responsible for archiving and providing access to them. It will not be enough to simply create "hard-copies" of these objects and allow users to access them within the confines of the library's physical space, however. Media created by the Web on the Web belongs on the Web, and libraries are already beginning to explore providing such through digital repository applications and digital asset management technologies. Yet these applications are generally separate from the library's catalogue, and this fracture will need to be mended. Library 2.0 will show no distinction between or among formats and the points at which they may be accessed.

Blogs and Wikis

Blogs and wikis are fundamentally 2.0, and their global proliferation has enormous implications for libraries. Blogs may indeed be an even greater milestone in the history of publishing than web-pages. They enable the rapid production and consumption of Web-based publications. In some ways, the copying of printed material is to web-pages as the printing press is to blogs. Blogs are HTML for the masses.

The most obvious implication of blogs for libraries is that they are another form of publication and need to be treated as such. They lack editorial governance and the security this provides, but many are nonetheless integral productions in a body of knowledge, and the absence of them in a library collection could soon become unthinkable. This will, of course, greatly complicate collection development processes, and the librarian will need to exercise a great deal of expertise and fastidiousness when adding a blog to a collection (or, perhaps, an automated blog-collection development system). Or, perhaps the very notions of "reliable" and "authoritative", so important to collection development, will need to be rethought in the wake of this innovation.

Wikis are essentially open web-pages, where anyone registered with the wiki can publish to it, amend it, and change it. Much as blogs, they are not of the same reliability as traditional resources, as the frequent discussions of Wikipedia (an online encyclopedia where any registered user can write, amend or otherwise edit articles) in the library world well note; but this of course does not eliminate their value, it merely changes librarianship, complicates collection development and information literacy instruction. The lack of peer review and editorship is a challenge to librarians, not in that users should avoid wikis, but only in that they should understand and be critical in depending on them. Wikis as items in a collection, and the associated instruction of users in the evaluation of them, are almost certainly part of the future of libraries. In addition, a library wiki as a service can enable social interaction among librarians and patrons, essentially moving the study group room online. As users share information and ask questions, answer questions, and librarians do the same within a wiki, a record of these transactions is archived perhaps for perpetuity. And these transcripts are in turn resources for the library to provide as reference. Furthermore, wikis and blogs will almost certainly evolve into a more multimedia environment as well, where both synchronous and asynchronous audio and video collaborations will take place. Blogs are new forms of publication, and wikis are new forms of group study rooms.

Ultimately, blogs and wikis are relatively quick solutions for moving library collections and services into Web 2.0. This beginning of Library 2.0 makes collections and services more interactive and user-centred, enable information consumers to contact information producers and become co-producers themselves. It could be that Library 2.0 blurs the line between librarian and patron, creator and consumer, authority and novice. The potential for this dramatic change is very real and immediate, a fact that places an incredible amount of importance on information literacy. In a world where no information is inherently authoritative and valid, the critical thinking skills of information literacy are paramount to all other forms of learning.

Social Networks

Social networks are perhaps the most promising and embracing technology discussed here. They enable messaging, blogging, streaming media, and tagging, discussed later. MySpace, FaceBook, Del.icio.us, Frappr, and Flickr are networks that have enjoyed massive popularity in Web 2.0. While MySpace and FaceBook enable users to share themselves with one another (detailed profiles of users' lives and personalities), Del.icio.us enables users to share Web resources and Flickr enables the sharing of pictures. Frappr is a bit of a blended network, using maps, chat rooms, and pictures to connect individuals.

Other social networks are noteworthy as well. LibraryThing enables users to catalogue their books and view what other users share those books. The implications of this site on how librarians recommend reading to users are apparent. LibraryThing enables users, thousands of them potentially, to recommend books to one another simply by viewing one another's collections. It also enables them to communicate asynchronously, blog, and "tag" their books.

It does not require much imagination to begin seeing a library as a social network itself. In fact, much of libraries' role throughout history has been as a communal gathering place, one of shared identity, communication, and action. Social networking could enable librarians and patrons not only to interact, but to share and change resources dynamically in an electronic medium. Users can create accounts with the library network, see what other users have in common to their information needs, recommend resources to one another, and the network recommends resources to users, based on similar profiles, demographics, previously-accessed sources, and a host of data that users provide. And, of course, these networks would enable users to choose what is public and what is not, a notion that could help circumvent the privacy issues Library 2.0 raises and which Litwin (2006) well enumerates.

Of all the social aspects of Web 2.0, it could be that the social network and its successors most greatly mirror that of the traditional library. Social networks, in some sense, are Library 2.0. The face of the library's web-presence in the future may look very much like a social network interface.

Tagging

Tagging essentially enables users to create subject headings for the object at hand. As Shanhi (2006) describes, tagging is essentially Web 2.0 because it allows users to add and change not only content (data), but content describing content (metadata). In Flickr, users tag pictures. In LibraryThing, they tag books. In Library 2.0, users could tag the library's collection and thereby participate in the cataloguing process.

Tagging simply makes lateral searching easier. The often-cited example of the U.S. Library of Congress's Subject Heading "cookery," which no English speaker would use when referring to "cookbooks," illustrates the problem of standardized classification. Tagging would turn the useless "cookery" to the useful "cookbooks" instantaneously, and lateral searching would be greatly facilitated.

Of course, tags and standardized subjects are not mutually exclusive. The catalogue of Library 2.0 would enable users to follow both standardized and user-tagged subjects; whichever makes most sense to them. In turn, they can add tags to resources. The user responds to the system, the system to the user. This tagged catalogue is an open catalogue, a customized, user-centred catalogue. It is library science at its best.

RSS Feeds

RSS feeds and other related technologies provide users a way to syndicate and republish content on the Web. Users republish content from other sites or blogs on their sites or blogs, aggregate content on other sites in a single place, and ostensibly distill the Web for their personal use. Such syndication of content is another Web 2.0 application that is already having an impact on libraries, and could continue to do so in remarkable ways.

Already libraries are creating RSS feeds for users to subscribe to, including updates on new items in a collection, new services, and new content in subscription databases. They are also republishing content on their sites. Varnum (2006) provides a blog that details how libraries use RSS feeds for patron use.

But libraries have yet to explore ways of using RSS more pervasively. A new product from a company called BlogBridge, BlogBridge: Library (BBL), "is a piece of software that you can install on your own server, inside your firewall. It's not the content of the library (the books), it's the software to organize the library (the building)." While BBL's potential for libraries has yet to be determine due to its being brand new, it is conceivable that this syndication will replace browsing and searching through library websites for content. BBL and similar RSS aggregator applications, installed in a library's system and coupled with the social network of the library, will enable users to have a single, customized, personal library page that syndicates all the library content of interest to them and their research, eliminating irrelevant information. And users will, of course, control that page and that content.

Mashups

Mashups are perhaps the single conceptual underpinning to all the technologies discussed in this article. They are ostensibly hybrid applications, where two or more technologies or services are conflated into a completely new, novel service. Retrivr, for example, conflates Flickr's image database and an experimental information architecture algorithm to enable users to search images not by metadata, but by the data itself. Users search for images by sketching images. In some ways, many of the technologies discussed above are mashups in their very nature. Another example is WikiBios, a site where users create online biographies of one another, essentially blending blogs with social networks.

Library 2.0 is a mashup. It is a hybrid of blogs, wikis, streaming media, content aggregators, instant messaging, and social networks. Library 2.0 remembers a user when they log in. It allows the user to edit OPAC data and metadata, saves the user's tags, IM conversations with librarians, wiki entries with other users (and catalogues all of these for others to use), and the user is able to make all or part of their profile public; users can see what other users have similar items checked-out, borrow and lend tags, and a giant user-driven catalogue is created and mashed with the traditional catalogue.

Library 2.0 is completely user-centred and user-driven. It is a mashup of traditional library services and innovative Web 2.0 services. It is a library for the 21st century, rich in content, interactivity, and social activity.

Conclusion

All together, the use of these Web 2.0 technologies and applications, along with others not here mentioned and others not yet invented, will constitute a meaningful and substantive change in the history of libraries. The library's collection will change, becoming more interactive and fully accessible. The library's services will change, focusing more on the facilitation of information transfer and information literacy rather than providing controlled access to it. This paper posits four conceptual underpinnings to Library 2.0: it is user-centred; a multimedia experience; socially rich; and communally innovative. It also espouses a focused definition for the term: "The application of interactive, collaborative, and multimedia web-based technologies to web-based library services and collections."

The best conception of Library 2.0 at this point in time would be a social network interface that the user designs. It is a personalized OPAC that includes access to IM, RSS feeds, blogs, wikis, tags, and public and private profiles within the library's network.

It is virtual reality of the library, a place where one can not only search for books and journals, but interact with a community, a librarian, and share knowledge and understanding with them. Library 1.0 moved collections and sparse services into the online environment, and Library 2.0 will move the full suite of library services into this electronic medium. The library has had a web-presence for many years, and with Library 2.0, its patrons will be joining it.

While Library 2.0 is a change, it is of a nature close to the tradition and mission of libraries. It enables the access to information across society, the sharing of that information, and the utilization of it for the progress of the society. Library 2.0, really, is merely a description of the latest instance of a long-standing and time-tested institution in a democratic society. Web 2.0 and libraries are well suited for marriage, and many librarians have recognized so.

Despite this change fitting so well with the history of libraries and their mission, it is still a major paradigmatic shift for librarianship to open not just access to their catalogues and collections, but access to their control. Library 2.0 demands libraries focus less on secured inventory systems and more on collaborative discovery systems.

There is perhaps a great synchronicity between librarianship and Web 2.0, but viewed holistically, Library 2.0 will revolutionize the profession. Rather than creating systems and services for patrons, librarians will enable users to create them for themselves. A profession steeped in decades of a culture of control and predictability will need to continue moving toward embracing facilitation and ambiguity. This shift corresponds to similar changes in library history, including the opening of book stacks and the inclusion of fiction and paperbacks in the early 20th century.

Library 2.0 is not about searching, but finding; not about access, but sharing. Library 2.0 recognizes that human beings do not seek and utilize information as individuals, but as communities. Some examples of the move from Library 1.0 to Library 2.0 include:

- Email reference/Q&A pages—> Chat reference
- Text-based tutorials—> Streaming media tutorials with interactive databases
- Email mailing lists, webmasters—> Blogs, wikis, RSS feeds
- Controlled classification schemes—> Tagging coupled with controlled schemes
- OPAC—> Personalized social network interface
- Catalogue of largely reliable print and electronic holdings—> Catalogue of reliable and suspect holdings, web-pages, blogs, wikis, etc.

It is, finally, also necessary to consider that the Web will continue to change rapidly for some time. Web 2.0 is an early one of many. Libraries must adapt to it, much as they did the Web originally, and must continually adapt for the foreseeable future. In this "perpetual beta" (O'Reilly, 2005), any stability other than the acceptance of instability is insufficient.

WEB-BASED SERVICES EXPECTED FROM LIBRARIES

Academic scenario, over the years, has undergone a tremendous change assuming new dimensions influenced by the technology driven applications. Management education is no exception to this. Traditional commerce and management education methods are observed to be inadequate.

Quality service package delivery is a formidable task for all institutions of business education (Gupta, 2003). The long-term sustainable advantages in the business education require more attention to the issue of service, quality and cost in the national and international markets.

Libraries are mainly entrusted with a host of predetermined tasks like acquiring, organizing, preserving, retrieving and disseminating information to the users. Right from ancient times to the present Internet era, the primary objective of library has always been this. However, the way this purpose has been achieved has drastically changed.

Information technology has influenced the very nature of business and management libraries. They are undergoing significant changes today not only in outlook but also in function, services, methods and techniques for collection development, processing and dissemination of information (Singh & Krishna, 2004). The conventional set up of brick and mortar libraries that store information within a constrained physical space have given way to data centres that integrate data sources around the globe by way of networking.

Libraries have not yet explored their full potential to the full (Miao, 2001). With the advancement in technology and its direct application to libraries, business and management libraries are becoming lean and agile libraries that streamline information supply. The pervasive nature of the Internet, coupled with platform independent database connectivity is turning library portals more and more effective.

The main purpose of this study is to study the availability of websites at management institutes and the extent of library information hosted on it. The study also aims to examine the reasons behind why websites have failed get the attention of majority of users and to identify the library services that they wish to carry through the internet.

WEB PORTALS AND LIBRARIES

A Web Portal can be defined as a website for a specific audience that aggregates an array of content and provides an array of services (Pienaar, 2003). They are the sites on the World Wide Web that typically provide personalized capabilities to their visitors.

They are designed to use distributed applications, different numbers and types of middleware, and hardware to provide services from a number of different sources. Content linked in library portal is superior to the open access content available on the Web (Joint, 2005). Authentication software, commonly known as Web Access Management (WAM) are available that allow the library to govern the access to licensed electronic content (Myhill, 2004). Commonly referred to as simply a portal, it is a website that offers access to a broad array of resources and services of libraries such as e-journals, online databases, Web OPAC, new additions and any other static information about library services.

The developments in information and communication technologies (ICT) and their subsequent absorption in library and information science (LIS) have forced information professionals to change the way they are functioning at present. Because of their popularity with the users, an overwhelming attention is being given to the web-based information services in libraries (Krishnamurthy & Chan, 2005).

LIS community has realized that the academic world is increasingly becoming web-based. Those institutes who wish to attract prospective students and the faculty members must show significant improvements in the institute's infrastructure.

Libraries with mere books and journals may no longer lend a credible support to the academic fraternity. Having a tech savvy library and information centre with exhaustive information resources in all formats has become unavoidable. Libraries are procuring more and more electronic sources like electronic journals, electronic books, online databases along with locally digitized theses and dissertations.

The efforts of libraries in providing users with an integrated way of checking the availability of a source in all possible formats have necessitated a properly designed web portal (Cox & Yeates, 2003). Management libraries are also supposed to define and redefine their services and continuously keep their efforts on value addition to the services offered by them. Proliferation of electronic resources has posed several challenges like multiple logins, multiple interfaces and resource discovery.

Web portal offers effective solutions to these challenges (Groenewegen & Huggard, 2003).

NEED FOR THE STUDY

Information and communication technologies (ICT) have brought a lot of conveniences to the library users (Gupta, 1996). Information being accessible at their desktop, the productivity of the students and faculty members has increased. As libraries continues to be flooded by more and more electronic resources, future students will become more and more dependent on them (McGeary, 2005). Libraries in business and management institutes use propriety or in-house software packages for library management. Even though there is a growing trend in libraries to move towards e-resources, some of the libraries still depend upon books and journals. Print sources continue to dominate the library environment in such cases. In this scenario, basic library services like online public access catalogue (OPAC), reservation, accessing current awareness bulletins, pay for the library dues and document delivery needs to be done at the convenience of users. A literature search on the LISA database and scanning the journal articles, conference and seminar proceedings revealed lack of availability of such literature which studies the web-based services expected from libraries in the management institutes. Hence, this need for the study.

OBJECTIVES OF THE STUDY

The objectives of the study are:

- to study the availability of institutes' websites and the extent of library information hosted on the websites;
- to study the regular use of the Internet by users and their frequency of visit to institutes' websites; and
- to identify the library transactions that users wish to carry out using the Internet.

HYPOTHESES

The hypotheses of the study are:

- Institutes have failed in attracting the library users to their websites as they provide only static information about library and its services.

- The majority of the users in management institutes use the Internet on a regular basis.
- Most of transactions users do at the library should be carried out through the Internet at their convenience.

SCOPE AND LIMITATIONS

The scope of the study is limited to studying the web-based services expected from libraries in All India Council of Technical Education (AICTE) approved management institutes affiliated to the University of Mumbai.The limitation is that this article covers only the day to day library transactions like online catalogue, reservations, etc. Access to online resources is not studied as it is understood that they will have to be web-based only.

METHODOLOGY

This article is based on part of a questionnaire survey conducted for the doctoral studies at Karnatak University, Dharwad. This survey covered the management institutes in Mumbai City, Maharashtra State, India to understand and measure the impact of information technology applications on library resources and services. In all 24 management institutes approved by All India Council of Technical Education (AICTE) and affiliated to the University of Mumbai (Appendix I) were surveyed. Different questionnaires were administered to librarians and users (faculty members and students) to understand the usage pattern of the Internet and the web-based library services that are expected. The questionnaire was designed to be quick and easy to complete. Among others, the questionnaire specifically contained questions on

- Availability of institute website
- Extent of library information on the website
- Regular use of the Internet by the users
- Frequency of visit to the institute website
- Web OPAC availability
- Library transactions wished to be carried out using the Web.

The questionnaire was piloted with few select management institutes and users and their comments were incorporated into the final version. For better results, questionnaire method was also followed by paying personal visits to the library so that the researchers can discuss with the librarian and users at the institutes.

Out of 24 management institutes, 22 institutes responded to the survey by returning the questionnaire, thus resulting into a response rate of 91.66%. The collected data has been duly analyzed and presented below.

Availability of institutes' websites

Management institutes, new or old, pay particular attention to design and host their own website to showcase and create awareness about their profile.

In this age, having a suitably designed website has become as important as their physical building itself. It is found that all the 22 institutes who have responded to this survey have their own website.

Extent of library information on institutes' websites

Presents data about the extent of information available about library on the institutes' websites. It is observed that almost all management institutes 20(90.91%) have only general information about library on their websites.

Extent of Library Information on Institutes' Websites

Extent of Information on Website/Portal	No. of Management Libraries
General Information	22 (100.00)
Library Rules and Regulations	2 (9.09)
Library Staff Details	0 (0.00)
Current Awareness Service / Selective Dissemination of Information Bulletins	0 (0.00)
OPAC	0 (0.00)
Any Other	0 (0.00)

Regular use of the Internet by users

Faculty members and students were asked about their Internet usage. Table mentions that an overwhelming number of faculty members 52(86.67%) and 175(92.11%) students have indicated the use of the Internet on a regular basis.

Regular Use of Internet

Regular use of Internet	Faculty Members	Students	Total
Yes	52 (86.67)	175 (92.10)	227 (90.80)
No	6 (10.00)	14 (7.37)	20 (8.00)
Not sure	2 (3.33)	1 (0.53)	3 (1.20)
Total	60 (100.00)	190 (100.00)	250 (100.00)

It is also observed that 6(10.00%) faculty members and 14(7.37%) students indicated that they do not use the Internet regularly. A negligible 2(3.33%) faculty members and 1(0.53%) student are not sure about their Internet usage habit.

Frequency of visit to institutes' websites

As an Institute Website/Portal is an access point for all resources and services, it is necessary to know the frequency of users' visit to the website. Table records the data about it.

Frequency of Visit to Institute's Website

Frequency of Visit to Institute's website	Faculty Members	Students	Total
Daily	7 (13.46)	19 (10.86)	26 (11.45)
Weekly	9 (17.30)	35 (20.00)	44(19.39)
Fortnightly	18 (34.62)	60 (34.28)	78 (34.36)
Monthly	18 (34.62)	61 (34.86)	79(34.80)
Not at all	00.00	00.00	00.00
Total	52(100.00)	175 (100.00)	227(100.00)

It is observed that about 7(13.46%) faculty members and 19(10.86%) students visit their institutes' websites daily. Nine (17.30%) faculty members and 35(20.00%) students prefer to visit weekly and about 18(34.62%) faculty members and 60(34.28%) students visit the website fortnightly. About 18 (34.62%) of faculty members and 61 (34.8%6) of students visit the website on a monthly basis.

The poor number of visits that the institute website receives is because not all institutes give any dynamic and useful information on the website. These websites contain some static information about history of the institute, faculty profile and some description about resource units like library and computer lab.

Web OPAC Availability: Online public access catalogue (OPAC), when made available on the Web is called Web OPAC. Information may be available in any media; it is the catalogue that ensures maximum exposure and subsequent use of information sources. Web OPAC's have provision of boolean operators.

While searching library collection using OPAC, we can use operators like AND, OR, NOT and make our query more specific. Web OPAC's also provide facilities like personalized onscreen display, save options, etc. It is surprising to know that none of the management libraries surveyed has its catalogue available on the Web.

Library Transactions and the Internet

Users were asked for an explanation as to what are the library transactions they wish to carry out at their convenience through the Internet. The observations are given in the table. About 40(66.67%) faculty members and 140(73.68%) students indicated that they wish to search books'. database.

Thirty five (58.33%) faculty members and 116(61.05%) students indicated they wish to know the availability of a particular document. About 47(78.33%) faculty members and 158(83.16%) students, highest number of users, wish to do a refined search of books, using all possible approaches.

Over 33(55%) faculty members and 140(73.68%) students indicated that they wish to reserve a book while 38 (63.33%) faculty members and 123 (64.74%) students indicated that they wish to access current awareness bulletins.

Library Transactions Wished to Be Carried Out Using the Internet

Category	Faculty Members	Students
To search the books database	40 (66.67)	140 (73.68)
To know the availability of a particular document	35 (58.33)	116 (61.05)
To search books using all approaches	47 (78.33)	158 (83.16)
To reserve a book	33 (55.00)	140 (73.68)
To access Current Awareness Bulletins	38 (63.33)	123 (64.74)
To pay library dues	11 (18.33)	54 (28.42)
To pay for fee based library services, if any	11 (18.33)	63 (33.16)
To know more about services rendered by library	41 (68.33)	150 (78.95)

About 41(68.33%) faculty members and 150(78.95%) would access the website to know more about services rendered by library. Relatively low preferences were given to activities like to pay library dues; to pay for fee based library services, if any. A close scrutiny and comparison of responses reveals that faculty members and students agree with each other on what transactions they wish to carry out using the Internet.

FINDINGS

- All the management institutes have their own website. However, the institutes' websites make a cursory mention of the library as a resource unit and provide only general information about library. Very insignificant number 2(9.09%) of libraries have provided library rules and regulations on the website. Important details like library staff details, Current Awareness Bulletins/ Selective Dissemination of Information (CAS/SDI) bulletins and OPAC is not made available on any institute website. Observations form table confirm the first hypotheses that the institutes have failed in attracting the library users to their websites as they provide only static information about library and its services.
- The majority of faculty members 52 (86.67%) and students 175 (92.10%) use the Internet on a regular basis. Observations from table confirm the second hypotheses that the majority of the users in management institutes use the Internet on a regular basis.
- In spite of the majority of users being regular users of the Internet, most of them do not visit institute website regularly. Their visits are scattered and range from daily to monthly.
- It was observed that users wish to carry out library transactions like searching for a document with all possible approaches, reservation, access library bulletins, pay for library dues and to know more about library resources and services. Observations from table confirm the third hypotheses that most of transactions users do at the library should be carried out through the Internet at their convenience.

Suggestions

The survey and the subsequent analysis of the data and the findings of the study have enabled the researchers to provide some practical suggestions about starting and improving the web-based services expected from management libraries.

The main suggestions for improvements are as follows:

- Websites should be developed into a more informative portal with detailed information like staff details with contact information, library bulletins like new additions, CAS and SDI bulletins, etc.
- Libraries should make the portal interactive by hosting the Web OPAC, announcements about new library resources and services, links to the websites of interest to the business and management studies.
- Library portal should provide a facility for users to access library databases and put a claim for document reservation.
- Every effort should be made on a consistent basis to update the library portal frequently. This will certainly entice users to library portal and then to the library resources and services.

Conclusion

Developments in information and communication technologies (ICT) have a profound impact on every sphere of academic activity. Library and information management is not an exception for this. Business and management libraries have so far not adapted the innovations of Internet and networking to the fullest extent. Earlier, card catalogue was called as the "*Mirror to the Library*". Now in this age of the Internet, it is the library portal that is being called as the "*Mirror of the Library*". Library portal reflects the strengths and weaknesses of the libraries very effectively. They are also the tool through which libraries are trying to reach out to the tech-savvy user. Libraries should make consistent efforts to provide web-based services to their users. The survey has revealed that management libraries in Mumbai city are lagging behind in exploiting the full potential of the library portal. It is hoped that libraries at the management institutes will attend to this lacunae by developing a fully functional web portal as soon as possible.

INFORMATION SEEKING STRATEGIES

Trends in a global information revolution and the spread in networked information and communication technologies (ICTs) around the world call for innovative strategies to promote information sharing across geographically dispersed and culturally disparate participants in a macro community (Anchan and Halli, 2003). Such efforts need to reflect social equity and global equality in representation and acknowledge the perspectives of under-represented cultural constituents in the contemporary globally intertwined environment (Castells and Himanen, 2003).

This is important to promote interconnectedness and interdependence and to project a more eco-centric (instead of an egocentric) world view in today's civil society (Mehra and Bishop, 2007). An eco-centric point of view will help develop cross-cultural bridges, facilitate information sharing, and build mutual trust and cross-cultural communication that may realize a shared dream of peaceful co-existence and reciprocal understanding (Hutton, 2003). In academic environments, building cross-cultural bridges begins with developing understanding of individuals of varied cultures and backgrounds, such as international students whose educational backgrounds and experiences may be totally alien to the normative American academic environments (Mehra and Papajohn, 2007).

Prior research shows that international students, particularly those from Asian countries, experience difficulties while in the United States in the areas of language barriers, academic performance, social adjustment, and adjustment to support services (Huntley, 1993). Many universities and colleges are making efforts to recognize the needs of international students and to internationalize their curricula and campuses to provide students with exposure to diversity (Hawkins and Haro, 1998). Current trends show that the United States remains the world leader in international student enrolment, hosting 565,039 international students in 2004-2005 and reaching nearly a quarter of all international students worldwide (UNESCO, 2006).

The University of Tennessee (UT) Fact Book, 2005-2006 (http://oira.tennessee.edu/factbook/) reports 1,146 international students (879 full-time and 267 part-time, 257 undergraduate and 889 graduate/professional) representing 4.028% in a total of 28,457 students on campus. Asian students represent a large proportion of international students at UT with China (301), India (187), South Korea (123), Canada (41), and Taiwan (38) as the five countries with highest student enrolment. UT recognizes the need to increase recruitment efforts to enroll and retain international students in order to compete with American universities and colleges.

UT's "Ready for the World: The International and Intercultural Awareness Initiative" (http://www.utk.edu/readyfortheworld/) is part of a long-term plan to transform the campus to a culture that appreciates and engages with diversity to effectively prepare students for a globalized workforce in the 21 st century via internationalizing the curriculum, developing global competency of faculty and staff, and concentrating on intercultural issues of specific concern to the university. Understanding the experiences of international students, especially in relation to information seeking strategies and information behaviours will provide reliable and valid datasets that are low-cost, authentic, and trustworthy towards pursuing the UT Ready for the World objectives. Institutional goals towards diversifying the student body and integrating multicultural academic curricula in American universities posits many questions about our understanding of how international students of varied cultures and backgrounds seek information and how they perceive their information needs and information seeking strategies. This study explored the information needs and information seeking strategies of ten Asian graduate students and assessed their experiences in using various ICTs to meet their needs during their academic study at UT.

RELEVANT LITERATURE

Existing literature on information seeking of international students has focused on adjustments to the American culture (Arthur, 2004), learning English as a second language (Liu, 1995), feelings of isolation (Hong, Fox, and Almarza, 2007), integration into the mainstream campus life (Andrade, 2006-2007), and on issues and challenges both inside and outside the classroom (Kwasi and Aman, 1998). A literature review on international students' experiences reveals a few studies relating to library use (Mehra, 2005a; Curry and Copeman, 2005; Liu and Redfern 1997).

Findings in these studies identified similarities and differences between native and non-native English-speaking students in terms of use of academic libraries. Unlike American students, non-native speakers experienced library anxiety, language/communications barriers, and problems adjusting to both the American educational and library system (Onwuegbuzie and Jiao, 1997; Conteh-Morgan, 2002). International students also faced many ICT challenges such as use of web search engines, online databases, and online catalogues (Badke, 2002).

Another study of incoming international students explored the students' library and computer experience (Jackson, 2005). Based on the findings, the author suggested that libraries offer specialized information competency and computer orientation programmes for the students. In fact, information literacy instruction has been shown to reduce the state of library anxiety among international students when given an assignment using library resources (Jiao and Onwuegbuzie, 2001; Battle, 2004). Additionally, information literacy programmes such as summer courses, special seminars, and mentoring and systematic instruction may prove significant in helping international students integrate information literacy skills into the research process in the American university (Korolev, 2001).

An important model for library skills training for international students proposes mapping the Association of College and Research Libraries (ACRL) Information Literacy Competency Standards with specific communication, educational, and cultural adjustments that international students experience when studying in the United States (Baron and Strout-Dapaz, 2001). For example, the Helping Hand Project, a collaborative effort between Oregon State University and the International Cultural Services Programme, translated a two-page handout about library services into fourteen different languages to acquaint non-native English speakers with these services in a language they understand. Such efforts help to lessen language barriers for international students during their initial library use and may contribute to their retention in academic institutions (Chau, 2002-2003).

Library use strategies have focused on definite areas of application, such as teaching bibliographic instruction to improve international students' performance in writing research papers (Tao, 2005; Abdullah, 2000). A quantitative study on the information seeking behaviours of international students employed a web-based anonymous survey to compare American and international graduate students' information needs, general information searching patterns, and participation in library activities. In addition, it examined the relationships between English language proficiency and both length of stay in the United States and information seeking behaviours (Liao, Finn, and Lu, 2005). Findings showed that language, culture communication, and technology barriers to international students' access to libraries plummeted with length of stay. Students used various web-based searching tools and resources as often as their American counterparts due in part to the effective role academic libraries played in educating international students in library use. The authors made recommendations for improving education about library services and information literacy skills.

Most existing research employed quantitative methods. While valuable, these methods do not provide a deep understanding of the complex nuances of the experience of cross-cultural students such as those from Asian countries, especially in relation to how they interact with library and information systems that are alien to them (Mehra, 2005b). Research that employes qualitative and quantitative approaches is needed to obtain a rich data for constructing a holistic and rich view of international students' perceptions, needs, and experiences. How do international students interact with various ICTs for academic work? What problems do international students experience in interacting with these ICTs? What influence, if any, do the educational processes in international students' home countries have on their study in the United States?

How do international students perceive their research skills and information needs? Specific deficiencies found in prior studies make this study relevant in the context of new trends in the contemporary global information society. For example, most research on international students addressed the cross-cultural learners in terms of a "deficit" model that treats their experiences solely in terms of problems and needs, and suggested solutions to improve the effectiveness of the learners' interactions with library and information systems without gaining understanding of their perspectives in the mode of analysis.

This is due to the fact that only quantitative methods were applied. Recent literature that employed surveys with open-ended questions has begun to offer more in-depth detail about the experiences of international students (Organization for Economic Cooperation and Development, 2006).

This study employed qualitative interviews to generate data that provides a rich view for constructing a profile of international students' information needs, research processes, and use of ICTs based on their day-to-day experiences and perceptions.

Results gained from this study will have implications for designing information literacy skills programmes, cross-cultural system interfaces, and services that are highly supportive of international students.

Research Questions

This study addressed the following research questions.

1. What are the information needs of Asian graduate students in the United States?
2. How do Asian graduate students perceive their information seeking strategies in using ICTs, such as web search engines and the Internet?
3. How do international students perceive their information seeking strategies in using ICTs offered by the academic library, such as library's website, OPAC, and online databases?
4. How do international students' educational experiences in their home countries influence their perceptions of information seeking strategies in the United States?

Methodology

This study employed both quantitative and qualitative research methods. Documenting the perceptions and experiences of Asian graduate students was grounded in critical theory, which recognizes perspectives of all stakeholders in a particular situation (Habermas, 1993). This includes points of view of the under-represented in order to "do justice to a diversity of socially defined perspectives while providing grounding for the evaluation of controversial problems" (Endres, 1996, #24). The application of critical theory becomes a methodological strategy to represent global diversity and facilitate cross-cultural exchange.

Participants: Ten Asian graduate students participated in this study. They were recruited via institutional contacts at the UT's Centre for International Education, through announcements in various electronic mailing lists and at popular student places (coffee shops, library), and through personal social networks and snowballing (asking initial participants to provide contact to other subjects who may participate in the study).

Instruments: Two instruments developed by the researchers were used for data collection: 1. an open-ended interview questionnaire that elicited qualitative data about the participants' use of ICTs, information seeking strategies, information needs, and the barriers and challenges they experienced during their academic study; and 2. a structured survey instrument that gathered demographic data about the participants' gender, age, length of stay in the United States, area of study, priority information needs, and the barriers and challenges they experienced in using ICTs to meet their needs.

Procedures: The data were collected in summer 2006 and spanned over ten days during the month of July. Each participant met with one of the researchers and was introduced to the purposes of the study and was asked to sign a consent form. Each interview took 60 to 90 minutes during which two data sets were collected, one set was generated from the open-ended interview questionnaire, and one set was gathered from the structured survey instrument. Both the researcher and a trained graduate teaching assistant in information sciences transcribed the participants' responses on the open-ended interview questionnaire. The participants completed the structured survey instrument. A monetary incentive was given to each participant as a token of appreciation for his/her efforts.

Data Analysis: Data were analyzed using grounded theory principles to generate themes and patterns from the participants' responses via open, axial, and selective coding that accounted for concepts and relationships between categories and subcategories within the context of interview questions (Glaser and Strauss, 1967). Findings were verified and analyzed based on a triangulation and cross-referencing of data that were collected from the two instruments. The broader perspectives of the participants were collectively threaded together as a mode of data analysis and representation. In addition, descriptive statistics generated from the structured survey instrument provided quantitative assessment of the participants' cross-cultural experiences (Mehra and Bilal, in press).

Findings

The findings in this study are reported within the context of the research questions posed. To gather background information about the participants, we asked them to provide demographic information in relation to different variables, such as age, length of stay, gender, area of study, and country of origin. The section below describes the participants' demographic information.

Participant Demographics: Five males and five females participated in this study. The youngest participant was 22 years old and the oldest was 39 years old. Three participants had been in the U.S. for nearly one year, four for one year, and three for two years. Fifty percent were majoring in electrical engineering, with one participant in each of the following disciplines: information sciences, management science, plant biotechnology, speech pathology, and child/family studies. Four participants were from China, three from India, and three from Taiwan.

Information Needs of Asian Students: Asian students were asked to articulate and rank their information needs. These needs were consolidated into eleven categories. These needs were ranked from highest to lowest as follows by the participants: 1. details about academic programmes and processes (*e.g.*, course information, stages of progress and how to fulfil requirements during various stages), 2. local information to facilitate day-to-day living (*e.g.*, grocery shopping, directions), 3. opportunities to experience American cultures and customs (*e.g.*, etiquette and norms of behaviour, lifestyle issues), 4. awareness of the American research processes and expectations (*e.g.*, how to conduct research, role of faculty in research), 5. international rules and immigration regulations (*e.g.*, visa requirements and time deadlines for special permissions), 6. language learning and conversational use (*e.g.*, classes to improve language skills), 7. career and professional development information (*e.g.*, financial aid opportunities), 8. familiarity with library services (*e.g.*, online databases), 9. awareness of additional support services and resources (*e.g.*, housing, health-related), 10. travel and leisure information (*e.g.*, recreational facilities and vacation planning), and 11. support in using computers and Internet facilities (*e.g.*, user accounts and user support services).

Information Needs and Recommendations for Meeting the Needs

Information Seeking Strategies in Using ICTs (Web Search Engines and the Internet): Table identifies and ranks key barriers and challenges the participants reported in using various ICTs (web search engines and the Internet). Ranked from highest to lowest, these barriers and challenges included: 1. lack of availability of multiple language interfaces, 2. poor searching skills, and limited vocabulary in the English language, 3. lack of critical reflection to become effective information consumers, 4. information clutter and low relevance of retrieved results, 5. distractive and time consuming search process, 6. unfriendliness of interfaces, 7. limited flexibility in search variation mechanisms, and.8. low speed access and limited computer availability. The participants perceived the web as a great resource for establishing connections with individuals and agencies in the United States before their arrival on campus. For example, three participants stated that securing housing at UT using the web and bulletin boards that were available in their native language (*e.g.*, Mandarin) had helped them meet UT students online who became their initial hosts upon arrival to the University.

Barriers and Challenges in Using ICTs (Web Search Engines and the Internet)

Information Seeking Strategies in Using ICTs in the Library: The participants felt moderately successful in using ICTs offered by UT main library (*e.g.*, library website, OPAC, and online databases). However, they faced barriers and challenges in using these ICTs effectively. The participants ranked these barriers and challenges, from highest to lowest as follows: 1. limited searching skills, 2. poor search functionalities of the interfaces, 3. unfriendly technology support, 4. limited relevant search results, 5. limited electronic journals and full-text, and 6. cultural and psychological problems.

All the participants expressed initial hesitancy and fear to speak with the librarian due to cultural factors. Seven participants expressed unfamiliarity and limited use of large-scale library systems and services in their home countries such as the one at UT main campus. Three participants felt intimidated asking a librarian for assistance and preferred to communicate via email reference instead of face-to-face interactions. Over fifty-percent reported using various kinds of library systems and services on their own even when they experience difficulty finding the information sought. In fact, self-efficacy and motivation were the driving forces in pursuing their information needs. The participants appreciated interlibrary loan services and the availability of library carrels and graduate study booths, which they used as personal spaces for academic study.

Barriers and Challenges in Using ICTs in the Library Prior Educational Experience and Information Seeking Strategies The participants were asked about the educational system in their home countries, information seeking behaviours and research processes and how they varied from those at UT. They reported differences in relation to: 1. role of faculty, 2. role of the library, 3. technology use, 4. research process, and 5. educational process. These are described below.

Role of Faculty: In the participants' home countries, faculty played a more significant role in describing, detailing, and explaining nuances of the research process in introductory courses in their field of study in their home countries, as compared to the United States. For example, three participants from India reported that faculty initiated the students' research process beyond identifying the research problem, offered lists of articles as a starting point, and worked with students continuously over the course of an academic year to ensure adequate progress. Conversely, in the United States, professors did not give as much initial help. The participants believed that this could be due to the level of the degree (graduate vs. undergraduate) rather than the educational process.

Role of the Library: All participants reported that the library did not play as instrumental role in supporting the research process in their home countries as it did in the United States. For example, lack of interlibrary loan programmes in home countries caused hardship because the participants had to physically visit the library holding an item of interest. Additional differences were: a. less frequent computer use and technology-related opportunities (*e.g.*, availability of fewer databases), b. lack of systematic training in using ICTs and library services for research, c. smaller collections and limited access to books (non-circulating collections), d. less friendly library staff, e. availability of interfaces in native languages, and f. limited use of the Internet.

Technology Use: The level of technology use in support of finding information for research purposes also varied between the participants' experiences in their home countries and the United States. Some differences included: a. slower and less effective online searching systems, b. less Internet-based research, c. less online availability of current research journals on different topics, d. limited access to computers, e. limited specialized databases, and f. limited technical and user support services.

Research Process: The participants noted similarities in the research process undertaken in their home countries and the United States. This was in relation to the large amount of time spent on searching and finding information. Their expected outcomes of the research process were also similar, especially in terms of finding relevant information that met their needs. Differences in the research process included a focus on using journal articles in the United States, as opposed to emphasis on class notes and textbooks. Since they had limited access to various ICTs in their home countries, the participants noted that information literacy skills such as searching online systems were not as critical as they were in the United States.

Educational Process: The main difference that influenced the participants' academic experiences concerned a lack of exposure to the semester-based academic programme. In their home countries, an academic programme spanned over nine months and the participants took only one final examination at the end of the programme. Under the semester-based system, the participants felt pressured and stressed out due to the cumulative work they had to achieve every semester. In order to cope with this new reality, the participants had to adjust their mental models to the new educational processes and seek help from peers, especially those from their own home countries and who had been in the same programme of study.

Discussion

This study revealed key aspects of the participants' information seeking strategies, information needs, and use of various ICTs. The participants needed greater support and guidance during their academic programme, from selecting courses to using information throughout the programme of study. This suggests that academic departments make efforts to communicate clear guidelines for academic advising. The participants experienced difficulty in conducting research due to limited familiarity with the research process, cultural differences, and lack of efforts on the part of faculty to establish a clear understanding of the process.

This implies that faculty needs to develop empathy for international students and recognize that they may need more assistance than their American counterparts. Similarly, library staff should make extra efforts to provide specialized training programmes for international students about the research process and how to use ICTs and library services. The participants reported that they often found information of interest by chance about local activities, events, directions, and resources.

These provided them with significant knowledge about daily life. They suggested dissemination of local information (*e.g.*, grocery store locations, entertainment venues such as cinema halls, and bus schedules) at various popular student meeting places (*e.g.*, coffee shops, library, sports facility) for awareness. Indeed, the UT International Student Association, the International House, and campus support units should provide such information online and across the campus.

Learning how to effectively communicate in the English language was critical to the participants. To enhance their language skills, they sought classes hosted by UT and participated in study groups, practice sessions, and role play experiences where students enacted different typical real-life situations such as visiting a restaurant, meeting a friend in a public place, and giving directions. They needed critical and frank assessment of their language speaking skills from academic advisors, peers, and friends, though most of them experienced situations where they did not obtain forthright opinions about this matter. The participants suggested a mentoring programme of international and American students to help them acclimatize to the new culturally-alien information environment, and to orchestrate as many formal and informal interactions with students of various cultures and backgrounds.

Career and professional development goals necessitated seeking financial aids to support their education. They sought opportunities for gaining professional skills that would assist them in their future careers. The participants lacked an adequate level of knowledge of how to find financial support and suggested that such information be available in their academic departments and through their advisors and other faculty members. The participants had limited awareness of the location of computer facilities, hours of operation, and how to benefit from existing computer services that support their cross-cultural and academic learning processes.

In addition, they experienced problems seeking information on campus support services such as housing, health-related services, counseling, and other benefits offered to students at UT. This suggests more effective dissemination strategies about support services available for international students, especially during admission to academic programmes and arrival on campus. The barriers and challenges the participants experienced in using various ICTs provide several directions for both training and system design improvement. In terms of training, library information professionals should provide information materials in various languages, especially in those that are spoken by most of the international student community on campus. In addition, they should establish outreach programmes with academic advisors in various departments to build awareness about library services available for international students.

Repeatedly, international students mentioned difficulty in using digital interfaces mainly due to their inadequate level of English language skills. Searching, browsing the hierarchical structure of web directories, understating the relationships between broad, narrow, and related terms, among others, were confusing to them. In addition, recalling keywords from limited vocabulary, and formulating effective search strategies surfaced as major problems.

The participants called for web-based systems that allow natural language searching and that provide interfaces in multiple languages. The participants used Google, Yahoo, and specialized search engines and websites. Apparently, they lacked awareness of the multiple language interfaces provided by Google and foreign language resources available on the web. It is unclear whether the language factor and/or whether the design of the interfaces they used impacted their information seeking strategies. Although the web is global in nature, the representation of information is based on western and European models of aesthetic and cultural values that limit its effective use by cross-cultural users around the world (Becker and Mottay, 2001).

Conclusions

Today's global information society presents opportunities and challenges in establishing intercultural awareness and appreciation of diversity. Documentation of international students' experiences and perceptions of their information needs, information seeking strategies, ICT use, and library and support services unveiled several problem areas faced by the students. Improving the quality of international students' experiences requires manifold efforts on the part of faculty, academic advisors, international student advisors, library staff, technology support staff, policy makers and administrators, and designers of web interfaces to provide appropriate and culturally-sensitive intervention programmes to identify and meet the information needs of international students.

This study investigated Asian graduate students' perceptions and experiences in using various ICTs. Additional data is being analyzed and will be reported in future research. Use of qualitative research methods provided a rich and holistic understanding of the complex reality of cross-cultural education and learning that international students encountered in the United States.

While valuable, the results of this study may not be generalized to the whole population of Asian students or the whole population of international students. Additional research that captures international students' naturalistic information seeking behaviours, and usability studies that assess the students' interaction with various ICTs are needed. Qualitative research is highly recommended to obtain deeper understanding of the experiences of international students. Future studies should include international students from different countries who are pursuing higher education at many other universities in the United States.

5

Information Literacy: Search Strategies, Tools and Resources

In the current Information Age, the speed at which we work makes us increasingly dependent on high-quality, accurate information. However, information is becoming more voluminous, fragmented into different formats and media, and duplicated in multiple physical locations. In order to access and use these myriad sources effectively, people must be information literate.

As defined by the American Library Association (ALA) in its mission statement for the global information society, 21st century information literacy is the ability to seek and effectively utilize information resources, including knowledge of how to use technologies and the forms in which information is stored (ALA, 1998). This means that asking a good question, as well as accessing, locating, evaluating, and using information, is critical not only in scholarly activities but in making daily decisions.

Having accurate, up-to-date information determines the difference between the rich and the poor in the Information Age. Community colleges can make a vital contribution toward closing this gap by equipping their students with the ability to access, retrieve, and utilize information.

As we strive to understand information literacy issues in a more holistic manner, the Information Literacy: Search Strategies, Tools & Resources (ST&R) Programme developed by Ercegovac (1997a) can provide invaluable guidance in a variety of information literacy environments. This Digest briefly describes challenges facing information literacy development as well as ST&R and its usefulness to community college faculty and students.

Information Technology

The growth of computer networks and information services has already enabled learners at all levels to share resources, collaborate with one another, and publish their results electronically. To use information sources effectively, we need both technology infrastructure (TI) and information literacy infrastructure (ILI) in place. While TI has been well-funded and developed, ILI is poorly applied in teaching and learning, and requires educators' attention.

Information technology is a tool for writing papers, communicating with colleagues worldwide, and exchanging experiments, ideas, and programmes internationally. As community colleges are considering distance learning and adding new technologies to their curriculum, ensuring students' information literacy becomes vital. However, this shift may challenge existing campus dynamics.

A Current Challenge

The proliferation of information sources and educational technology have created a dysfunctional relationship between community college faculty and librarians that is based on an outdated teaching/learning paradigm (Tompkins, 1996). Traditionally, teaching has been the purview of faculty while librarians were viewed as merely custodians of printed information resources. In the current Information Age however, librarians have become the primary instructors in community colleges to teach research methods and critical thinking skills as applied to information access (Academic Senate for California Community Colleges, 1996). As such, there is increasing support for community college librarians to be seen as key instructional team members and as partners with faculty (Tompkins, 1996; McHenry, Stewart & Wu, 1992).

Especially as libraries are transformed into integrated library/high technology centres, resource-based learning (*i.e.*, drawing on resources beyond textbooks and lectures) and information literacy can be adopted as goals across academic disciplines. At Central Seattle Community College, for example, faculty linked an English composition course with one in library science to teach students how to use information literacy skills in the context of cultural pluralism (McHenry, Stewart & Wu, 1992). By working together, librarians and faculty were able to teach content as well as the valuable skill of navigating through complex data bases and information resources.

While faculty may know how to teach English composition or other standard courses, they may not be as comfortable teaching information literacy. Fortunately, an abundance of resources has emerged from sources including the Department of Education (1996), the ERIC Clearinghouse on Information and Technology (Eisenberg & Johnson, 1996) and independent authors (for example see Mendrinos, 1994). These publications state information literacy goals, review literacy tools, provide case studies, and present adaptable models of information literacy curricula.

The Star Programme

One recently developed aid is the Information Literacy: Search Strategies, Tools & Resources (ST&R) Programme that can be tailored to the local needs of colleges. It is comprised of three integrated instructional components: the ST&R book, a PowerPoint presentation for classroom use, and an HTML version of the book for installation on institutional servers.

Implemented at the intersection of learners and Web-ready information resources, ST&R can initiate students to the world of information literacy. It is a comprehensive and flexible tool that has been developed to enable students to become self-sustained seekers and users of information sources and digital libraries. This can be especially useful in the community colleges where many students are from disadvantaged or lower socioeconomic backgrounds and previously may not have had access to such sources.

The programme has been designed for anyone interested in the critical and effective use of all types of information sources regardless of their format (*e.g.*, books, journal articles, manuscripts, log diaries, visual elements, and other artifacts) and medium (*e.g.*, printed, electronic, and networked digital libraries). ST&R takes a user-centred perspective and focuses on the intellectual aspects of locating, evaluating, interpreting, and communicating information sources rather than on the technical aspects of these activities.

Furthermore, ST&R is comprehensive because it contains references to a variety of sources and digital repositories, introduces effective search strategies and tools for the use of these sources, and covers critical evaluation of these sources. In this one-stop "literacy mall," ST&R also offers exercises, a glossary of introduced terms and concepts, and Internet addresses of numerous sources available on the Web. In particular, the electronic version of ST&R allows students to connect automatically with Internet addresses and explore various search engines in an orderly and guided manner. Instructors are equipped with the "ST&R Show," based on the Microsoft PowerPoint 97 presentation programme, that features links to selected Internet digital libraries and resources.

The ST&R Programme also is flexible because its content is divided into a series of nine interrelated yet independent chapters. Students can expand each chapter by doing more exercises and searches, tracking new Web addresses, updating the existing ones, and developing their own portfolio of annotated information sources.

This programme is the first attempt to translate research from the fields of information seeking, information retrieval, and educational psychology into a practical information literacy programme. It can be utilized in a variety of academic settings including libraries, media centres, and classrooms. In addition, different academic departments may wish to incorporate individual parts of ST&R into their curricula to fit their own information literacy mission, students, and collections. Also, the programme is scalable to the different academic abilities of community college students.

In summary, ST&R represents an accumulation of over 10 years of teaching, in-class testing with undergraduates at the University of California, Los Angeles, and feedback from real learners and users. It is based on understanding the user, active learning, a conceptual approach in teaching, and modularity (Ercegovac, 1995; 1997b). While the programme is a very practical information literacy tool, it also is based on solid research and conceptual foundations. For example, it recognizes the importance of the information life cycle (*e.g.*, information need, search and interpretation, evaluation, and use) as well as the user (National Academy of Sciences, 1998).

Conclusion

In this Information Age, we browse and query the world's repositories without ever having to leave our workplaces and communities. Thus, it is not surprising that the traditional sense of a library as a confined space with local dimensions has introduced ambiguities to the way people interpret library collections and uses. As a result, the value of a library as a store has been questioned, and the library's role as a service is largely misunderstood.

Another concern is the ease with which untrained users can directly search sources, resulting in their continued difficulty with utilizing information retrieval systems. Furthermore, definitions of access and information are not agreed upon universally.

All these changes have created the need to rethink information literacy and to educate students in the lifelong quest for knowledge. ST&R helps in this regard.

NON-LINEAR INFORMATION RETRIEVAL SEARCH STRATEGIES FOR USERS

Humans think associatively. Yet information retrieval tools in library and information centres are linear, such as Online Access Catalogue systems (OPACs), online and electronic databases. There is an urgent need for associational retrieval tools which would be more suitable for the thinking processes of the mind.

As a non-linear linking device, or as a communication tool, a hypermedia search tool can be used as a search strategy formulation guide in library and information centres. At the heart of reference service is the search strategy—it should be possible to design an information mapping device to basic reference tools, in addition to providing an excellent reference service. There are various expert systems and hypertext packages for specific information packages (*e.g.*, Thomas, 1990;

Garrison, 1989; and Vickery and Brooks, 1987. It should also be possible to design one for t whole host of key reference sources. The unfolding of information sources along the path of a search strategy would be a potentially powerful device.

From a cognitive point of view, such a device would be desirable. Daniels points out that human interaction with information systems ought to be viewed "as an adaptive, cognitive system, in order for effective interfaces and even whole systems to be designed." (1986; 273) Such information retrieval systems could include reference tools in library and information centres.

"In traditional text, the model assumes a linear form. Yet the models in the mind are more like networks than lines. Would a medium not be more powerful were it to allow the representation of networks directly? Hypertext is a new medium which represents text (and nontext) in networks rather than in lines." (Rada, 1991)

Hypermedia, a non-linear linking device, can be used as a search strategy formulation tool in libraries/information centres. But before the application of non-linear technology to information retrieval in libraries we need to develop theories on users interaction with information systems.

At present, there is a paucity of search strategy theories for users, even in the use of linear retrieval systems. Such a dynamic search strategy needs to be designed or an existing one adapted. This paper proposes that as a starting point we can consider the one developed by Gerald Jahoda and Judith Schiek Braunagel in *The Librarian and Reference Queries: A Systematic Approach* (1980). Although the search strategies developed in their text is mainly for training new reference librarians, it can be argued that a hypermedia version of such a search strategy would also be useful in guiding new users. An important dimension of Jahoda and Braunagel's search strategy is the topology of reference questions. Is it possible that a user's reference queries can be categorized into a neat topology as follows?

On the other hand, answer-providing tools can be listed in twelve categories (Jahoda & Braunagel, 1980): Users will be responsible for selecting their "message categories" based on each query; as well as information source categories. Tutorial packages could be built into the system to assist users in developing skills in this very crucial task. It goes without saying that some of these categories in both of the above lists have to be spelled out in terms more meaningful for the user.

The terminology used by Jahoda and Braunagel can be summarized as follows: "We characterized the message of each query as the subject of the query, the given, and the information needed about the subject, the wanted. Next, the specific message words used by the requestor in a query have been translated into generic tags called given and wanted descriptors. Each query can be divided into these components." (Jahoda & Braunagel, 1980, p. 14)

They admit that not all queries may be indexed with the list of descriptors on the checklist (1980; 14). A hypermedia package has to build the necessary bridges between the possible questions (*i.e.*, the checklist of descriptors) and the answer providing tools. Users have to make the initial choice of wanted information, as follows:

ACADEMIC LIBRARIES IN INDIA: A PRESENT-DAY SCENARIO

The Educational System

India has a large higher education system. The growth rate of educational institutions in India was very slow before independence in 1947. Today there are a total of 237 universities, including 116 general universities, 12 science and technology universities, 7 open universities, 33 agricultural universities, 5 women's universities, 1 language universities and 11 medical universities along with 12,600 colleges that provide education in all disciplines. The number of teachers is 3.1 million, and 7.8 million students are enrolled in higher education.

University Grants Commission (UGC)

UGC, established by an act of parliament in 1956, coordinates and monitors the higher education system in India and provides grants to the universities and colleges. Two hundred ninety four universities/institutions in the country are directly under the purview of UGC. It also advises the union and state governments on measures to university education. It frames rules and regulations for overall teaching and research at higher education.

As a result, it also looks after the academic libraries, *i.e.*, sets various standards for library education, library staff, library services, etc. A number of committees have been set up by the UGC for the support of higher education in general and the library services in academic libraries in particular. UGC has also set up three information centres covering different disciplines—the National Centre for Science Information (NCSI) at Indian Institute of Science Bangalore, SNDT Women's University Mumbai, and National Social Science Information Centre at M.S. University at Baroda, to provide the document delivery services to students, teachers, and researchers.

Information and Library Network (INFLIBNET)

The University Grants Commission has set up an autonomous Inter-University Centre in 1991 called INFLIBNET. It is involved in modernizing university libraries in India and connects them through a nation-wide high-speed data network. It promotes automation of libraries, develops standards, creates union catalogues of serials, theses, books, monographs and non-book materials; provides access to bibliographic information sources; creates database of projects, institutions, specialists; provides training, etc. Almost all academic libraries, especially university libraries, are members of INFLIBNET. It has also developed library automation software called SOUL (Software for University Libraries) and has distributed the same free of cost to its member libraries.

Other Networks

Besides INFLIBNET, a number of other national networks and various library networks have also been developed including NICNET (National Informatic Center's network), INDONET, ERNET (Education and Research Network), CALIBNET (Calcutta Library Network), DELNET(Developing Library

Network), etc. ADINET is associated with INFLIBNET, DELNET with NIC and MALIBNET with CFTRI. A number of educational institutions are members of such networks. These networks, especially DELNET (which has 752 member libraries including 742 from India and 10 from outside), are engaged in compiling union catalogues, creating various databases of experts, providing training to library staff, ILL, online facilities, reference service, assistance in retrospective conversion, etc.

Library Consortia

Due to a financial crunch and the rising costs of journals, many Indian university and college libraries cannot subscribe to all the required journals and databases. To overcome this problem, libraries are forming consortia. Some special libraries and organizations like the Indian Institute of Astrophysics (IIA) Library, Inter-university Centre for Astronomy and Astrophysics (IUCAA) Library, National Centre for Radio Astrophysics (NCRA) Library, Physical Research Laboratory (PRL) Library, Raman Research Institute (RRI) Library, Tata Institute of Fundamental Research (TIFR) Library, Council of Scientific and Industrial Research, Department of Atomic Energy, etc., have established consortia to share electronic access to journal literature. NISCAIR (formed by the merger of INSDOC and NISCOM) is developing a consortium for CSIR labs for accessing e-journals.

Consortia in India are still a new concept that requires proper guidelines and methodologies. In a survey by UGC in 2001, it was noted that although 142 university libraries had computer and Internet facilities and were interlinked to INFLIBNET, they were subscribing to printed journals only. In order to solve this problem, UGC launched a major initiative called UGC-INFONET that provides high speed Internet connections so as to have electronic access to professional literature including research journals, abstracts, review publications, and databases from all areas in science and technology, as well as in social sciences and humanities. Today, a number of professional journals are available over UGC-INFONET to all universities. The e-subscription initiative under UGC-Infonet is an important portal for sharing print as well as electronic resources amongst university libraries. INFLIBNET functions as a resource centre with an aim to cater to the needs of its members for resources not accessible to them in electronic media or are available in print media.

INDEST Consortium

The Ministry of Human Resource Development (MHRD) has set up the "Indian National Digital Library in Science and Technology (INDEST) Consortium". The ministry provides funds required for the subscription to electronic resources for 38 academic institutions, including the Indian Institute of Sciences, Indian Institute of Technology, Regional Engineering Colleges, Indian Institute of Managements, and about 60 centrally-funded/ aided government institutions through the consortium. The INDEST consortium is the most ambitious initiative so far in the area of engineering and technology disciplines.

The primary objective of libraries is to organize and provide access to information, and it remains the same although the format and methods have changed drastically. Under the present scenario of declining budgets and higher subscription costs of journals in India, it is becoming very difficult to meet the demands of library/information users. The only solution to the problem is the pooling and sharing of resources—print as well as electronic—by way of consortia. New technology has provided great opportunities for delivery of services within consortia. More and more libraries must unite, which of course requires a change in the attitudes, practices, and policies to get the maximum benefit.

ACADEMIC LIBRARIES IN A DIGITAL AGE

"I don't need the library, it's too big, too complicated, and anyway, everything worth having is on the Internet," the bright eager undergraduate answered the ancient faculty member who recommended using the library.

"Anyway, the library's catalogue is on-line, and I can look at it if I need stuff," she concluded.

"But maybe you'll need one of the real books that they have in the library," the old professor suggested.

"Maybe," she conceded, "but probably not, and anyway, if there's a source on line, I'll always use it before anything in the library."

Conversations like this appear with increasing frequency among academics bridging the generational divides. Students increasingly see the library as mostly irrelevant, while faculty and librarians of a certain age cling to the security of an authoritative collection and familiar classification systems. Brought up on the web and the endless flow of marginally organized information that is CNN, MTV or ESPN—a flow that makes almost no distinction between the important and the trivial, fact and speculation, authority and gossip—students have little patience with the formal organizational structure of the library and the authority of the librarian.

We, whose introduction to libraries preceded the computerized card catalogue and thus truly obsolete dinosaurs of the emerging digital age, live by a hierarchical information model. We think of information as organized and structured taxonomies of sources; we understand the difference between government documents and rare books, between the US history and Latin American history sources, and we expect to find these materials in their appropriate, separately structured locations in our libraries. We think that science and art, business and literature inhabit different information spaces. Educated in a world dominated by the physicality of libraries, from the neighbourhood public libraries to college libraries and the great international research libraries, we think of information as residing in a particular place.

I know about the New York Public Library, the Lilly Library, the Bancroft Library, the Nettie Lee Benson Library, the Library of Congress, and the Bodelian Library. Each one is in my imagination as a physical place with its own personality that tells me what sources I can expect to find within its walls. I have a mental map of each one's physical layout, a memory of its organizational peculiarities and cataloguing quirks. The advent of the computerized card catalogue did not disabuse me of this mental map for these digital artifacts simply reproduced in a more convenient way most of the same information that resided on what now appears charming and quaint library cards. To my students, this recitation is as picturesque, decorative, and ultimately useless as the artifacts scattered about the restaurant chains of America, the washboards and kerosene lanterns, the *Chew Mail Pouch Tobacco* signs, and the other impedimenta of a lost age. They indulge my reminiscence, for after all, I will give them a grade, but I can see in their eyes the same bemused tolerance I gave my grandparents when they talked about the procedure for hand cranking their Model T.

Nonetheless, for all of the digital progress we have seen, this generation and the next (and in universities the time span for generational change is four to six years) will continue to find that libraries remain imposing buildings that house relics of a past age. These library monuments already serve as places to study, places to get online at a computer laboratory, places for the social rituals of female-male bonding that constitute so much of college life. Some students pursuing difficult projects will ask a librarian for help, others will use reserve books forced on them by old fashioned professors, and advanced graduate students may actually recognize the value of the materials collected and managed within their university's physical library.

Yet the activity of the traditional library takes place within uneasy hearing distance of the current trendy mantra anticipating the total digitization of human knowledge, whatever its original form (print, manuscript, picture, sound, or digital representation). The library, we hear, is pretty much over unless it can remake itself into an academic *Yahoo*, an intellectual *Google*, or some other competitive hyper-textualized, multi-threaded, linked, digital resource.

What are librarians to do and what should their universities think? For one thing, we stopped building the buildings. In most universities, this aversion to physical library space began in the mid 1980s at least and grew into a full-blown phobia by the end of the 1990s. Talk to a university president about expanding the library, and you get this conversation.

Laments the librarian, *"We need more library space, the books are filling our existing space and the patrons have no place to sit and study or read. We will be out of space by June two years hence."*

"How much new space do we need?" asks a cautious president.

"Oh," says the librarian with confidence, recounting the results of endless planning committees and design workshops, *"x-zillion square feet at multi-hundred of dollars a square foot. After all, library buildings require good air conditioning, strong foundations, special shelves and lighting, and lots of security."*

"So, this is what, $80 million, $100 million?" asks the president, now fully alert.

"Something on that order," responds the librarian.

"And this new space," the president asks, *"How long will it be adequate for the library's needs?"*

This honest if foolish librarian responds, *"Oh, until the time the building is built and occupied, then we'll need to plan for more space."*

Desperate to exit this conversation, the president asks, *"And how much of the collection housed in this space is used in any one year?"*

"About 1/3," reports the still honest librarian.

Seeing an escape route, the president proposes, *"Let's put the unused 2/3's of the collection in a warehouse and get it when someone wants it. Then we won't need the new space."*

Familiar with the ways of university politics, the librarian admonishes the president, *"Oh, but the faculty won't like it. When they want a book they want it now, and they want to browse the stacks."*

No amateur in university politics either, the president counters, *"OK, I'll take the library building plan to the faculty and ask the following questions and we will see what the faculty think."*

Herewith the questionnaire to the faculty:

"The University has $80 million in construction funds. Which one of the following projects should have the highest priority?

A. The Library at a minimum of $80 million

B. A science building at $30 million

C. A general faculty office building at $20 million

D. A classroom building at $20 million

E. Renovation of our old space at $10 million

F. All of the above except for the Library building"

Recognizing defeat for the moment, the librarian begins planning to expand remote storage. We do not build new library space much anymore unless for computer centres, for computer labs, for classroom and seminar space, or for study halls. The books go into remote storage, the computer catalogue lets us recall them on a 24-hour or better turnaround, and complaints about this policy barely rise to the audible.

Every year I take my students in an advanced history class to the library for a show and tell. You might think they would know where it is and how it works, but in fact, for many, it is new news.

Sure, they know where it is, they have been there to get a reserve book or meet their boyfriend, but the book part of the library is not much relevant to their academic lives. We do the show and tell, and each year it has more and more computer content, more and more computer indices, digitized finding aids, digital representations of journal articles, online access to newspapers, whatever you can imagine.

My librarian friend, who does this for me every year, now brings in at least two physical items. One is a periodical index (bound, real pages, small print, authoritative, structured) and one is a government document of some kind. He does a great job, and when it is over, some of the students come up and look at these physical objects, with the curiosity of the museum visitor. "What quaint things," they seem to say, but out of respect for my white hair, they do not speak these thoughts aloud. They pick the books up and handle them, as you would look at a hand powered wringer washer in the local museum: interested, curious, but not relevant to your daily life.

Then they go on with their work, on-line, on the Internet, each year the density of their digital experiences and abilities greater and greater, and their familiarity with the physical library less and less.

Do they read physical books? Of course they do. They buy and read paperbacks of all kinds, they read the student newspaper, they buy how-to-do-it and self-improvement books. The library, though, that is something else again. It is there, it can be useful, but it is not at the centre of their understanding of knowledge and information.

What then, does this mean for the university library, the academic librarian? Is it the end of the world, as we know it? Is the digital revolution likely to eliminate the art, craft, and science of librarianship? Not likely, but it certainly has and will continue to change it. Fortunately, it is expensive to digitize the world. The rate of change previously limited by bandwidth (the capacity for storing and manipulating digital representations of knowledge) now faces the barriers raised by the cost of converting the old touchable stuff into virtual digital stuff. Politics and power also create their own barriers.

The digital landscape belongs to no one and everyone. Property rights to digital space hardly exist because anyone can create new digital territory. I have a virtual server located somewhere (I'm not sure exactly where). I own two domain names, each one creating completely new digital space. It cost me perhaps $50 to set this up, and I pay about $90 a month to maintain this reasonably sized plot of digital real estate. This space not only belongs exclusively to me, but it came without limiting anyone else's ability to create more digital space. Since digital real estate, unlike the limited physical land I grew up with, is close to being a free good, it complicates the relationships of power and authority, all of which depend on the management of scarcity.

Books and their publishers represent this power and authority. We deliver books to the world within a system that centralizes and controls the distribution of intellectual content on behalf of various powerful groups. We like to think that this is all done in the service of true and unfettered knowledge but of course that is not so. All physical book and journal publishing involves gatekeeper processes that enforce certain standards of content and marketability on the production and distribution of content. Many people and organizations live off this gatekeeper function, the basis of which is the scarcity and high cost of intellectual bandwidth. Paper, printing, binding, distribution, and the rest of the physical process of information production serve to limit the bandwidth for delivering content. Librarians also limit the content available to their clients under the name of collection development (another gatekeeper function) selecting the physically available subset of information accessible to their publics. Much effort, expense, and rationalization goes into this rationing process

The digital imperative changes the structures of cost and power that underlie these transactions. The cost of producing a book on the Internet is close to zero (leaving aside the cost of generating the intellectual content). I put two books on line, both of them out-of-print, both previously produced at considerable expense by reputable houses, sold to tiny audiences, and surely resulted in significant financial losses to the publishers. I put them on line for free, with the exception of the sweat equity of my own work, a minimal investment compared to what it would have taken me to produce these books in physical form. They now live on my digital real estate, they cost me very little to maintain there, and they remain available to anyone at any time for no cost. I am my own gatekeeper.

It is the physicality of the information medium that made possible the rationing, gate keeping, and in the case of for-profit scientific journals, profit gouging that are key characteristics of the paper-based information age. With the dramatic decline in the cost of bandwidth (disk drives, internet access, personal computers, and other forms of digital transmission and storage), the threat to the monopoly of physical media grows exponentially. We only need to look at MP3, Napster, and their offspring to recognize the collapse of old rationing paradigms with their attendant power and authority systems.

So where, in this wonderful new world, is the library? We do not know for sure. Many smart people work overtime to translate traditional library strengths into digital age essential resources. We see the mega catalogue movement in search of the virtual union catalogue. These efforts take the core finding aid of the library and attempt to construct a monster computer searchable file that will contain records for all the media recorded in all the library catalogues of the known universe.

Well, I exaggerate slightly, but not by much. Like most such visions, the critical challenges come from the most mundane of human foibles: territoriality and resistance to common standards. Librarians have many standards, but the wonderful human need to make common things our own causes each library or librarian to modify or use the standard in slightly different ways. These differences, not easily reconciled, create a significant challenge to the implementation of the megavision.

Another effort seeks to digitize unique subsets of the physical assets of libraries or groups of libraries. Rare books, photographs, manuscripts, and similar special collections yield to digitization and publication within the infinitely expanding space of the Internet. These projects leverage the unique physical assets of individual libraries into unique digital assets, thereby preserving the identity and presence of the institution in knowledge space.

Others, observing the rise of the portal boom, seek to transform the library into an information utility for a specific set of customers, usually faculty, students, and staff of the academic institution. With exactly the same purpose as Yahoo and the Microsoft Network, the library portals create a central location where patrons begin their search for the information that their lives require. Successful library portals must compete not only against the commercial portal sites but also against other portals within their own institution for athletic programmes, alumni associations, or the university's own homepage.

Then we have the dynamic and competitive business of electronic library catalogues. I have looked through the sites of many of these companies. They all promise to serve us better, solve our technological problems, and adapt to any changes in the electronic universe. They promise low costs, user friendliness, and the ability to do everything and anything you might want with the catalogue resources of your library, and they announce the capacity to link your systems seamlessly to everything on the net.

How then does a library, in real time and with real money and serving real people, deal with infinite possibilities of the digital age?

The digital world has forced us to think somewhat differently about the value of the library. Once we valued the library for the duplication it could sustain, as represented in the annual ranking of library volumes and acquisition expenditures. These data points told me that the book I wanted that I knew to be in the University of Illinois library was likely to also be in the Bancroft Library. It told me that most of what I had used as a graduate student in New York, I could probably find in the UCLA library. Physical duplication of common titles proved to be the touchstone of library quality. Indeed, I can still remember the impressive repetition of the major university library acronyms in the entries of the National Union Catalogue. Those eight or ten libraries whose initials always appeared under every citation were surely the best for they duplicated the most.

In a digital world, no one cares who has the copy we find on line. The existence of duplicate copies gives no one an advantage when the digital copy is infinitely reproducible. If I find the journal article in JHU's Project Muse, I do not care if it also exists in my home library or if it exists in Berkeley's library. I have it if Project Muse has it. I only need the library to facilitate my access to this digital resource.

The key to this shift in emphasis, of course, is the recognition that physical copies of expensive but common artifacts have little value if a digital version exists. The trick is to find the digital version, and to find all those that are like it, or related to it, or suggestive of it.

Who among us has not used *Google* or *Yahoo* or *Altavista*? For us old people, these services are a miracle and a threat. Where are the subject headings? Where is the authority that classifies this as Latin American history and that as Latin American literature? I search for Bolívar, and I get endless amounts of stuff. Some junk, some interesting, some unanticipated. I browse around, I find serendipitously wonderful things about Don Simón, but when I am done, I do not know if I am done. What did the search miss? What did I skip over in skimming through the endless Bolívarian items, most of which have nothing to do with the historical Bolívar of my work? The Internet search engine is a miracle, but it also finds more junk than stuff. I go to Project Muse, I search there and get a big list of articles, some relevant, some not, but again, unstructured, free form text. I love it; I worry about it.

Librarians should be in this game in a big way, and many are. As the Internet becomes so large an information space that it requires systematic and authoritative management, the librarian's skills, properly translated, will become crucial for ensuring me that I do indeed have all that I should on Bolívar. The ownership of the physical space or the artifacts matters much less than the ability to find the right digitally stored knowledge. I do not care where Bolívar's *Carta de Jamaica* is stored; I care that I can read the authoritative annotated text on line.

Will all this become free? No; money will change hands, and probably more money than we now spend on libraries, but we will spend the money differently. We will spend it on hardware, software, and the gurus who manage them. We will spend it on translating content into digital form; we will spend it on search engines and the research that builds them. The construction of these tools, currently in the earliest stages, will require us to waste much money. We will build the tools, anticipating one kind of bandwidth and capacity and as soon as our tools appear, the bandwidth will expand to such an extent that we will need to begin again.

Libraries and librarians will do two things most. They will maintain and manage unique collections of objects (sheet music from Hoagy Carmichael or the Letters of Thomas Jefferson), many of which they will digitize and deliver into the world. They will provide their constituents with help and assistance, as they always have, in finding, evaluating, and understanding the universe of information that the digital world has provided us.

They will spend less time and energy developing collections and much more developing on-line guides to subjects, topics, and resources. They will buy fewer materials. No one will care what volume of material each library owns, only what volume of materials each library's clients can access.

Can we predict this development, its pace and content? Probably not. But let me offer you *Lombardi's Rules for Digital Survival* created from 30 years of engagement in the academic computer revolution.

1. The objects are not as important as the content. Collection development becomes access development. Access to content is the primary mantra of all library work. Geography becomes increasingly irrelevant.
2. Helping clients find resources in a digitally chaotic world is the first priority. Digitizing the rare book collection might be the second.
3. If a vendor promises you seamless access and modular compatibility with any future developments, expect expensive upgrades.
4. If others spend money on a similar project, let them finish before you start yours. Being first to invent large scale digital library projects is for those with money to lose, tolerant customers, and tenure. If it will take ten years to deliver value, let someone else invest in it.
5. If someone else has a service you need, buy it, do not invent it. If someone has 80% of the service you need, buy it; do not invent it.
6. Nothing currently defining the Internet will remain recognizable after 5 years.
7. There is safety in numbers; join consortia and urge others to take the lead.
8. Invest in unique products only when you have a comparative advantage and someone else pays for it.
9. For the next ten years, if it works well, is reliable, and you know how to use it, it is obsolete.

6

Open Archival Information System

An Open Archival Information System (or OAIS) is an archive, consisting of an organization of people and systems, that has accepted the responsibility to preserve information and make it available for a Designated Community.

OAIS is the ISO reference model for Open Archival Information System.

The information being maintained has been deemed to need "long term preservation", even if the OAIS itself is not permanent. "Long term" is long enough to be concerned with the impacts of changing technologies, including support for new media and data formats, or with a changing user community. "Long term" may extend indefinitely. In this reference model there is a particular focus on digital information, both as the primary forms of information held and as supporting information for both digitally and physically archived materials. Therefore, the model accommodates information that is inherently non-digital (*e.g.*, a physical sample), but the modelling and preservation of such information is not addressed in detail.

THE REFERENCE MODEL

The reference model:

- provides a framework for the understanding and increased awareness of archival concepts needed for long term digital information preservation and access.
- provides the concepts needed by non-archival organizations to be effective participants in the preservation process.

- provides a framework, including terminology and concepts, for describing and comparing architectures and operations of existing and future archives.
- provides a framework for describing and comparing different long term preservation strategies and techniques.
- provides a basis for comparing the data models of digital information preserved by archives and for discussing how data models and the underlying information may change over time.
- provides a foundation that may be expanded by other efforts to cover long-term preservation of information that is *not* in digital form (*e.g.*, physical media and physical samples).
- expands consensus on the elements and processes for long-term digital information preservation and access, and promotes a larger market which vendors can support.
- guides the identification and production of OAIS-related standards.

REQUIREMENTS OF THE SYSTEM

The OAIS must:

- Negotiate for and accept appropriate information from information producers.
- Obtain sufficient control of the information provided to the level needed to ensure long term preservation.
- Determine, either by itself or in conjunction with other parties, which communities should become the *designated community* and, therefore, should be able to understand the information provided.
- Ensure that the information to be preserved is *independently understandable* to the designated community. In other words, the community should be able to understand the information without needing the assistance of the experts who produced the information.

- Follow documented policies and procedures which ensure that the information is preserved against all reasonable contingencies, and which enable the information to be disseminated as authenticated copies of the original, or as traceable to the original.
- Make the preserved information available to the designated community.

PRESERVATION (LIBRARY AND ARCHIVAL SCIENCE)

Preservation is a branch of Library and Information Science concerned with maintaining or restoring access to artifacts, documents and records through the study, diagnosis, treatment and prevention of decay and damage.

It should be distinguished from conservation which refers to the treatment and repair of individual items to slow decay or restore them to a usable state. Conservation is occasionally used interchangeably with preservation, particularly outside the professional literature.

HISTORY

Antecedents

Although preservation as a formal profession in libraries and archives dates from the twentieth century, its philosophy and practice has roots in many earlier traditions. In library science, preservation is treated as an active and intentional process, as opposed to the passive sense of preservation that might be applied to paleontological or archaeological finds. The survival of these items is a matter of chance, from an information science perspective, while the preservation of them after their discovery is a matter of intentional activity.

Human record-keeping arguably dates back to the cave painting boom of the upper paleolithic, some 32,000-40,000 years ago. More direct antecedents are the writing systems that developed in the 4th millennium B.C. Written record keeping and information sharing practices, along with oral tradition, sustain and transmit information from one group to another. This level of preservation has been supplemented over the last century with the professional practice of preservation and conservation in the cultural heritage community.

1. Oral tradition or oral culture, the transmission of information from one generation to the next without a writing system.
2. Antiquarian practices, including scribal practice, burial practice, the libraries at Pergamum, Alexandria and other ancient archives.
3. Medieval practices, including the scriptorium and relic collection
4. Renaissance and the changing conception of artists and works of art
5. Enlightenment and the Encyclopedists
6. Romantic movement's imperative to preserve

Significant Events

- 1933: William Barrow introduces the field of conservation to paper deacidification when he publishes a paper on the acid paper problem. In later studies, Barrow tested paper from American books made between 1900 and 1949 and learned that after forty years the books had lost on average 96 percent of their original strength; after less than ten years, they had already lost 64 percent. Barrow determined that this rapid deterioration was not the direct result of using wood-pulp fibers, since rag papers of this period were also aging rapidly, but rather due to the residual sulfuric acid produced in both rag and wood pulp papers. Manufacturing methods used after 1870 employed sulfuric acid for sizing and bleaching the paper. Earlier papermaking methods left the final product only mildly alkaline or even neutral. Such paper has maintained its strength for 300 to 800 years, despite sulfur dioxide and other air pollutants. Barrow's 1933 article on the fragile state of wood pulp paper predicted the shelf life of this paper was approximately 40-50 years. At that point the paper would begin to show signs of deterioration, and he concluded that research for a new media on which to write and print was needed.

- 1966: The Flood of the River Arno in Florence, Italy damaged or destroyed millions of rare books and lead to the development of restoration laboratories and new methods in conservation. Instrumental in this process was conservationist Peter Waters, who lead a group of volunteers, called "mud angels", in restoring thousands of books and papers. This event awakened many historians, librarians, and other professionals to the importance of having a preservation plan. Many consider this flood to be one of the worst disasters since the burning of the Alexandria Library in ancient Rome. It spurred a resurgence in the profession of preservation and conservation worldwide.
- 1987: Terry Saunders releases the film Slow Fires: On the Preservation of the Human Record which examines paper embrittlement resulting from acid decay

Significant Preservationists

- William Barrow (1904 – 1967) was an American chemist and paper conservator, and a pioneer of library and archives conservation. He introduced the field of conservation to paper deacidification through alkalization.
- Paul N. Banks (1934-2000) was Conservator and Head of the Conservation Department at the Newberry Library from 1964 to 1981, and published regularly on bookbinding, book and paper conservation and problems related to conservation. He designed and implemented a curriculum for Columbia University's School of Library Science that dealt directly with preservation training.
- Pamela Darling, author and historian, was Preservation Specialist for the Association of Research Libraries. Her works include materials to aid libraries in establishing their own comprehensive preservation programmes.
- Carolyn Harris worked as head of Columbia University Libraries' Preservation Division from 1981 until 1987, where she worked closely with Paul Banks. She published extensive research throughout her career,

especially dealing with mass deacidification of wood-pulp paper.

- Peter Waters, former Conservation Officer at the Library of Congress in Washington, DC, worked in the areas of disaster recovery and preparedness, and the salvaging of water-damaged paper goods.
- Nicholson Baker is a contemporary American novelist and author of *Double Fold,* a criticism of libraries' destruction of paper-based media.
- Patricia Battin, as the first president of the Commission on Preservation and Access, worked to organize a national campaign both for the use of alkaline paper in publishing companies and for a national programme of preservation microfilming.
- John F. Dean, Preservation and Conservation Librarian at Cornell University, has made contributions towards improving preservation efforts in developing countries. Specifically, Dean has created online tutorials for library conservation and preservation in Southeast Asia and Iraq and the Middle East.

The Paul Banks and Carolyn Harris Preservation Award for outstanding preservation specialists in library and archival science, is given annually by the Association for Library Collections & Technical Services, a subdivision of the American Library Association. It is awarded in recognition of professional preservation specialists who have made significant contributions to the field. Banks/Harris award winners:

- Sally Buchanan 2001-Buchanan received the award in recognition of years of service in the preservation field while an associate professor at the University of Pittsburgh School of Information Science
- Ellen McCrady 2002-Since 1975, McCrady has edited and published the "Abbey Newsletter", covering important information for preservation professionals. She also conducts research regarding papermaking and acid testing.
- John F. Dean 2003-Since its inception in 1985, Dean has led the Department of Preservation and Conservation at Cornell University.

- Jan Merrill-Oldham 2004-As the Malloy-Rabinowitz Preservation Librarian at Harvard University, Merrill-Oldham oversees the Weissman Preservation Centre and the Preservation and Imaging Department.
- Paul Conway 2005-Conway is an associate professor in the University of Michigan School of Information and has worked with Yale and Duke University after beginning his career at the Gerald R. Ford Presidential Library. His research and educational work focuses primarily on digital preservation and electronic media.
- Gary Frost 2006-Currently a conservator at the University of Iowa Libraries, Frost has been an educator and practitioner in the field of library preservation for over 35 years.

PRACTICES

Care and Handling

1. Exhibitions
2. Circulating collections
3. Special collections

Research and Testing

With old media deteriorating or showing their vulnerabilities and new media becoming available, research remains active in the field of conservation and preservation. Everything from how to preserve paper media to creating and maintaining electronic resources is being explored by students and professionals in library and information science.

The two main issues that most libraries tend to face are the rapid disintegration of acidic paper and water damage (due to flooding, plumbing problems, etc.). Therefore, these areas of preservation, as well as new digital technologies, receive much of the research attention.

The American Library Association has many scholarly journals that publish articles on preservation topics, such as *College and Research Libraries, Information Technology and Libraries,* and *Library Resources and Technical Services.*

Scholarly periodicals in this field from other publishers include *International Preservation News, Journal of the American Institute for Conservation*, and *Collection Management* among many others.

Regional Centres

- The Conservation Centre for Art and Historic Artifacts in Philadelphia, PA. CCAHA is a non-profit conservation laboratory specializing in the treatment of art and historic artifacts on paper. The Centre also trains museum and library professionals in disaster planning, records and archives management.
- The Northeast Document Conservation Centre in Andover, MA. Since its inception in 1973, the Centre has instructed institutions and organizations, as well as librarians, conservators, preservationists and museum professionals in preservation care and procedures.

Vendor Services

Many private entities have provide preservation and conservation services and supplies. Listed here are many of these businesses.

Conservation Supplies

- ArchapeX
- Archivart
- Carr McLean
- Conservation Resources
- Demco
- Gaylord
- Light Impressions
- Hollinger Corp.
- Metal Edge
- Paige Company
- Talas
- University Products

Library Binding

Library binding is a common preservation practice. The Library Binding Institute is the trade organization for library binders, and works with the American Library Association to maintain the Library Binding Standard, ANSI Z39.78-2000.

- Library Binding Institute
- The HF Group
- ICI Binding Corporation
- Bridgeport Library Binding Services
- Ocker & Trapp Library Binding, Inc.
- Acme Bookbinding

Conservators in Private Practice and Conservation Centres

- Conservators in Private Practice from the American Institute for Conservation.
- Conservation Centre for Art and Historic Artifacts
- Northeast Document Conservation Centre

Exhibition and Storage

- Benchmark
- Casewerks
- Delta Design Cabinets
- Glasbau Hahn
- Helmut Guenschel, Inc.
- Small Corp

BRANCHES OF PRESERVATION

Standard Functions of Preservation Programmes

- Collections Care refers to the general maintenance and preventive care of a collection as a whole. This can include activities such as security, environmental monitoring, preservation surveys and more specialized activities such as mass deacidification.
- Conservation refers to the treatment and repair of individual items to slow decay or restore them to a

usable state. Conservation is occasionally used interchangeably with preservation, particularly outside the professional literature.

- Digital preservation refers to the maintenance of digitally stored information. This should not be confused with digitization, which is a process of creating digital information which must, in turn, be digitally preserved. Means of digital preservation include refreshing, migration, replication and emulation.
- Disaster Preparedness refers to the practice of arranging for the necessary resources and planning the best course of action to prevent or minimize damage to a collection in the event of a disaster of any level of magnitude.
- Reformatting refers to the practice of creating copies of an object in another type of data storage device. Reformatting processes include microfilming and digitization.

Media Specific Issues and Treatments

- Books
  - Sizing
- Ephemera and Realia
- Paper
  - Acid-free paper
  - Japanese tissue
  - Mummy paper
- Parchment
  - Parchment repair
  - Preservation of Illuminated Manuscripts
- Moving image
  - Moving Image Preservation Education
- Recorded sound
  - Preservation of magnetic audiotape
- Oral history preservation
- Language Preservation

- Visual materials
  - o Colour photography
  - o Architectural reprography, a variety of technologies and media used to make multiple copies of original drawings or records created by architects, engineers, mapmakers and related professionals.
- Optical media preservation
- Ink

EDUCATION

One of the biggest challenges in the field of preservation today is educating a library's community, especially librarians and other staff, in the best ways to handle materials as well as the conditions in which particular materials will decay the least. This challenge is exacerbated by the fact that preservation is a peripheral element of most library science curricula; indeed, there are few places where one can receive a specialized education in preservation.

The primary degree granting institution for library and archival preservation is the University of Texas at Austin's School of Information Science. The conservation and preservation programme is offered in partnership with the Kilgarlin Centre for Preservation of the Cultural Record and trains both conservators and preservation administrators. Other conservation programmes in the United States focus on Art Conservation and are considered to be more museum focused than library focused. These programmes are all part of the Association of North American Graduate Programmes in the Conservation of Cultural Property (ANAGPIC).

The Rutgers Preservation Management Institute provides post-graduate training in preservation administration for working librarians who have already completed a Master's degree. UT Austin also offers certificates of advanced study in conservation and preservation to librarians who already hold their MLS.

Another educational resource available to preservationists is the Northeast Document Conservation Centre or NEDCC. This institution was founded in 1973 as a reaction to the growing problem of paper deterioration occurring in repositories in the New England area. The Centre provides institutions and organizations, as well as librarians, conservators, preservationists, and museum professionals, with help in learning proper care and procedures to better preserve the integrity of their collections. The institution provides a variety of services such as imaging, surveys and consultations, and digitation.

They also assist with disaster planning. The educational opportunities it provides include provision of workshops, conferences, and specialized trainings. Additional online courses are also available. For instance, some of the workshops offered by the NEDCC include: Basic Preservation, Collections Care, Emergency Preparedness, Integrated Pest Management (IPM), Identification and Care of Photographs, Basic and Intermediate Book Repair, Basic Paper Repair, Preservation of Scrapbooks, Preservation Technologies, Holdings Maintenance, Creating and Maintaining Digital Collections, Scanning Training, and Grant Writing.

Additional preservation education is available to librarians through various professional organizations, such as:

- American Institute for Conservation of Historic and Artistic Works
- American Library Association
- Amigos Library Services Preservation Service
- Association for Information and Image Management (AIIM)
- Association for Recorded Sound Collections
- Buffalo State College. Art Conservation Department, Buffalo, NY
- Campbell Centre for Historic Preservation Studies, Mount Carroll, IL.
- George Eastman House. School of Film & Video Preservation Rochester, NY
- The Kilgarlin Centre for Preservation of the Cultural Record
- Library Binding Institute

- New York University. Conservation Centre, Institute of Fine Arts, New York, NY
- North Bennet Street School. Boston, MA
- Northeast Document Conservation Centre (NEDCC)
- The Conservation Centre for Art and Historic Artifacts in Philadelphia, PA
- Queen's University. Master of Art Conservation Programme, Ont, Canada
- Rare Book School (RBS) at the University of Virginia
- Society of American Archivists
- Southeastern Library Network (SOLINET)
- University of Delaware. Winterthur Art Conservation Programme, Newark, DE
- The National Archives

NON-ACADEMIC FACILITIES AND PRESERVATION

Public Libraries: Limited, tax-driven funding can often interfere with the ability for public libraries to engage in extensive preservation activities. Materials, particularly books, are often much easier to replace than to repair when damaged or worn. Public libraries usually try to tailor their services to meet the needs and desires of their local communities, which could cause an emphasis on acquiring new materials over preserving old ones. Librarians working in public facilities frequently have to make complicated decisions about how to best serve their patrons. Commonly, public library systems work with each other and sometimes with more academic libraries through interlibrary loan programmes. By sharing resources, they are able to expand upon what might be available to their own patrons and share the burdens of preservation across a greater array of systems.

Archival Repositories and Special Collections: Archival facilities focus specifically on rare and fragile materials. With staff trained in appropriate techniques, archives are often available to many public and private library facilities as an alternative to destroying older materials. Items that are unique, such as photographs, or items that are out of print, can be preserved in archival facilities more easily than in many library settings.

Museums: Because so many museum holdings are unique, including print materials, art, and other objects, preservationists are often most active in this setting.

LEGAL ISSUES

Reformatting, or in any other way copying an item's contents, raises obvious copyright issues. In many cases, a library is allowed to make a limited number of copies of an item for preservation purposes.

CRITICISM

There is a long-standing tension between preservation of and access to library materials, particularly in the area of special collections. Handling materials promotes their progression to an unusable state, especially if they are handled carelessly. On the other hand, materials must be used in order to gain any benefit from them. In a collection with valuable materials, this conflict is often resolved by a number of measures which can include heightened security, requiring the use of gloves for photographs, restricting the materials researchers may bring with them into a reading room, and restricting use of materials to patrons who are not able satisfy their research needs with less valuable copies of an item. These measures can seem intimidating to less experienced researchers who might feel that these preservation measures are in place solely to keep materials out of the hands of the public.

There is also controversy surrounding preservation methods. A major controversy at the end of the twentieth century centred on the practice of discarding items that had been microfilmed. A similar concern persists over the retention of original documents reformatted by any means, analog or digital. Concerns include a scholarly needs and legal requirements for authentic or original records as well as questions about the longevity, quality and completeness of reformatted materials. Retention of originals as a source or fail-safe copy is now a fairly common practice.

Many digitized items, such as back issues of periodicals, are provided by publishers and databases on a subscription basis. If these companies were to cease providing access to their digital information, facilities that elected to discard paper copies of these periodicals could face significant difficulties in providing access to these items. Discussion as to the best ways to utilize digital technologies is therefore ongoing, and the practice continues to evolve.

LIBRARIAN

A librarian is an information professional trained in library science and information science: the organization and management of information and service to people with information needs. The word is also used for those in charge of collections in general. Librarians work typically in one of the many types of library or school media centres, and increasingly in other information-provision settings; the term is also used sometimes in a popular sense to refer to anyone who works in a library.

Although librarians have been traditionally associated with collections of books, as seen by the etymology of the word "librarian," modern librarians deal with information in many formats, including books, magazines, newspapers, audio recordings in various formats (both music recordings and audiobooks), video recordings in various formats, maps, photographs and other graphic material, bibliographic databases, and Internet resources in general. They often provide other information services, including computer provision and training, coordination of public programmes, basic literacy education, and help with finding and using community resources.

In most western nations the librarian is a professional with a Masters degree in library science who is educated to analyze information needs and provide patrons in a variety of settings with information resources appropriate to meet those needs.

In a library, there are many positions other than that of librarian; such positions include library associate, library technician, library assistant, clerk, page, shelver, and volunteer. There are also professional positions such as managers.

LIBRARIAN ROLES AND DUTIES

Olivia Crosby described librarians as "Information experts in the information age". Specific duties vary depending on the size and type of library. Most librarians spend their time working in one of the following areas of a library:

- *Public service librarians* work with the public, frequently at the reference desk of lending libraries. Some specialize in serving adults or children. Children's librarians provide appropriate material for children at all age levels, include pre-readers, conduct specialized programmes and work with the children (and often their parents) to help foster interest and competence in the young reader. (In larger libraries, some specialize in teen services, periodicals, or other special collections.)
- *Reference or research librarians* help people doing research to find the information they need, through a structured conversation called a reference interview. The help may take the form of research on a specific question, providing direction on the use of databases and other electronic information resources; obtaining specialized materials from other sources; or providing access to and care of delicate or expensive materials. These services are sometimes provided by other library staff that have been given a certain amount of special training; some have criticized this trend.
- *Technical service librarians* work "behind the scenes" ordering library materials and database subscriptions, computers and other equipment, and supervise the cataloguing and physical processing of new materials.
- *Collections development librarians* monitor the selection of books and electronic resources. Large libraries often use approval plans, which involve the librarian for a specific subject creating a profile that allows publishers to send relevant books to the library without any additional vetting. Librarians can then see those books when they arrive and decide if they will become part of the collection or not. All collections librarians also have a certain amount of funding to allow them to

purchase books and materials that don't arrive via approval.

- Archivists can be specialized librarians who deal with archival materials, such as manuscripts, documents and records, though this varies from country to country, and there are other routes to the archival profession.
- *Systems Librarians* develop, troubleshoot and maintain library systems, including the library catalogue and related systems.
- *Electronic Resources Librarians* manage the databases that libraries license from third-party vendors.
- *School Library Media Specialists* work in school libraries and perform duties as teachers, information technology specialists, and advocates for literacy.

Experienced librarians may take administrative positions such as library or information centre director. Similar to the management of any other organization, they are concerned with the long-term planning of the library, and its relationship with its parent organization (the city or county for a public library, the college/university for an academic library, or the organization served by a special library). In smaller or specialized libraries, librarians typically perform a wide range of the different duties. Representative examples of specific tasks:

- Researching topics of interest for their constituencies.
- Referrals to other community organizations and government offices.
- Suggesting appropriate books ("readers' advisory") for children of different reading levels, and recommending novels for recreational reading.
- Supervising and promoting reading clubs.
- Developing programmes for library users of all ages and backgrounds.
- Managing access to electronic information resources.

WORKPLACES

Basic categories of workplace settings for librarians are routinely classified around the world as: public, academic, school, and special. Some librarians will start and operate their own business. They often call themselves information brokers, research specialists, knowledge management, competitive intelligence or independent information professionals. Below are the basic differences between the types of libraries.

Public Library: These institutions are created through legislation within the jurisdiction they serve. Accordingly, they are given certain benefits, such as taxpayer funding, but must adhere to service standards and meet a wide group of client needs. They are usually overseen by a board of directors or library commission from the community. Mission statements, service and collection policies are the fundamental administrative features of public libraries. Occasionally private lending libraries serve the public in the manner of public libraries. In the United States, public librarians and public libraries are represented by the Public Library Association.

Academic Library: Libraries that serve a post-secondary institution. Depending upon the institution, the library may serve a particular faculty or the entire institution. Many different types, sizes, and collections are found in academic libraries and some academic librarians are specialists in these collections and archives. A University librarian, or Chief librarian, is responsible for the library within the college structure, and may also be called the Dean of Libraries. Some post-secondary institutions treat librarians as faculty, and they may be called professor or other academic ranks. Some universities make similar demands of academic librarians for research and professional service as are required of faculty. Academic librarians administer various levels of service and privilege to faculty, students, alumni and the public.

School Library Media Centre: Libraries which exclusively serve the needs of a public or private school. The primary purpose is to support the students, teachers, and curriculum of the school or school district. In addition to library administration, certificated teacher-librarians instruct individual students, groups and classes, and faculty in effective research methods, often referred to as information literacy skills. Audiovisual equipment service and/or textbook circulation may also be included in a school librarian's responsibilities.

Often, teacher-librarians are qualified teachers who take academic courses for school library certification and/or earn a Master's degree in Library Science.

Special Library: News, law, medical, government, nongovernmental organization, prison, corporate, museum or any other type of library owned and operated by an organization are considered as special library. They can be highly specialized, serving a discrete user group with a restricted collection area. In an increasingly global and virtual workplace, many special librarians may not even work in a library at all but instead manage and facilitate the use of electronic collections. Funding for special libraries varies widely.

Librarians in some types of special libraries may be required to have additional training, such as a law degree for a librarian in an academic law library or appropriate subject degrees for subject specialties such as chemistry, engineering, etc. Many belong to the Special Libraries Association. There are also more specific associations such as the American Association of Law Libraries, Art Libraries Society of North America, the Medical Library Association, or the Visual Resources Association.

EDUCATION

In the United States and Canada, a librarian normally has a one or two-year master's degree in library and information science, library science or information science (called an MLS, MALIS, MSLS, MIS, MS-LIS, MISt, MLIS, or MILS) from an accredited university. These degrees are accredited by the American Library Association and can have specializations within fields such as archiving, records management, information architecture, public librarianship, medical librarianship, law librarianship, special librarianship, academic librarianship, or school (K-12) librarianship. School librarians often are required to have a teaching credential, as well as a library science degree. Many, if not most, academic librarians also have a second, subject-based master's degree.

In the UK and some other countries, a librarian can have a three-or four-year bachelor's degree in library and information studies or information science; separate master's degrees in librarianship, archive management, and records management are also available. In the United Kingdom, these degrees are accredited by the Chartered Institute of Library and Information Professionals and the Society of Archivists. In Germany and some other countries, the first step for an academic librarian is a PhD in a subject field, followed by additional training in librarianship.

Librarians in Australia can take one of two routes; an undergraduate degree in Library and Information Studies or a Graduate Diploma in Library and Information Studies after the completion of a Bachelor's Degree in another discipline. The Australian Library and Information Association (ALIA)is responsible for accreditation of library specific qualifications for both librarians and library technicians.

It is also possible to earn a doctorate in library and information science. Graduates with PhDs usually become teaching faculty in schools of library and information science, or sometimes occupy the directorship or deanship of university libraries. Those undertaking research at the doctoral level can pursue a very wide range of interests including information technology, government information policy, social research into information use among particular segments of society, information in organizations and corporate settings, and the history of books and printing.

It is common in academic and other research libraries to require the librarians to obtain Master's degrees in some academic subject, sometimes but not necessarily related to their professional responsibilities; in major research libraries, some of the librarians will hold Ph. D degrees in subject fields.

Other advanced degrees often taken in conjunction with a degree in librarianship are law, management, or public administration.

Library associates, library technicians, and library assistants often have college diplomas but usually do not hold library-related degrees. Occasionally they also hold undergraduate or graduate degrees in other disciplines. These workers, sometimes referred to as para-professionals, perform duties such as database management, cataloguing, ready reference, and serials and monograph processing.

PROFESSIONAL ORGANIZATIONS AND ACTIVITIES

The two largest library associations in the United States are the American Library Association (ALA) and the Special Libraries Association. Many U.S. states have their own library association as well. Librarians may also join such organizations as the Association of College and Research Libraries and the Public Library Association and the Art Libraries Society. The Canadian Library Association serves Canada and there are provincial associations as well, such as the Ontario Library Association. In the United Kingdom, the professional body for Librarians is the Chartered Institute of Library and Information Professionals (formerly known as the Library Association). The International Federation of Library Associations and Institutions (IFLA) represents the interests of libraries and librarians internationally.

Recent issues of concern for U.S. libraries include implementation of the Patriot Act and the Children's Internet Protection Act. Many librarians around the world share American librarians' concern over ethical issues surrounding censorship and privacy. Some librarians join activist organizations like the UK-based Information for Social Change and the North American-based Progressive Librarians Guild. Within the American Library Association (ALA), some also join the Social Responsibilities Round Table. SRRT came into being amid the social ferment of the 1960s and is often critical of the American Library Association for not living up to its professed ideals. Another important activist organization is the Social Responsibilities Special Interest Section of the American Association of Law Libraries (AALL). These activist organizations are viewed as controversial by some librarians, while others view them as a natural extension and outgrowth of their own deeply-held library ethics.

TECHNOLOGY IN LIBRARIES

The increasing role of technology in libraries has a significant impact on the changing roles of librarians. New technologies are dramatically increasing the accessibility of information, and librarians are adapting to the evolving needs of users that emerge from the adoption of these new technologies.

The most significant example of how technology has changed the role of librarians in the last 50 years has been the move from traditional card catalogues to online public access catalogues (OPACs). Librarians had to develop software and the MARC standards for cataloguing records electronically. They had to purchase and run the computers necessary to use the software. They had to teach the public how to use the new technologies and move to more virtual working environments.

The same could be said of other technology developments, from electronic databases (including the Internet), to logistical functions such as barcodes (or in the near future RFID). Many librarians provide virtual reference services (via web-based chat, instant messaging, text messaging, and e-mail), work in digitalization initiatives for works in the public domain, teach technology classes to their users, and work on the development of information architectures for improving access and search functionality.

These examples illustrate some of the ways in which librarians are using technology to fulfil and expand upon their historical roles.

Increasing technological advance has presented the possibility of automating some aspects of traditional libraries. In 2004 a group of researchers in Spain developed the UJI Online Robot. This robot is able to navigate the library, look for the specified book, and upon its discovery, carefully take it from the shelf and deliver it to the user. Because of the robot's extremely limited function, its introduction into libraries poses little risk of the employment of librarians, whose duties are not defined by menial tasks such as the retrieval of books.

LIBRARIANS IN POPULAR CULTURE

Stereotypes of librarians in popular culture are frequently negative: bookish characters who may be prim and introverted if female, or timid and mild if male. Such stereotypes are likely to have a negative impact on the attractiveness of librarianship as a profession to young people. This article provides a collection of descriptions of librarians in popular culture, *i.e.*, literature, film, television, and games.

LITERATURE

Children's literature has a generally positive portrayal of librarians as young, helpful and friendly, becoming more positive over the course of the 20th century. Adult literature, however, portrays the profession more negatively. Between these, portrayals of librarians in young adult fiction are neutral to negative.

Here librarians are predominantly female, middle-aged, usually unattractive in some way, and mostly unmarried. Personality is mixed between positive traits such as intelligence, likeability, and kind-heartedness; and negative traits such as strictness, timidity, and eccentricity. While some provide assistance to the main characters, several are the villains of the book. Duties generally include reference, but may only show housekeeping tasks; however the amount of technology used by librarian characters has increased over time.

A disproportionate number of the librarians represented in novels are in the detective fiction genre, frequently as an amateur detective and protagonist. Although the stereotype of the librarian as "passive bore" does not seem reconcilable with the intensity of a mystery, the stereotypical librarian does share many traits with the successful detective. Their mindset is focused, calm, unbiased in considering viewpoints, and interested in the world around them.

By personality they are industrious perfectionists-and eccentric. The drab and innocuous look of the stereotypical librarian is perfect for avoiding suspicion, while their research skills and ability to ask the right questions allow them to procure and put together the information necessary to solve the case.

The knowledge they have gained from wide reading successfully competes with a private investigator's personal experience. For example, Jacqueline Kirby is drawn into the mystery in Elizabeth Peters' novel *The Seventh Sinner* (1972) due to her awareness of her surroundings. Wearing the stereotypical bun, glasses and practical clothes-together with an eccentrically large purse-she is self-possessed and resourceful, knowledgeable in a variety of fields and skilled at research.

A sampling of librarians featured in works of literature include:

- Neal Stephenson's novel, *Snow Crash* features both the "Central Information Congress" (a commercialized melding of the Central Intelligence Agency and the Library of Congress) and a virtual librarian which assists the main character, Hiro Protagonist.
- In the *Discworld* book series by Terry Pratchett there is a librarian who has been magically turned into an orangutan. In these stories, librarians frequently have supernatural powers related to books and library work, including access to a form of hyperspace known as L-Space.
- In the comic book series *Batman*, Barbara Gordon is a computer-savvy librarian using the name Oracle. Before she was shot by the Joker, restricting the use of her legs, she was known as Batgirl.
- Lucien, from Neil Gaiman's comic book series The Sandman, tends to The Dreaming's library, where all the books that are dreamt of, but never written, are contained.
- Henry De Tamble (from the novel *The Time Traveller's Wife*) is a Chicago librarian with "Chrono Displacement" disorder; at random times, he suddenly disappears without warning and finds himself in the past or future, usually at a time or place of importance in his life.
- Jack and Annie in *The Magic Treehouse* series of children's books become "Master Librarians".
- Irma Pince is the librarian in several of the Harry Potter novels. She is a minor character as a disciplinarian in the Hogwarts library.
- Malachi is the scholarly librarian in Umberto Eco's medieval murder mystery The Name of the Rose who unlocks the secrets of a labyrinthine library to the novel's protagonists.
- In Jo Dereske novels, Helma Zukas of Bellehaven, Washington (her way of swearing is "Oh, Faulkner!").

- Laurali R. Wright has a series of crime novels set in British Columbia featuring Cassandra Mitchell, librarian and partner of a Royal Canadian Mountie.
- In "It" by Stephen King the central narrator is Mike Hanlon, a librarian in the small town of Derry, Maine. He is described as "the keeper of the lighthouse".
- In Kingsley Amis' comic novel *That Uncertain Feeling*, a Welsh librarian bored with his marriage casts his eye upon a new girl in town. In the film version, *Only Two Can Play*, the librarian was played by Peter Sellers.
- The manga series *Read or Die* (a.k.a. R.O.D.) features protagonist bibliophile Yomiko Readman, who works for the Library of England in search of rare and powerful books.
- Richard Peck's book, *Here Lies the Librarian*. "This book is dedicated to Living librarians everywhere And to my Dean Beth Mehalick Paskoff", who is Dean of Library and Information Sciences at Louisiana State University. On the cover is a cemetery with a gravestone that reads, "SHH!".
- Lilian Jackson Braun's popular mystery series *The Cat Who...* features Polly Duncan, head of the Pickax Library and companion of the main character, James Qwilleran. This series also features Qwilleran's two bibliocats, Kao K'o Kung (Koko) and Yum Yum.
- In the novel *The Da Vinci Code* by Dan Brown, Robert Langdon (Tom Hanks) and Sophie Neveu (Audrey Tautou) visit a library to determine the importance of "A. Pope".
- Charlaine Harris, who writes the Southern Vampire Mysteries, writers another series called the "Southern Librarian" mysteries, about librarian Aurora "Ro" Teagarden, who solves murder mysteries.
- The eponymous character in Garth Nix's Lirael (2001) is an assistant librarian whose curiosity about the library she works in leads her into trouble and whose research skills save her. The head librarian is intimidating and the library itself a dangerous place.

FILM

According to Ann Seidl, director of the documentary The Hollywood Librarian, librarians in film are often portrayed as meek, timid, and unassertive in nature. After indexing hundreds of appearances of librarians in film, she found that "the shorter the reference to a librarian in a film, the worse the stereotype." By the 1950s, movies had established the stereotype of librarians as "spinsters" and "eggheads". Thus, female movie librarians are usually unmarried, prim and introverted. They are usually young and may be attractive, but dress drably and are sexually repressed: in movies such as It's a Wonderful Life and The Music Man their career is characterised as a "fate worse than death". Male movie librarians-mild, intelligent and timid-have fewer and less important roles. Seidl's documentary discusses such stereotypes as:

- A wretched alternate fate is revealed for Mary Hatch Bailey (played by Donna Reed) in the movie *It's a Wonderful Life' (1946)': "She's just about to close up the library!"*
- "Do you want me to draw you a map?!" barks a staggeringly rude and unhelpful librarian (John Rothman) at Sophie Zawistowski (Meryl Streep) in Sophie's Choice (1982).

In contrast with the more well-rounded characters in:

- Librarian Bunny Watson (played by Katharine Hepburn) teaches Richard Sumner (played by Spencer Tracy) a few things about modern research methods in the movie *Desk Set* (1957).
- Shirley Jones stars as the no-nonsense "Marian the Librarian" in the movie *The Music Man.*

Librarians are usually every-man characters caught up in circumstances, rather than being heroes; likewise they are rarely villainous although they have flaws, such as racism in Goodbye, Columbus. Other appearances of librarians in film include:

- In *No Man of Her Own* (1932), Clark Gable is a big city con man who falls for a local librarian (Carole Lombard) while on the lam.

- Virginia Mayo plays a librarian in Wonder Man (film) (1945), but the great quote is from Danny Kaye who plays the bookworm Edwin Dingle: "I enjoy it here very much... uh, I love the smell of leather bindings."
- As a librarian in a small town, Alicia Hull (Bette Davis) befriends Freddie Slater (Kevin Coughlin) – while being ostracised for refusing to remove a book on Communism from the public library during the height of the Red Scare – in Storm Centre (1956).
- Ingrid Pitt plays a "nymphomaniac librarian" (as she described it) in the classic British movie The Wicker Man (1973), who is found naked by Edward Woodward's virginal Christian policeman.
- Debbie gets friendly with a librarian in Debbie Does Dallas (1978).
- Goldie Hawn dons cat-eyed glasses when she plays San Francisco librarian Gloria Mundy who helps Chevy Chase solve an assassination plot in the comedy *Foul Play* (1978).
- Alice Drummond plays the librarian in Ghostbusters (1984) who first encounters the book-stacking ghost of a former librarian in the famous New York Public Library.
- "Weird Al" Yankovic plays Conan the Librarian, in a brief segment of the 1989 film *UHF*.
- "Books are my life now," explains librarian Lynn Weslin (Rene Russo) to her ex-boyfriend and baseball player Jake Taylor (Tom Berenger) in Major League (1989).
- Circulation desk worker Charlie Simms (Chris O'Donnell) breaks the rules and lets his fair-weathered friend George Willis, Jr. (Philip Seymour Hoffman) take a reserve book out of the library. From Scent of a Woman (1992).
- In Philadelphia (1993), a librarian (Tracey Walter) encourages an ailing Andrew Beckett (Tom Hanks) to use a private study room.
- A librarian assists Thora Birch's character in the 1994 film *Monkey Trouble* with information on a monkey she has found.

- Richard Tyler (Macaulay Culkin) is led on a fantastical adventure through a library by Mr. Dewey (Christopher Lloyd), AKA The Pagemaster (1994).
- Mary (played by Parker Posey) is the ultimate *Party Girl* (1995) who discovers, "I want to be a librarian!" in an exception to the prim librarian stereotype.
- In *A Very Brady Sequel* (1996), Roy Martin (Tim Matheson) informs Greg Brady (Christopher Daniel Barnes) that he should date someone more of his "own speed", suggesting a librarian as an example.
- Jet Li's character in the movie *Black Mask (film)* (1996) works as a librarian.
- Evelyn Carnahan is proud to be a librarian in the movies *The Mummy* (1999) and *The Mummy Returns.*
- Heather Stephens plays Jill, the awkward librarian (and closet dominatrix), in the movie *Tomcats* (2001).
- Vox (played by Orlando Jones), a holographic entity possessing a "compendium of all human knowledge", works at a futuristic New York Public Library in the movie *The Time Machine* (2002).
- Jocasta Nu is an archivist in the film *Star Wars Episode II: Attack of the Clones* (2002).
- *Last Life in the Universe* (2003) is an intriguing tale about a male Japanese librarian.
- Michelle Williams plays a small part as a young, blonde, out-of-wedlock-pregnant, love-torn local librarian in The Station Agent (2003).
- Noah Wyle's character in the television movie *The Librarian: Quest for The Spear* (2004) and *The Librarian: Return to King Solomon's Mines.* His mother: "Sixteen years of college and they've got you putting books on shelves?"

TELEVISION

The portrayal of librarians on the small screen has usually followed the same stereotypes as those found in motion pictures. For example, in most animated cartoon series (such as Baby

Looney Tunes or Rugrats) the librarian is often shown silencing the main/pivotal characters-especially younger children-when they're in a library area. Some even ban the characters from the libraries for making rude or strange noises.

In creating the Australian miniseries *The Librarians*, however, co-producers and-writers Wayne Hope and Robyn Butler consulted with real librarians for research, and took their advice to avoid shooshing and cardigan-wearing librarian characters.

- On the television series *All That*, there are several sketches that feature a silence-obsessed librarian (known as "The Loud Librarian" to some) that scolds someone for even making a coughing sound. She is eventually "fired" when Lori Beth Denberg leaves the cast in 1998.
- In the television series *Buffy the Vampire Slayer*, Anthony Stewart Head played the role of Rupert Giles, school librarian in earlier episodes and Buffy's watcher.
- In a *Star Trek* episode *All Our Yesterdays*, Ian Wolfe plays librarian Mr. Atoz: "The library serves no purpose unless someone is using it." Mr. Atoz's name apparently derives from the phrase "A to Z", a reference to his occupation as a librarian.
- In the 1967 episode of The Avengers (TV series), "Murdersville", a gun is used with a silencer after the librarian points to the SILENCE sign.
- In an episode of *Seinfeld*, Cosmo Kramer (Michael Richards) dates a librarian from the New York Public Library, much to the chagrin of the "library cop."
- In one episode of Monty Python's Flying Circus wild animals are interviewed for the position of librarian.
- In one episode of The Simpsons a librarian questions Reverend Lovejoy about a Bible he has checked out every weekend for the past 12 years, asking wouldn't it be easier just to buy one, to which the Reverend replies, "Perhaps...on a Librarian's salary..."
- The television series Once Upon A Time centres around a librarian trapped in a witch's tower, who is forced to

produce stories with a machine called 1Z2Z, and then read them.

- In an Orwellian future, a librarian (played by Burgess Meredith) fills the title role of "The Obsolete Man" (1961) in an episode from The Twilight Zone.
- Al Bundy (Ed O'Neill) pulls off a typical claims returned trick on an old and bitter librarian in the Married... with Children episode "He Thought He Could" (1988).
- In a few episodes of That 70s Show, Shannon Elizabeth played Kelso's librarian girlfriend.
- On the May 24, 2007 episode of the Colbert Report, Colbert interviewed Wikipedia co-founder Jimmy Wales. During the interview, he showed on the screen the statement "Librarians are hiding something" and asked Wales how he would stop or prevent vandalism to Wikipedia based on that statement.

COMPUTER AND VIDEO GAMES

There have been several characters associated with the library field in the realm of interactive entertainment, often portrayed as guides and/or purveyors of knowledge who help the user progress within the game:

- Miss Bluegarden, from the game *Secret of Evermore.*
- Myrna Bookbottom, the stereotypical meek English librarian, from the game *Freaky Flyers.*
- Brisketta, from the game *Brave Fencer Musashi.*
- The Daguerreo Librarian, the unnamed overseer of the Daguerreo Library in *Final Fantasy IX.*
- Darian, an anthropomorphic car from the children's educational game *Putt-Putt Travels Through Time.*
- Alan Dinsdale, Velma's former school librarian, from the game *Scooby Doo: Mystery Mayhem.*
- Eike, the librarian of Budehuc Castle, from the game *Suikoden III.*
- Geelo, from the game *Icewind Dale.*

- Aldus T. Giles, Assistant Correspondence Clerk of the Tarantian Library, from the game *Arcanum: Of Steamworks and Magick Obscura.*
- Grendor, a Rhynoc, from the game *Spyro: Season of Ice.*
- Mayumi Himuro, from the game *Divi-Dead.*
- Jaard, from the game *Soulbringer.*
- Kairn, a librarian/vampire, from the game *Veil of Darkness.*
- Manaka Komaki, from the game *ToHeart2.*
- Kordava Librarian, the unnamed librarian of the city of Kordava, from the game *Conan: The Dark Axe.*
- Lady, from the game *Boktai 2: Solar Boy Django.*
- Lex, the bespectacled green worm caretaker of the Great Library, from the puzzle games *Bookworm* and *Bookworm Adventures.*
- Librari, the Elder of the Town Minish, from the game *The Legend of Zelda: The Minish Cap.*
- Marcus, from the game *Siege of Avalon.*
- Maria, from the game *Harvest Moon 64.*
- Mary, from the game *Harvest Moon: Friends of Mineral Town.*
- Master Librarian, the caretaker of Dracula's Long Library, from the game *Castlevania: Symphony of the Night.*
- Mop Top Island Librarian, an anthropomorphic onion, from the children's educational game *Pajama Sam 3: You Are What You Eat From Your Head To Your Feet.*
- Nightshade, the super-hero alter ego of librarian Mark Gray, from the game *Nightshade.*
- Natsume Oguro, a 15-year-old girl, from the game *.hack//INFECTION.*
- Onett Librarian, the unnamed caretaker of the Onett Library, from the game *EarthBound.*
- Phatt Island Librarian, the unnamed lady in charge of the library on Phatt Island, from the game *Monkey Island 2: LeChuck's Revenge.*

- Hester Primm, from the game *The Sims Bustin' Out.*
- Victorian Principles, from the game *Leisure Suit Larry 7: Love for Sail!.*
- Mrs. Stapleton, from the game *Fallout.*
- Mr. Sullivan, from the game *Clock Tower.*
- Swofford, from the game *Geneforge 2.*
- Tar-Meena, an Argonian located within the Arcane University, from the game *Elder Scrolls IV.*
- Trish, from the game *Wild Arms Alter Code: F.*
- Sherman Trout, head of the Library of Congress, from the game *The Final Scene.*
- Cedrin Zil, from the game *Icewind Dale II.*
- *World of Warcraft* features several librarian characters: Mae Paledust, Brother Paxton, Donyal Tovald, and Milton Sheaf.

TOYS AND HOBBIES

- In 2003, Archie McPhee brought out a librarian action figure, modelled on Seattle Public Library librarian Nancy Pearl. Wearing a suit, bun and glasses, the action figure sparked controversy. particularly for the button-triggered shushing motion. Many librarians took it in a light-hearted spirit, while others felt it perpetuated negative stereotypes.
- Space Marine Librarians are characters from the collectible miniatures game *Warhammer 40,000* ; these superhuman fighters come equipped with potent psychic powers, rather than just being deskbound intellects. Wielding force staffs and psychic abilities, they are found on the battlefield battling alongside their non-psychic battle brothers delivering justice to the Emperor's enemies, while at the same time advising the Space Marine Commander.

MUSIC

- Sweet Librarian by Railroad Jerk, from The Third Rail album

- The Librarian's Nightmare by Phil Hammon from The Librarian's Nightmare album
- "Love in the Library" by Jimmy Buffett, from the Fruitcakes album
- " Librarian" by New Zealand band Haunted Love
- "Karen" by the Go-Betweens, from the Lee Remick/ Karen 7" single
- Tales of a Librarian, album by Tori Amos
- The Librarians, defunct Californian power pop band
- Librarians, rock band from West Virginia
- Librarian by Jonathan Rundman, from Public Library album
- Library by Cursor Minor, from Library/Our Day Will Come

COMIC STRIPS

- Unshelved is an online daily comic strip set in Mallville Public Library reflecting changes in the real world of libraries and with an eye for popular culture.
- Questionable Content is another webcomic that recently began featuring a character who works in an academic library setting.
- One Big Happy often features Ruthie at Story Time at her local library. The Library Lady is often despairing of Ruthie's non-sequtorial interruptions.

LIBRARY TECHNICIAN

A library technician is a person who uses their clerical skills to assist librarians acquire, prepare and organize information. They also assist library patrons in finding information although this is usually part of their required duties. The widespread use of computerized information storage and retrieval systems has resulted in library technicians handling technical services (such as derivative cataloguing) that were once performed by librarians. Because libraries are increasingly using new technologies (such as automated databases, CD-ROM, the Internet and virtual libraries), the role of the library technician is expanding and evolving accordingly. In addition, library managers find hiriing library technicians attractive because their wages are slightly lower than that of librarians.

Library technicians may be graduates of a library diploma programme (commonly called "Library and Information Technician") from a community college or institute. Duties can vary with the type and size of the library but can include: cataloguing and classifying of materials, data input to assist in acquiring print and nonprint materials, and circulation procedures. In a larger library, they may be responsible for clerical staff in a certain section or department. In smaller libraries, where the foundations of organization and operation are already established, they may serve as the manager.

Using the latest information technologies, their goal is to bring together people, information and materials and meet the challenges of a constantly changing information environment. Library technicians work in environments as diverse as business corporations, professional firms, financial institutions, cultural organizations, public libraries and schools.

LIBRARY CATALOGUE

A library catalogue (or library catalogue) is a register of all *bibliographic items* found in a particular library or group of libraries, such as those belonging to a university system spread out over several geographic locations. A bibliographic item can be any information entity (*e.g.*, books, computer files, graphics, realia, cartographic materials, etc.), that is considered library material (*e.g.*, a single novel in an anthology), or a group of library materials (*e.g.*, a trilogy), or linked from the catalogue (*e.g.*, a webpage) as far as it is relevant to the catalogue and to the users (patrons) of the library.

The card catalogue was a familiar sight to library users for generations, but it has been effectively replaced by the Online Public Access Catalogue (OPAC). Some still refer to the online catalogue as a "card catalogue", but this is incorrect. Some libraries with OPAC access still have card catalogues on site, but these are now strictly a secondary resource and are seldom updated. Many of the libraries that have retained their physical card catalogue post a sign advising the last year that the card catalogue was updated. Some libraries have eliminated their card catalogue in favour of the OPAC for the purpose of saving space for other use, such as additional shelving.

GOAL OF A LIBRARY CATALOGUE

Charles Ammi Cutter made the first explicit statement regarding the objectives of a bibliographic system in 1876. According to Cutter, those objectives were:

1. to enable a person to find a book of which either (Finding objective)
    - the author
    - the title
    - the subject is known.
2. to show what the library has (Collocating objective)
    - by a given author
    - on a given subject
    - in a given kind of literature
3. to assist in the choice of a book (Choice objective)
    - as to its edition (bibliographically)
    - as to its character (literary or topical)

These objectives can still be recognized in more modern definitions formulated throughout the 20th century. 1960/61 Cutter's objectives were revised by Lubetzky and Lubetzky and the Conference on Cataloguing Principles (CCP) in Paris. The latest attempt to describe a library catalog's goals and functions was made in 1998 with Functional Requirements for Bibliographic Records (FRBR) which defines four user tasks: find, identify, select, and obtain.

CATALOGUE TYPES

Traditionally, there are the following types of catalogue:

- *Author* catalogue: a formal catalogue, sorted alphabetically according to the authors' or editors' names of the entries.

- *Title* catalogue: a formal catalogue, sorted alphabetically according to the title of the entries.
- *Dictionary* catalogue: a catalogue in which all entries (author, title, subject, series) are interfiled in a single alphabetical order. This was the primary form of card catalogue in the Anglo-American world just prior to the introduction of the computer-based catalogue.
- *Keyword* catalogue: a subject catalogue, sorted alphabetically according to some system of keywords.
- Mixed alphabetic catalogue forms: sometimes, one finds a mixed author/title, or an author/title/keyword catalogue.
- *Systematic* catalogue: a subject catalogue, sorted according to some systematic subdivision of subjects. Also called a *Classified* catalogue.
- *Shelf list* catalogue: a formal catalogue with entries sorted in the same order as bibliographic items are shelved. This catalogue may also serve as the primary inventory for the library.

HISTORY

Library catalogues originated as manuscript lists, arranged by format (folio, quarto, etc.) or in a rough alphabetical arrangement by author. Printed catalogues, sometimes called *dictionary catalogues* enabled scholars outside a library to gain an idea of its contents. These would sometimes be interleaved with blank leaves on which additions could be recorded, or bound as *guardbooks* in which slips of paper were bound in for new entries. Slips could also be kept loose in cardboard or tin boxes, stored on shelves. The first card catalogues appeared in the nineteenth century, enabling much more flexibility, and towards the end of the twentieth century the OPAC was developed

- 1595: *Nomenclator* of Leiden University Library appears, the first printed catalogue of an institutional library.
- 1674: Thomas Hyde's catalogue for the Bodleian Library.

More about the early history of library catalogues has been collected in 1956 by Strout.

CATALOGUING RULES

Cataloguing (or cataloguing) rules have been defined to allow for consistent cataloguing of various library materials across several persons of a cataloguing team and across time. Users can use them to clarify how to find an entry and how to interpret the data in an entry. Cataloguing rules prescribe

- which information from a bibliographic item is included in the entry;
- how this information is presented on a catalogue card or in a cataloguing record;
- how the entries should be sorted in the catalogue.

The larger a collection, the more elaborate cataloguing rules are needed. Users cannot and do not want to examine hundreds of catalogue entries or even dozens of library items to find the one item they need.

Currently, most cataloguing rules are similar to, or even based on, the International Standard Bibliographic Description (ISBD), a set of rules produced by the International Federation of Library Associations (IFLA) to describe a wide range of library materials.

These rules organize the bibliographic description of an item in the following areas: title and statement of responsibility (author or editor), edition, material-dependent information (for example, the scale of a map), publication and distribution, physical description (for example, number of pages), series, note, and standard number (ISBN). The most commonly used set of cataloguing rules in the English speaking world are the Anglo-American Cataloguing Rules, 2nd Edition, or AACR2 for short. In the German-speaking world there exists the *Regeln für alphabetische Katalogisierung*, abbreviated RAK. AACR2 has been translated into many languages, however, for use around the world. AACR2 provides rules for *descriptive cataloguing* only and does not touch upon *subject cataloguing.*

Library items that are written in a foreign script are, in some cases, transliterated to the script of the catalogue.

Sorting

In a title catalogue, one can distinguish two sort orders:

- In the *grammatic* sort order (used mainly in older catalogues), the most important word of the title is the first sort term. The importance of a word is measured by grammatic rules; for example, the first noun may be defined to be the most important word.
- In the *mechanic* sort order, the first word of the title is the first sort term. Most new catalogues use this scheme, but still include a trace of the grammatic sort order: they neglect an article (The, A, etc.) at the beginning of the title.

The grammatic sort order has the advantage that often, the most important word of the title is also a good keyword (question 3), and it is the word most users remember first when their memory is incomplete. However, it has the disadvantage that many elaborate grammatic rules are needed, so that only expert users may be able to search the catalogue without help from a librarian. In some catalogues, person's names are standardized, i. e., the name of the person is always (catalogued and) sorted in a standard form, even if it appears differently in the library material. This standardization is achieved by a process called authority control. An advantage of the authority control is that it is easier to answer question 2 (which works of some author does the library have?). On the other hand, it may be more difficult to answer question 1 (does the library have some specific material?) if the material spells the author in a peculiar variant. For the cataloguer, it may incur (too) much work to check whether *Smith, J.* is *Smith, John* or *Smith, Jack*. For some works, even the title can be standardized. The technical term for this is *uniform title*. For example, translations and reeditions are sometimes sorted under their original title. In many catalogues, parts of the Bible are sorted under the standard name of the book(s) they contain. The plays of William Shakespeare are another frequently cited example of the role played by a *uniform title* in the library catalogue.

Many complications about alphabetic sorting of entries arise. Some examples:

- Some languages know sorting conventions that differ from the language of the catalogue. For example, some Dutch catalogues sort *IJ* as *Y*. Should an English catalogue follow this suit? And should a Dutch catalogue sort non-Dutch words the same way?

- Some titles contain numbers, for example *2001: A Space Odyssey*. Should they be sorted as numbers, or spelled out as *Two thousand and one*?
- *de Balzac, Honoré* or *Balzac, Honoré de*? *Ortega y Gasset, José* or *Gasset, José Ortega y*?

For a fuller discussion, see collation.

In a subject catalogue, one has to decide on which classification system to use. The cataloguer will select appropriate subject headings for the bibliographic item and a unique classification number (sometimes known as a "call number") which is used not only for identification but also for the purposes of shelving, placing items with similar subjects near one another, which aids in browsing by library users, who are thus often able to take advantage of serendipity in their search process.

ONLINE CATALOGUES

Online cataloguing has greatly enhanced the usability of catalogues, thanks to the rise of Machine Readable Cataloguing = MARC standards in the 1960s. Rules governing the creation of catalogue MARC records include not only formal cataloguing rules like AACR2 but also special rules specific to MARC, available from the Library of Congress and also OCLC. MARC was originally used to automate the creation of physical catalogue cards; Now the MARC computer files are accessed directly in the search process. OPACs have enhanced usability over traditional card formats because:

1. The online catalogue does not need to be sorted statically; the user can choose author, title, keyword, or systematic order dynamically.
2. Most online catalogues offer a search facility for any word of the title; the goal of the grammatic word order (provide an entry on the word that most users would look for) is reached even better.
3. Many online catalogues allow links between several variants of an author name. So, authors can be found

both under the original and the standardised name (if entered properly by the cataloguer).

SEARCHING WITH AN OPAC

As noted above, the acronym OPAC means Online Public Access Catalogue.

Many libraries have their catalogue accessible via Internet; some of them can be queried using a simple browser, other using a special version of browser (with Javascript and CSS features), some others using Z39.50 clients.

If you are looking for a book or another item, you can access to the OPAC of your nearest library and search for it there. If you cannot find a particular book in the catalogue, it may be obtainable through interlibrary loan, also known to librarians as I.L.L. Ask the nearest Reference librarian for assistance.

If you want to look if a book exists and you have few elements to identify it, you can use a meta-searcher: you can fill the query form once and spread you search over many library catalogues. A service such as MultiOpac does this task for you.

Another option is to use a union catalogue, in which many libraries have combined their entire holdings into one database. The largest union catalogue is OCLC's WorldCat.

ARCHIVIST

An Archivist surveying an unprocessed collection of materials. Surveying is commonly done to determine priorities for preservation and/or conservation of materials before an archivist begins arrangement and description.

An archivist is a professional who assesses, collects, organizes, preserves, maintains control over, and provides access to information determined to have long-term value.

The information maintained by an archivist can be any form of media (photographs, video or sound recordings, letters, documents, electronic records, etc.). As Richard Pearce-Moses wrote, *"Archivists keep records that have enduring value as reliable memories of the past, and they help people find and understand the information they need in those records."*

Determining what records have enduring value is not always easy. Archivists must also select records valuable enough to justify the costs of storage and preservation, plus the labour intensive expenses of arrangement, description, and reference service. The theory and scholarly work underpinning archives practices is called archival science.

DUTIES AND WORK ENVIRONMENT

Archivists' duties include acquiring and appraising new collections, arranging and describing records, providing reference service, and preserving materials. In arranging records, archivists apply two important principles: provenance and original order, sometimes referred to as *respect des fonds*. Provenance refers to the origin of records, essentially who created them.

The idea of *respect des fonds* is applied by keeping records in their original order as established and maintained by the creator(s). This also means that records from one corporate body should not be mixed with records from another. Original order is not always the best way to maintain some collections though, and archivists must use their own experience and current best practices to determine the correct way to keep collections of mixed media or those lacking a clear original arrangement.

American archivists are also guided in their work by a code of ethics. Alongside their work behind the scenes arranging and caring for collections, archivists assist users in interpreting collections and answering inquiries. This reference work can be just part of an archivist's job in a smaller organization, or consist of most of their occupation in a larger archive where specific roles (such as processing archivist and reference archivist) may be delineated.

Archivists work for a variety of organizations, including government agencies, local authorities, museums, hospitals, historical societies, businesses, charities, corporations, colleges and universities, and any institution whose records may potentially be valuable to researchers, exhibitors, genealogists, or others. Alternatively, they could also work on the collections of a large family or even of an individual. Applicants for archives jobs usually outnumber positions available.

Archivists are often educators as well; it is not unusual for an archivist employed at a university or college to lecture in a subject related to their collection. Archivists employed at cultural institutions or for local government frequently design educational or outreach programmes to further the ability of archive users to understand and access information in their collections. This might include such varied activities as exhibitions, promotional events or even media coverage.

The advent of Encoded Archival Description, along with increasing demand for materials to be made available online, has required archivists to become more tech-savvy in the past decade. Many archivists are now acquiring basic XML skills in order to make their finding aids available to researchers online.

SKILLS

Because of the varied nature of the job and organisations and work environment, archivists need to have a wide range of skills:

- Those who work in reference and access-oriented positions need to be good with people, so that they are able to help them with their research.
- An ability to apply some basic knowledge of conservation is needed to help extend the useful life of cultural artifacts. Many different types of media (such as photographs, acidic papers, and unstable copy processes) can deteriorate if not stored and maintained properly.
- Although many archival collections are comprised of paper records, increasingly archivists must confront the new challenges posed by the preservation of electronic records, so they need to be forward-looking and technologically proficient.
- Because of the amount of sorting and listing, they need to be very logical and organised and be able to pay attention to detail.

- When cataloguing records, or when assisting users, archivists need to have some research skills.

EDUCATIONAL PREPARATION

The educational preparation for archivists varies from country to country.

Colombia

In Colombia, the Universidad de La Salle offers the degree of Professional in Information Systems, Library and Archival Sciences. It is a vocational training programme, within existing legal standards aimed at providing knowledge, skills and abilities required for the design and management of information systems and documentation of various sorts.

Its projection for the future is based on the application of new information technologies and communications for the management of information services economically viable. The programme was created in 1971.

Graduates of this programme have founded the Colombian College of Archivists-CCA, and the Colombian Society of Archivists-SCA; comprising the Alumni Association of Librarian and Archival Science (Asociación de Egresados de Bibliotecología y Archivística de la Universidad de La Salle-ASEBIAR); are officials of the General Archives of the Nation, the Archives of Bogota and the most prestigious public and private companies.

Other institutions that offers a degree in Archival Science are:

- Universidad del Quindío-Professional degree: Professional in Information and Documentation, Library and Archival Sciences.
- Escuela Interamericana de Bibliotecología-Technological degree: Technologist in Archival Science.
- Universidad Católica de Manizales-Technological degree: Technologist in Documentation and Archival Science.
- Servicio Nacional de Aprendizaje-SENA in chain training with the Tecnológico de Antioquia-Technical degree: Professional Technical in Archives.

Some institutions, tech colleges and universities offers assignatures about Archival Science, but don't offers title of Archivist.

Republic of Ireland

In Ireland, the University College Dublin School of History and Archives offers a Higher Diploma in Archival Studies, recognised by the Society of Archivists.

United Kingdom

In the United Kingdom, there are currently five full-or part-time professional Masters courses in archives administration or management which are recognised by the Society of Archivists. Students are expected to have relevant paid or voluntary work experience before obtaining a place on the UK courses; many undertake a year's traineeship. Also, in Great Britain, certification can be pursued via the Registration Scheme offered by the Society of Archivists.

United States

According to the most recent professional census of American Archivists published, most of those in the United States have earned a Masters degree. However, the exact type of degree can vary; the most common sorts of advanced degrees held by archivists are in archival science, history, library science, or library and information science. It is also possible for archivists to earn a doctorate in library, or library and information, science. Archivists with a Ph. D. often work as teaching faculty or deans and directors of archival programmes. In 2002, the Society of American Archivists published Guidelines for a Graduate Programme in Archival Studies.

Also in the United States, the Academy of Certified Archivists offers supplemental archival training by means of a certification programme. Critics of ACA certification object to its yearly membership fees, the theoretical versus practical nature of its tests, and the need for members to re-certify every five years. Many positions in government archives require certification from the ACA, but due to its controversial nature, the ACA is not required by all employers in the United States.

7

Computer Science Education for Library Services

Some universities teach computer science as a theoretical study of computation and algorithmic reasoning. These programmes often feature the theory of computation, analysis of algorithms, formal methods, concurrency theory, databases, computer graphics and systems analysis, among others. They typically also teach computer programming, but treat it as a vessel for the support of other fields of computer science rather than a central focus of high-level study.

Other colleges and universities, as well as secondary schools and vocational programmes that teach computer science, emphasize the practice of advanced computer programming rather than the theory of algorithms and computation in their computer science curricula. Such curricula tend to focus on those skills that are important to workers entering the software industry. The practical aspects of computer programming are often referred to as software engineering. However, there is a lot of disagreement over what the term "software engineering" actually means, and whether it is the same thing as programming.

COMPUTER

Computers take numerous physical forms. The first devices that resemble modern computers date to the mid-20th century (around 1940-1941), although the computer concept and various machines similar to computers existed prior. Early electronic computers were the size of a large room, consuming as much power as several hundred modern personal computers. Modern computers are based on comparatively tiny integrated circuits and are millions to billions of times more capable while occupying a fraction of the space.

Today, simple computers may be made small enough to fit into a wrist watch and be powered from a watch battery. Personal computers in various forms are icons of the information age and are what most people think of as "a computer". However, the most common form of computer in use today is by far the embedded computer. Embedded computers are small, simple devices that are often used to control other devices — for example, they may be found in machines ranging from fighter aircraft to industrial robots, digital cameras, and even children's toys.

The ability to store and execute lists of instructions called *programmes* makes computers extremely versatile and distinguishes them from calculators. The Church–Turing thesis is a mathematical statement of this versatility: Any computer with a certain minimum capability is, in principle, capable of performing the same tasks that any other computer can perform. Therefore, computers with capability and complexity ranging from that of a personal digital assistant to a supercomputer are all able to perform the same computational tasks given enough time and storage capacity.

HISTORY OF COMPUTING

It is difficult to identify any one device as the earliest computer, partly because the term "computer" has been subject to varying interpretations over time.

Originally, the term "computer" referred to a person who performed numerical calculations (a human computer), often with the aid of a mechanical calculating device. Examples of early mechanical computing devices included the abacus, the slide rule and arguably the astrolabe and the Antikythera mechanism (which dates from about 150-100 BC). The end of the Middle Ages saw a re-invigoration of European mathematics and engineering, and Wilhelm Schickard's 1623 device was the first of a number of mechanical calculators constructed by European engineers.

However, none of those devices fit the modern definition of a computer because they could not be programmed. In 1801, Joseph Marie Jacquard made an improvement to the textile loom that used a series of punched paper cards as a template to allow his loom to weave intricate patterns automatically. The resulting Jacquard loom was an important step in the development of computers because the use of punched cards to define woven patterns can be viewed as an early, albeit limited, form of programmability.

In 1837, Charles Babbage was the first to conceptualize and design a fully programmable mechanical computer that he called "The Analytical Engine". Due to limited finance, and an inability to resist tinkering with the design, Babbage never actually built his Analytical Engine.

Large-scale automated data processing of punched cards was performed for the U.S. Census in 1890 by tabulating machines designed by Herman Hollerith and manufactured by the Computing Tabulating Recording Corporation, which later became IBM. By the end of the 19th century a number of technologies that would later prove useful in the realization of practical computers had begun to appear: the punched card, Boolean algebra, the vacuum tube (thermionic valve) and the teleprinter. During the first half of the 20th century, many scientific computing needs were met by increasingly sophisticated analog computers, which used a direct mechanical or electrical model of the problem as a basis for computation. However, these were not programmable and generally lacked the versatility and accuracy of modern digital computers.

A succession of steadily more powerful and flexible computing devices were constructed in the 1930s and 1940s, gradually adding the key features that are seen in modern computers. The use of digital electronics (largely invented by Claude Shannon in 1937) and more flexible programmability were vitally important steps, but defining one point along this road as "the first digital electronic computer" is difficult (Shannon 1940). Notable achievements include:

EDSAC was one of the first computers to implement the stored programme (von Neumann) architecture.

- Konrad Zuse's electromechanical "Z machines". The Z3 (1941) was the first working machine featuring binary arithmetic, including floating point arithmetic and a measure of programmability. In 1998 the Z3 was proved to be Turing complete, therefore being the world's first operational computer.
- The non-programmable Atanasoff – Berry Computer (1941) which used vacuum tube based computation, binary numbers, and regenerative capacitor memory.
- The secret British Colossus computer (1944), which had limited programmability but demonstrated that a device using thousands of tubes could be reasonably reliable and electronically reprogrammable. It was used for breaking German wartime codes.
- The Harvard Mark I (1944), a large-scale electromechanical computer with limited programmability.
- The U.S. Army's Ballistics Research Laboratory ENIAC (1946), which used decimal arithmetic and is sometimes called the first general purpose electronic computer (since Konrad Zuse's Z3 of 1941 used electromagnets instead of electronics). Initially, however, ENIAC had an inflexible architecture which essentially required rewiring to change its programming.

Several developers of ENIAC, recognizing its flaws, came up with a far more flexible and elegant design, which came to be known as the stored programme architecture or von Neumann architecture. This design was first formally described by John von Neumann in the paper "First Draft of a Report on the EDVAC", published in 1945. A number of projects to develop computers based on the stored programme architecture commenced around this time, the first of these being completed in Great Britain. The first to be demonstrated working was the Manchester Small-Scale Experimental Machine (SSEM) or "Baby". However, the EDSAC, completed a year after SSEM, was perhaps the first practical implementation of the stored programme design. Shortly thereafter, the machine originally described by von Neumann's paper — EDVAC — was completed but did not see full-time use for an additional two years. Nearly all modern computers implement some form of the stored programme architecture, making it the single trait by which the word "computer" is now defined. By this standard, many earlier devices would no longer be called computers by today's definition, but are usually referred to as such in their historical context. While the technologies used in computers have changed dramatically since the first electronic, general-purpose computers of the 1940s, most still use the von Neumann architecture. The design made the universal computer a practical reality.

Vacuum tube-based computers were in use throughout the 1950s, but were largely replaced in the 1960s by transistor-based devices, which were smaller, faster, cheaper, used less power and were more reliable. These factors allowed computers to be produced on an unprecedented commercial scale. By the 1970s, the adoption of integrated circuit technology and the subsequent creation of microprocessors such as the Intel 4004 caused another leap in size, speed, cost and reliability. By the 1980s, computers had become sufficiently small and cheap to replace simple mechanical controls in domestic appliances such as washing machines. Around the same time, computers became widely accessible for personal use by individuals in the form of home computers and the now ubiquitous personal computer. In conjunction with the widespread growth of the Internet since the 1990s, personal computers are becoming as common as the television and the telephone and almost all modern electronic devices contain a computer of some kind.

STORED PROGRAMME ARCHITECTURE

The defining feature of modern computers which distinguishes them from all other machines is that they can be programmed. That is to say that a list of instructions (the programme) can be given to the computer and it will store them and carry them out at some time in the future.

In most cases, computer instructions are simple: add one number to another, move some data from one location to another, send a message to some external device, etc. These instructions are read from the computer's memory and are generally carried out (executed) in the order they were given. However, there are usually specialized instructions to tell the computer to jump ahead or backwards to some other place in the programme and to carry on executing from there. These are called "jump" instructions (or branches). Furthermore, jump instructions may be made to happen conditionally so that different sequences of instructions may be used depending on the result of some previous calculation or some external event. Many computers directly support subroutines by providing a type of jump that "remembers" the location it jumped from and another instruction to return to the instruction following that jump instruction.

Programme execution might be likened to reading a book. While a person will normally read each word and line in sequence, they may at times jump back to an earlier place in the text or skip sections that are not of interest. Similarly, a computer may sometimes go back and repeat the instructions in some section of the programme over and over again until some internal condition is met. This is called the flow of control within the programme and it is what allows the computer to perform tasks repeatedly without human intervention.

Comparatively, a person using a pocket calculator can perform a basic arithmetic operation such as adding two numbers with just a few button presses. But to add together all of the numbers from 1 to 1,000 would take thousands of button presses and a lot of time — with a near certainty of making a mistake. On the other hand, a computer may be programmed to do this with just a few simple instructions. For example:

```
mov #0,sum; set sum to 0
mov #1,num; set num to 1
loop: add num,sum; add num to sum
add #1,num; add 1 to num
cmp num,#1000; compare num to 1000
ble loop; if num <= 1000, go back to 'loop'
halt; end of programme. stop running
```

Once told to run this programme, the computer will perform the repetitive addition task without further human intervention.

It will almost never make a mistake and a modern PC can complete the task in about a millionth of a second.

However, computers cannot "think" for themselves in the sense that they only solve problems in exactly the way they are programmed to. An intelligent human faced with the above addition task might soon realize that instead of actually adding up all the numbers one can simply use the equation

and arrive at the correct answer (500,500) with little work. In other words, a computer programmed to add up the numbers one by one as in the example above would do exactly that without regard to efficiency or alternative solutions.

Programmes

In practical terms, a computer programme might include anywhere from a dozen instructions to many millions of instructions for something like a word processor or a web browser. A typical modern computer can execute billions of instructions every second and nearly never make a mistake over years of operation.

Large computer programmes may take teams of computer programmers years to write and the probability of the entire programme having been written completely in the manner intended is unlikely. Errors in computer programmes are called bugs. Sometimes bugs are benign and do not affect the usefulness of the programme, in other cases they might cause the programme to completely fail (crash), in yet other cases there may be subtle problems. Sometimes otherwise benign bugs may be used for malicious intent, creating a security exploit. Bugs are usually not the fault of the computer. Since computers merely execute the instructions they are given, bugs are nearly always the result of programmer error or an oversight made in the program's design.

In most computers, individual instructions are stored as machine code with each instruction being given a unique number (its operation code or opcode for short). The command to add two numbers together would have one opcode, the command to multiply them would have a different opcode and so on. The simplest computers are able to perform any of a handful of different instructions, the more complex computers have several hundred to choose from — each with a unique numerical code. Since the computer's memory is able to store numbers, it can also store the instruction codes.

This leads to the important fact that entire programmes (which are just lists of instructions) can be represented as lists of numbers and can themselves be manipulated inside the computer just as if they were numeric data. The fundamental concept of storing programmes in the computer's memory alongside the data they operate on is the crux of the von Neumann, or stored programme, architecture. In some cases, a computer might store some or all of its programme in memory that is kept separate from the data it operates on. This is called the Harvard architecture after the Harvard Mark I computer. Modern von Neumann computers display some traits of the Harvard architecture in their designs, such as in CPU caches.

While it is possible to write computer programmes as long lists of numbers (machine language) and this technique was used with many early computers, it is extremely tedious to do so in practice, especially for complicated programmes. Instead, each basic instruction can be given a short name that is indicative of its function and easy to remember — a mnemonic such as ADD, SUB, MULT or JUMP. These mnemonics are collectively known as a computer's assembly language. Converting programmes written in assembly language into something the computer can actually understand (machine language) is usually done by a computer programme called an assembler. Machine languages and the assembly languages that represent them (collectively termed low-level programming languages) tend to be unique to a particular type of computer. For instance, an ARM architecture computer (such as may be found in a PDA or a hand-held videogame) cannot understand the machine language of an Intel Pentium or the AMD Athlon 64 computer that might be in a PC.

Though considerably easier than in machine language, writing long programmes in assembly language is often difficult and error prone. Therefore, most complicated programmes are written in more abstract high-level programming languages that are able to express the needs of the computer programmer more conveniently (and thereby help reduce programmer error).

High level languages are usually "compiled" into machine language (or sometimes into assembly language and then into machine language) using another computer programme called a compiler.

Since high level languages are more abstract than assembly language, it is possible to use different compilers to translate the same high level language programme into the machine language of many different types of computer. This is part of the means by which software like video games may be made available for different computer architectures such as personal computers and various video game consoles.

The task of developing large software systems is an immense intellectual effort. It has proven, historically, to be very difficult to produce software with an acceptably high reliability, on a predictable schedule and budget. The academic and professional discipline of software engineering concentrates specifically on this problem.

Example

Suppose a computer is being employed to drive a traffic light. A simple stored programme might say:

1. Turn off all of the lights
2. Turn on the red light
3. Wait for sixty seconds
4. Turn off the red light
5. Turn on the green light
6. Wait for sixty seconds
7. Turn off the green light
8. Turn on the yellow light
9. Wait for two seconds
10. Turn off the yellow light
11. Jump to instruction number

With this set of instructions, the computer would cycle the light continually through red, green, yellow and back to red again until told to stop running the programme. However, suppose there is a simple on/off switch connected to the computer that is intended be used to make the light flash red while some maintenance operation is being performed. The programme might then instruct the computer to:

1. Turn off all of the lights
2. Turn on the red light
3. Wait for sixty seconds
4. Turn off the red light
5. Turn on the green light
6. Wait for sixty seconds
7. Turn off the green light
8. Turn on the yellow light
9. Wait for two seconds
10. Turn off the yellow light
11. If the maintenance switch is NOT turned on then jump to instruction number 2
12. Turn on the red light
13. Wait for one second
14. Turn off the red light
15. Wait for one second
16. Jump to instruction number 11

In this manner, the computer is either running the instructions from number (2) to (11) over and over or its running the instructions from (11) down to (16) over and over, depending on the position of the switch.

HOW COMPUTERS WORK

A general purpose computer has four main sections: the arithmetic and logic unit (ALU), the control unit, the memory, and the input and output devices (collectively termed I/O). These parts are interconnected by busses, often made of groups of wires.

The control unit, ALU, registers, and basic I/O (and often other hardware closely linked with these) are collectively known as a central processing unit (CPU). Early CPUs were composed of many separate components but since the mid-1970s CPUs have typically been constructed on a single integrated circuit called a *microprocessor*.

Control Unit

The control unit (often called a control system or central controller) directs the various components of a computer. It reads and interprets (decodes) instructions in the programme one by one. The control system decodes each instruction and turns it into a series of control signals that operate the other parts of the computer. Control systems in advanced computers may change the order of some instructions so as to improve performance.

A key component common to all CPUs is the programme counter, a special memory cell (a register) that keeps track of which location in memory the next instruction is to be read from.

The control system's function is as follows — note that this is a simplified description and some of these steps may be performed concurrently or in a different order depending on the type of CPU:

1. Read the code for the next instruction from the cell indicated by the programme counter.
2. Decode the numerical code for the instruction into a set of commands or signals for each of the other systems.
3. Increment the programme counter so it points to the next instruction.
4. Read whatever data the instruction requires from cells in memory (or perhaps from an input device). The location of this required data is typically stored within the instruction code.
5. Provide the necessary data to an ALU or register.
6. If the instruction requires an ALU or specialized hardware to complete, instruct the hardware to perform the requested operation.
7. Write the result from the ALU back to a memory location or to a register or perhaps an output device.
8. Jump back to step (1).

Since the programme counter is (conceptually) just another set of memory cells, it can be changed by calculations done in the ALU. Adding 100 to the programme counter would cause the next instruction to be read from a place 100 locations further down the programme. Instructions that modify the programme counter are often known as "jumps" and allow for loops (instructions that are repeated by the computer) and often conditional instruction execution (both examples of control flow). It is noticeable that the sequence of operations that the control unit goes through to process an instruction is in itself like a short computer programme-and indeed, in some more complex CPU designs, there is another yet smaller computer called a microsequencer that runs a microcode programme that causes all of these events to happen.

Arithmetic/logic Unit (ALU)

The set of arithmetic operations that a particular ALU supports may be limited to adding and subtracting or might include multiplying or dividing, trigonometry functions (sine, cosine, etc.) and square roots. Some can only operate on whole numbers (integers) whilst others use floating point to represent real numbers — albeit with limited precision. However, any computer that is capable of performing just the simplest operations can be programmed to break down the more complex operations into simple steps that it can perform. Therefore, any computer can be programmed to perform any arithmetic operation — although it will take more time to do so if its ALU does not directly support the operation. An ALU may also compare numbers and return boolean truth values (true or false) depending on whether one is equal to, greater than or less than the other ("is 64 greater than 65?").

Logic operations involve Boolean logic: AND, OR, XOR and NOT. These can be useful both for creating complicated conditional statements and processing boolean logic.

Superscalar computers contain multiple ALUs so that they can process several instructions at the same time. Graphics processors and computers with SIMD and MIMD features often provide ALUs that can perform arithmetic on vectors and matrices.

Memory

A computer's memory can be viewed as a list of cells into which numbers can be placed or read. Each cell has a numbered "address" and can store a single number. The computer can be instructed to "put the number 123 into the cell numbered 1357" or to "add the number that is in cell 1357 to the number that is in cell 2468 and put the answer into cell 1595". The information stored in memory may represent practically anything. Letters, numbers, even computer instructions can be placed into memory with equal ease. Since the CPU does not differentiate between different types of information, it is up to the software to give significance to what the memory sees as nothing but a series of numbers.

In almost all modern computers, each memory cell is set up to store binary numbers in groups of eight bits (called a byte). Each byte is able to represent 256 different numbers; either from 0 to 255 or-128 to +127. To store larger numbers, several consecutive bytes may be used (typically, two, four or eight). When negative numbers are required, they are usually stored in two's complement notation. Other arrangements are possible, but are usually not seen outside of specialized applications or historical contexts. A computer can store any kind of information in memory as long as it can be somehow represented in numerical form. Modern computers have billions or even trillions of bytes of memory. The CPU contains a special set of memory cells called registers that can be read and written to much more rapidly than the main memory area. There are typically between two and one hundred registers depending on the type of CPU. Registers are used for the most frequently needed data items to avoid having to access main memory every time data is needed. Since data is constantly being worked on, reducing the need to access main memory (which is often slow compared to the ALU and control units) greatly increases the computer's speed.

Computer main memory comes in two principal varieties: random access memory or RAM and read-only memory or ROM. RAM can be read and written to anytime the CPU commands it, but ROM is pre-loaded with data and software that never changes, so the CPU can only read from it. ROM is typically used to store the computer's initial start-up instructions. In general, the contents of RAM is erased when the power to the computer is turned off while ROM retains its data indefinitely.

In a PC, the ROM contains a specialized programme called the BIOS that orchestrates loading the computer's operating system from the hard disk drive into RAM whenever the computer is turned on or reset. In embedded computers, which frequently do not have disk drives, all of the software required to perform the task may be stored in ROM. Software that is stored in ROM is often called firmware because it is notionally more like hardware than software. Flash memory blurs the distinction between ROM and RAM by retaining data when turned off but being rewritable like RAM. However, flash memory is typically much slower than conventional ROM and RAM so its use is restricted to applications where high speeds are not required.

In more sophisticated computers there may be one or more RAM cache memories which are slower than registers but faster than main memory. Generally computers with this sort of cache are designed to move frequently needed data into the cache automatically, often without the need for any intervention on the programmer's part.

Input/output (I/O)

I/O is the means by which a computer receives information from the outside world and sends results back. Devices that provide input or output to the computer are called peripherals. On a typical personal computer, peripherals include input devices like the keyboard and mouse, and output devices such as the display and printer. Hard disk drives, floppy disk drives and optical disc drives serve as both input and output devices. Computer networking is another form of I/O.

Often, I/O devices are complex computers in their own right with their own CPU and memory. A graphics processing unit might contain fifty or more tiny computers that perform the calculations necessary to display 3D graphics. Modern desktop computers contain many smaller computers that assist the main CPU in performing I/O.

Multitasking

While a computer may be viewed as running one gigantic programme stored in its main memory, in some systems it is necessary to give the appearance of running several programmes simultaneously. This is achieved by having the computer switch rapidly between running each programme in turn. One means by which this is done is with a special signal called an interrupt which can periodically cause the computer to stop executing instructions where it was and do something else instead. By remembering where it was executing prior to the interrupt, the computer can return to that task later.

If several programmes are running "at the same time", then the interrupt generator might be causing several hundred interrupts per second, causing a programme switch each time. Since modern computers typically execute instructions several orders of magnitude faster than human perception, it may appear that many programmes are running at the same time even though only one is ever executing in any given instant. This method of multitasking is sometimes termed "time-sharing" since each programme is allocated a "slice" of time in turn.

Before the era of cheap computers, the principle use for multitasking was to allow many people to share the same computer. Seemingly, multitasking would cause a computer that is switching between several programmes to run more slowly-in direct proportion to the number of programmes it is running.

However, most programmes spend much of their time waiting for slow input/output devices to complete their tasks. If a programme is waiting for the user to click on the mouse or press a key on the keyboard, then it will not take a "time slice" until the event it is waiting for has occurred. This frees up time for other programmes to execute so that many programmes may be run at the same time without unacceptable speed loss.

Multiprocessing

Some computers may divide their work between one or more separate CPUs, creating a multiprocessing configuration.

Traditionally, this technique was utilized only in large and powerful computers such as supercomputers, mainframe computers and servers. However, multiprocessor and multi-core (multiple CPUs on a single integrated circuit) personal and laptop computers have become widely available and are beginning to see increased usage in lower-end markets as a result.

Supercomputers in particular often have highly unique architectures that differ significantly from the basic stored-programme architecture and from general purpose computers. They often feature thousands of CPUs, customized high-speed interconnects, and specialized computing hardware.

Such designs tend to be useful only for specialized tasks due to the large scale of programme organization required to successfully utilize most of a the available resources at once. Supercomputers usually see usage in large-scale simulation, graphics rendering, and cryptography applications, as well as with other so-called "embarrassingly parallel" tasks.

Networking and the Internet

Computers have been used to coordinate information in multiple locations since the 1950s, with the U.S. military's SAGE system the first large-scale example of such a system, which led to a number of special-purpose commercial systems like Sabre.

In the 1970s, computer engineers at research institutions throughout the United States began to link their computers together using telecommunications technology. This effort was funded by ARPA (now DARPA), and the computer network that it produced was called the ARPANET. The technologies that made the Arpanet possible spread and evolved.

In time, the network spread beyond academic and military institutions and became known as the Internet. The emergence of networking involved a redefinition of the nature and boundaries of the computer.

Computer operating systems and applications were modified to include the ability to define and access the resources of other computers on the network, such as peripheral devices, stored information, and the like, as extensions of the resources of an individual computer.

Initially these facilities were available primarily to people working in high-tech environments, but in the 1990s the spread of applications like e-mail and the World Wide Web, combined with the development of cheap, fast networking technologies like Ethernet and ADSL saw computer networking become almost ubiquitous.

In fact, the number of computers that are networked is growing phenomenally. A very large proportion of personal computers regularly connect to the Internet to communicate and receive information. "Wireless" networking, often utilizing mobile phone networks, has meant networking is becoming increasingly ubiquitous even in mobile computing environments.

FURTHER TOPICS

Hardware

The term hardware covers all of those parts of a computer that are tangible objects. Circuits, displays, power supplies, cables, keyboards, printers and mice are all hardware.

History of computing hardware		
First Generation (Mechanical/Electromechanical)	Calculators	Antikythera mechanism, Difference Engine, Norden bombsight
	Programmable Devices	Jacquard loom, Analytical Engine, Harvard Mark I, Z3
Second Generation (Vacuum Tubes)	Calculators	Atanasoff–Berry Computer, IBM 604, UNIVAC 60, UNIVAC 120
	Programmable Devices	ENIAC, EDSAC, EDVAC, UNIVAC I, IBM 701, IBM 702, IBM 650, Z22
Third Generation (Discrete transistors and SSI, MSI, LSI Integrated circuits)	Mainframes	IBM 7090, IBM 7080, System/360, BUNCH
	Minicomputer	PDP-8, PDP-11, System/32, System/36
Fourth Generation (VLSI integrated circuits)	Minicomputer	VAX, AS/400
	4-bit microcomputer	Intel 4004, Intel 4040
	8-bit microcomputer	Intel 8008, Intel 8080, Motorola 6800, Motorola 6809, MOS Technology 6502, Zilog Z80
	16-bit microcomputer	8088, Zilog Z8000, WDC 65816/65802
	32-bit microcomputer	80386, Pentium, 68000, ARM architecture
	64-bit microcomputer[15]	x86-64, PowerPC, MIPS, SPARC
	Embedded computer	8048, 8051
	Personal computer	Desktop computer, Home computer, Laptop computer, Personal digital assistant (PDA), Portable computer, Tablet computer, Wearable computer
Theoretical/experimental	Quantum computer, Chemical computer, DNA computing, Optical computer, Spintronics based computer	

Computer Software

Operating system	Unix/BSD	UNIX System V, AIX, HP-UX, Solaris (SunOS), IRIX, List of BSD operating systems
	GNU/Linux	List of Linux distributions, Comparison of Linux distributions
	Microsoft Windows	Windows 95, Windows 98, Windows NT, Windows XP, Windows Vista, Windows CE
	DOS	86-DOS (QDOS), PC-DOS, MS-DOS, FreeDOS
	Mac OS	Mac OS classic, Mac OS X
	Embedded and real-time	List of embedded operating systems
	Experimental	Amoeba, Oberon/Bluebottle, Plan 9 from Bell Labs
Library	Multimedia	DirectX, OpenGL, OpenAL
	Programming library	C standard library, Standard template library
Data	Protocol	TCP/IP, Kermit, FTP, HTTP, SMTP
	File format	HTML, XML, JPEG, MPEG, PNG
User interface	Graphical user interface (WIMP)	Microsoft Windows, GNOME, KDE, QNX Photon, CDE, GEM
	Text user interface	Command line interface, shells
	Other	
	Office suite	Word processing, Desktop publishing, Presentation program, Database management system, Scheduling & Time management, Spreadsheet, Accounting software
	Internet Access	Browser, E-mail client, Web server, Mail transfer agent, Instant messaging
	Design and manufacturing	Computer-aided design, Computer-aided manufacturing, Plant management, Robotic manufacturing, Supply chain management
	Graphics	Raster graphics editor, Vector graphics editor, 3D modeler, Animation editor, 3D computer graphics, Video editing, Image processing
	Audio	Digital audio editor, Audio playback, Mixing, Audio synthesis, Computer music
	Software Engineering	Compiler, Assembler, Interpreter, Debugger, Text Editor, Integrated development environment, Performance analysis, Revision control, Software configuration management
	Educational	Edutainment, Educational game, Serious game, Flight simulator

Peripheral device (Input/output)	Input	Mouse, Keyboard, Joystick, Image scanner
	Output	Monitor, Printer
	Both	Floppy disk drive, Hard disk, Optical disc drive, Teleprinter
Computer busses	Short range	RS-232, SCSI, PCI, USB
	Long range (Computer networking)	Ethernet, ATM, FDDI

Software

Software refers to parts of the computer which do not have a material form, such as programmes, data, protocols, etc. When software is stored in hardware that cannot easily be modified (such as BIOS ROM in an IBM PC compatible), it is sometimes called "firmware" to indicate that it falls into an uncertain area somewhere between hardware and software.

Programming Languages

Programming languages provide various ways of specifying programmes for computers to run. Unlike natural languages, programming languages are designed to permit no ambiguity and to be concise. They are purely written languages and are often difficult to read aloud.

They are generally either translated into machine language by a compiler or an assembler before being run, or translated directly at run time by an interpreter.

Sometimes programmes are executed by a hybrid method of the two techniques. There are thousands of different programming languages — some intended to be general purpose, others useful only for highly specialized applications.

Lists of programming languages	Timeline of programming languages, Categorical list of programming languages, Generational list of programming languages, Alphabetical list of programming languages, Non-English-based programming languages
Commonly used Assembly languages	ARM, MIPS, x86
Commonly used High level languages	BASIC, C, C++, C#, COBOL, Fortran, Java, Lisp, Pascal
Commonly used Scripting languages	Bourne script, JavaScript, Python, Ruby, PHP, Perl

PROFESSIONS AND ORGANIZATIONS

As the use of computers has spread throughout society, there are an increasing number of careers involving computers. Following the theme of hardware, software and firmware, the brains of people who work in the industry are sometimes known irreverently as wetware or "meatware".

Hardware-related	Electrical engineering, Electronics engineering, Computer engineering, Telecommunications engineering, Optical engineering, Nanoscale engineering
Software-related	Human-computer interaction, Information technology, Software engineering, Scientific computing, Web design, Desktop publishing

The need for computers to work well together and to be able to exchange information has spawned the need for many standards organizations, clubs and societies of both a formal and informal nature.

Organizations

Standards groups	ANSI, IEC, IEEE, IETF, ISO, W3C
Professional Societies	ACM, ACM Special Interest Groups, IET, IFIP
Free/Open source software groups	Free Software Foundation, Mozilla Foundation, Apache Software Foundation

HISTORY OF COMPUTING

Concrete Devices

Computing is intimately tied to the representation of *numbers*. But long before abstractions like *number* arose, there were mathematical concepts to serve the purposes of civilization. These concepts are implicit in concrete practices such as :

- *one-to-one correspondence*, a rule to count *how many* items, say on a tally stick, which was eventually abstracted into *number*;
- *comparison to a standard*, a method for assuming *reproducibility* in a measurement, for example, the number of coins;
- the *3-4-5* right triangle was a device for assuring a *right angle*, using ropes with 12 evenly spaced knots, for example.

NUMBERS

Eventually, the concept of numbers became concrete and familiar enough for counting to arise, at times with sing-song mnemonics to teach sequences to others. All the known languages have words for at least "one" and "two", and even some animals like the blackbird can distinguish a surprising number of items.

Advances in the numeral system and mathematical notation eventually led to the discovery of mathematical operations such as addition, subtraction, multiplication, division, squaring, square root, and so forth. Eventually the operations were formalized, and concepts about the operations became understood well enough to be stated formally, and even proven. See, for example, Euclid's algorithm for finding the greatest common divisor of two numbers.

By the High Middle Ages, the positional Hindu-Arabic numeral system had reached Europe, which allowed for systematic computation of numbers. During this period, the representation of a calculation on paper actually allowed calculation of mathematical expressions, and the tabulation of mathematical functions such as the square root and the common logarithm (for use in multiplication and division) and the trigonometric functions. By the time of Isaac Newton's research, paper or vellum was an important computing resource, and even in our present time, researchers like Enrico Fermi would cover random scraps of paper with calculation, to satisfy their curiosity about an equation. Even into the period of programmable calculators, Richard Feynman would unhesitatingly compute any steps which overflowed the memory of the calculators, by hand, just to learn the answer.

NAVIGATION AND ASTRONOMY

Starting with known special cases, the calculation of logarithms and trigonometric functions can be performed by looking up numbers in a mathematical table, and interpolating between known cases. For small enough differences, this linear operation was accurate enough for use in navigation and astronomy in the Age of Exploration. The uses of interpolation have thrived in the past 500 years: by the twentieth century Leslie Comrie and W.J. Eckert systematized the use of interpolation in tables of numbers for punch card calculation.

In our time, even a student can simulate the motion of the planets, an N-body differential equation, using the concepts of numerical approximation, a feat which even Isaac Newton could admire, given his struggles with the motion of the Moon.

WEATHER PREDICTION

The numerical solution of differential equations, notably the Navier-Stokes equations was an important stimulus to computing, with Lewis Fry Richardson's numerical approach to solving differential equations. To this day, some of the most powerful computer systems of the Earth are used for weather forecasts.

SYMBOLIC COMPUTATIONS

By the late 1960s, computer systems could perform symbolic algebraic manipulations well enough to pass college-level calculus courses. Using programmes like *Maple*, *Macsyma (now Maxima)* and *Mathematica*, including some open source programmes like *Yacas*, it is now possible to visualize concepts such as modular forms which were only accessible to the mathematical imagination before this.

HISTORY OF COMPUTING HARDWARE

Computers can be separated into software and hardware. Computing hardware is the physical machine that, under the direction of a programme, stores and manipulates data. Since first concieved, there has been a constant drive to make computer hardware faster, cheaper, and store more data.

Before the development of the general-purpose computer, most calculations were done by humans. Tools to help humans calculate are generally called calculators. Calculators continue to develop, but computers have overshadowed them and become ubiquitous, due to their incredible flexibility. Computer technology has undergone profound changes every decade since the 1940s.

This article covers major developments in the history of computing hardware, and attempts to put them in context. For a detailed timeline of events, see the computing timeline article. The history of computing article is a related overview and treats methods intended for pen and paper, with or without the aid of tables. Since all computers rely on digital storage, and tend to be limited by the size and speed of memory, the history of computer data storage is tied to the development of computers.

EARLIEST CALCULATORS

Humanity has used devices to aid in computation for millennia. The earliest counting device was probably some form of tally stick; later record keeping aids include Phoenician clay shapes which represented counts of items, probably livestock or grains, in containers. Another example is a device for establishing the checkered cloths of the counting houses served as simple for enumerating stacks of coins, by height. A more arithmetic-oriented machine is the abacus. The earliest form of abacus, the dust abacus, is thought to have been invented in Babylonia. The ancient Egyptian bead and wire abacus dates from 500 BC.

A number of analog computers were constructed in ancient and medieval times to perform astronomical calculations. These include the Antikythera mechanism from ancient Greece (c. 150-100 BC); the Planisphere; some of the inventions of Abû Rayhân al-Bîrûnî (c. AD 1000); the Equatorium of Abû Ishâq Ibrâhîm al-Zarqâlî (c. AD 1015); and the astronomical analog computers of other medieval Muslim astronomers and engineers.

John Napier (1550–1617) noted that multiplication and division of numbers can be performed by addition and subtraction, respectively, of logarithms of those numbers. While producing the first logarithmic tables Napier needed to perform many multiplications, and it was at this point that he designed Napier's bones, an abacus-like device used for multiplication and division.

Since real numbers can be represented as distances or intervals on a line, the slide rule was invented in the 1620s to allow multiplication and division operations to be carried out significantly faster than was previously possible. Slide rules were used by generations of engineers and other mathematically inclined professional workers, until the invention of the pocket calculator. The engineers in the Apollo programme to send a man to the moon made many of their calculations on slide rules, which were accurate to three or four significant figures.

In 1623, Wilhelm Schickard built the first digital mechanical calculator and thus became the father of the computing era. Since his machine used techniques such as cogs and gears first developed for clocks, it was also called a 'calculating clock'. It was put to practical use by his friend Johannes Kepler, who revolutionized astronomy.

An original calculator by Pascal (1640) is preserved in the Zwinger Museum. Machines by Blaise Pascal (the Pascaline,

1642), and Gottfried Wilhelm von Leibniz (1671) followed. Around 1820, Charles Xavier Thomas created the first successful, mass-produced mechanical calculator, the Thomas Arithmometer, that could add, subtract, multiply, and divide. It was mainly based on Leibniz's work. Mechanical calculators, like the base-ten addiator, the comptometer, the Monroe, the Curta and the Addo-X remained in use until the 1970s.

Leibniz also described the binary numeral system, a central ingredient of all modern computers. However, up to the 1940s, many subsequent designs (including Charles Babbage's machines of the 1800s and even ENIAC of 1945) were based on the harder-to-implement decimal system.

1801: PUNCHED CARD TECHNOLOGY

As early as 1725 Basile Bouchon used a perforated paper loop in a loom to establish the pattern to be reproduced on cloth, and in 1726 his co-worker Jean-Baptiste Falcon improved on his design by using perforated paper cards attached to one another for efficiency in adapting and changing the programme. The Bouchon-Falcon loom was semi-automatic and required manual feed of the programme.

In 1801, Joseph-Marie Jacquard developed a loom in which the pattern being woven was controlled by punched cards. The series of cards could be changed without changing the mechanical design of the loom. This was a landmark point in programmability. In 1833, Charles Babbage moved on from developing his difference engine to developing a more complete design, the analytical engine, which would draw directly on Jacquard's punched cards for its programming..

In 1835 Charles Babbage described his analytical engine. It was the plan of a general-purpose programmable computer, employing punch cards for input and a steam engine for power. One crucial invention was to use gears for the function served by the beads of an abacus. In a real sense, computers all contain automatic abacuses (technically called the arithmetic logic unit or floating-point unit).

His initial idea was to use punch-cards to control a machine that could calculate and print logarithmic tables with huge precision (a specific purpose machine). Babbage's idea soon developed into a general-purpose programmable computer, his analytical engine.

While his design was sound and the plans were probably correct, or at least debuggable, the project was slowed by various problems. Babbage was a difficult man to work with and argued with anyone who didn't respect his ideas. All the parts for his machine had to be made by hand. Small errors in each item can sometimes sum up to large discrepancies in a machine with thousands of parts, which required these parts to be much better than the usual tolerances needed at the time. The project dissolved in disputes with the artisan who built parts and was ended with the depletion of government funding.

Ada Lovelace, Lord Byron's daughter, translated and added notes to the "*Sketch of the Analytical Engine*" by Federico Luigi, Conte Menabrea. She has become closely associated with Babbage. Some claim she is the world's first computer programmer, however this claim and the value of her other contributions are disputed by many.

A reconstruction of the Difference Engine II, an earlier, more limited design, has been operational since 1991 at the London Science Museum. With a few trivial changes, it works as Babbage designed it and shows that Babbage was right in theory.

The museum used computer-operated machine tools to construct the necessary parts, following tolerances which a machinist of the period would have been able to achieve. Some feel that the technology of the time was unable to produce parts of sufficient precision, though this appears to be false. The failure of Babbage to complete the engine can be chiefly attributed to difficulties not only related to politics and financing, but also to his desire to develop an increasingly sophisticated computer. Today, many in the computer field term this sort of obsession *creeping featuritis*.

In 1890, the United States Census Bureau used punched cards, sorting machines, and tabulating machines designed by Herman Hollerith, to handle the flood of data from the decennial census mandated by the Constitution. Hollerith's company eventually became the core of IBM. IBM developed punched card technology into a powerful tool for business data-processing and produced an extensive line of specialized unit record equipment. By 1950, the IBM card had become ubiquitous in industry and government. The warning printed on most cards intended for circulation as documents (checks, for example), "Do not fold, spindle or mutilate," became a motto for the post-World War II era.

Following in the footsteps of Babbage, although unaware of his earlier work, was Percy Ludgate, an accountant from Dublin, Ireland. He independently designed a programmable mechanical computer, which he described in a work that was published in 1909.

Leslie Comrie's articles on punched card methods and W.J. Eckert's publication of *Punched Card Methods in Scientific Computation* in 1940, described techniques which were sufficiently advanced to solve differential equations, perform multiplication and division using floating point representations, all on punched cards and unit record machines. The Thomas J. Watson Astronomical Computing Bureau, Columbia University performed astronomical calculations representing the state of the art in computing.

In many computer installations, punched cards were used until (and after) the end of the 1970s. For example, science and engineering students at many universities around the world would submit their programming assignments to the local computer centre in the form of a stack of cards, one card per programme line, and then had to wait for the programme to be queued for processing, compiled, and executed. In due course a printout of any results, marked with the submitter's identification, would be placed in an output tray outside the computer centre. In many cases these results would comprise solely a printout of error messages regarding programme syntax *etc.*, necessitating another edit-compile-run cycle. *Also see* Computer programming in the punch card era.

Punched cards are still used and manufactured to this day, and their distinctive dimensions (and 80-column capacity) can still be recognized in forms, records, and programmes around the world.

1930S–1960S: DESKTOP CALCULATORS

By the 1900s earlier mechanical calculators, cash registers, accounting machines, and so on were redesigned to use electric motors, with gear position as the representation for the state of a variable. Companies like Friden, Marchant Calculator and Monroe made desktop mechanical calculators from the 1930s that could add, subtract, multiply and divide. The word "computer" was a job title assigned to people who used these calculators to perform mathematical calculations. During the Manhattan project, future Nobel laureate Richard Feynman was the supervisor of the roomful of human computers, many of them women mathematicians, who understood the differential equations which were being solved for the war effort. Even the renowned Stanis³aw Ulam was pressed into service to translate the mathematics into computable approximations for the hydrogen bomb, after the war.

In 1948, the Curta was introduced. This was a small, portable, mechanical calculator that was about the size of a pepper grinder. Over time, during the 1950s and 1960s a variety of different brands of mechanical calculator appeared on the market.

The first all-electronic desktop calculator was the British ANITA Mk.VII, which used a Nixie tube display and 177 subminiature thyratron tubes. In June 1963, Friden introduced the four-function EC-130. It had an all-transistor design, 13-digit capacity on a 5-inch CRT, and introduced reverse Polish notation (RPN) to the calculator market at a price of $2200. The model EC-132 added square root and reciprocal functions. In 1965, Wang Laboratories produced the LOCI-2, a 10-digit transistorized desktop calculator that used a Nixie tube display and could compute logarithms.

With development of the integrated circuits and microprocessors, the expensive, large calculators were replaced with smaller electronic devices.

ADVANCED ANALOG COMPUTERS

Before World War II, mechanical and electrical analog computers were considered the "state of the art", and many thought they were the future of computing. Analog computers use continuously varying amounts of physical quantities, such as voltages or currents, or the rotational speed of shafts, to represent the quantities being processed. An ingenious example of such a machine was the water integrator built in 1928; an electrical example is the Mallock machine built in 1941. Unlike modern digital computers, analog computers are not very flexible, and need to be reconfigured (*i.e.*, reprogrammed) manually to switch them from working on one problem to another. Analog computers had an advantage over early digital computers in that they could be used to solve complex problems while the earliest attempts at digital computers were quite limited. But as digital computers have become faster and used larger memory (*e.g.*, RAM or internal store), they have almost entirely displaced analog computers, and computer programming, or coding has arisen as another human profession.

Since computers were rare in this era, the solutions were often *hard-coded* into paper forms such as graphs and nomograms, which could then allow analog solutions to problems, such as the distribution of pressures and temperatures in a heating system. Some of the most widely deployed analog computers included devices for aiming weapons, such as the Norden bombsight and Fire-control systems for naval vessels. Some of these stayed in use for decades after WWII. One example is the Mark I Fire Control Computer, deployed by the United States Navy on a variety of ships from destroyers to battleships. Other examples included the Heathkit EC-1, and the hydraulic MONIAC Computer.

The art of analog computing reached its zenith with the differential analyzer, invented in 1876 by James Thomson and built by H. W. Nieman and Vannevar Bush at MIT starting in 1927. Fewer than a dozen of these devices were ever built; the most powerful was constructed at the University of Pennsylvania's Moore School of Electrical Engineering, where the ENIAC was built. Digital electronic computers like the ENIAC spelled the end for most analog computing machines, but hybrid analog computers, controlled by digital electronics, remained in substantial use into the 1950s and 1960s, and later in some specialized applications.

EARLY DIGITAL COMPUTERS

The era of modern computing began with a flurry of development before and during World War II, as electronic circuits, relays, capacitors, and vacuum tubes replaced mechanical equivalents and digital calculations replaced analog calculations. Machines such as the Atanasoff–Berry Computer, the Z3, the Colossus, and ENIAC were built by hand using circuits containing relays or valves (vacuum tubes), and often used punched cards or punched paper tape for input and as the main (non-volatile) storage medium. In this era, a number of different machines were produced with steadily advancing capabilities. At the beginning of this period, nothing remotely resembling a modern computer existed, except in the long-lost plans of Charles Babbage and the mathematical musings of Alan Turing and others. At the end of the era, devices like the EDSAC had been built, and are universally agreed to be digital computers. Defining a single point in the series as the "first computer" misses many subtleties.

Alan Turing's 1936 paper proved enormously influential in computing and computer science in two ways. Its main purpose was to prove that there were problems (namely the halting problem) that could not be solved by any sequential process. In doing so, Turing provided a definition of a universal computer, a construct that came to be called a Turing machine, a purely theoretical device that formalizes the concept of algorithm execution, replacing Kurt Gödel's more cumbersome universal language based on arithmetics. Except for the limitations imposed by their finite memory stores, modern computers are said to be Turing-complete, which is to say, they have algorithm execution capability equivalent to a universal Turing machine. This limited type of Turing completeness is sometimes viewed as a threshold capability separating general-purpose computers from their special-purpose predecessors.

For a computing machine to be a practical general-purpose computer, there must be some convenient read-write mechanism, punched tape, for example. For full versatility, the Von Neumann architecture uses the same memory both to store programmes and data; virtually all contemporary computers use this architecture (or some variant). While it is theoretically possible to implement a full computer entirely mechanically (as Babbage's design showed), electronics made possible the speed and later the miniaturization that characterize modern computers.

There were three parallel streams of computer development in the World War II era, and two were either largely ignored or were deliberately kept secret. The first was the German work of Konrad Zuse. The second was the secret development of the Colossus computer in the UK. Neither of these had much influence on the various computing projects in the United States. After the war, British and American computing researchers cooperated on some of the most important steps towards a practical computing device.

Konrad Zuse's Z-series: The First Programme-controlled Computers

Working in isolation in Germany, Konrad Zuse started construction in 1936 of his first Z-series calculators featuring memory and (initially limited) programmability. Zuse's purely mechanical, but already binary Z1, finished in 1938, never worked reliably due to problems with the precision of parts.

Zuse's subsequent machine, the Z3, was finished in 1941. It was based on telephone relays and did work satisfactorily. The Z3 thus became the first functional programme-controlled, all-purpose, digital computer. In many ways it was quite similar to modern machines, pioneering numerous advances, such as floating point numbers. Replacement of the hard-to-implement decimal system (used in Charles Babbage's earlier design) by the simpler binary system meant that Zuse's machines were easier to build and potentially more reliable, given the technologies available at that time. This is sometimes viewed as the main reason why Zuse succeeded where Babbage failed.

Programmes were fed into Z3 on punched films. Conditional jumps were missing, but since the 1990s it has been proved theoretically that Z3 was still a universal computer (ignoring its physical storage size limitations). In two 1936 patent applications, Konrad Zuse also anticipated that machine instructions could be stored in the same storage used for data – the key insight of what became known as the Von Neumann architecture and was first implemented in the later British EDSAC design (1949).

Zuse also claimed to have designed the first higher-level programming language, (Plankalkül), in 1945 (which was published in 1948) although it was implemented for the first time in 2000 by a team around Raul Rojas at the Free University of Berlin–five years after Zuse died.

Zuse suffered setbacks during World War II when some of his machines were destroyed in the course of Allied bombing campaigns. Apparently his work remained largely unknown to engineers in the UK and US until much later, although at least IBM was aware of it as it financed his post-war startup company in 1946 in return for an option on Zuse's patents.

American Developments

In 1937, Claude Shannon produced his master's thesis at MIT that implemented Boolean algebra using electronic relays and switches for the first time in history. Entitled *A Symbolic Analysis of Relay and Switching Circuits*, Shannon's thesis essentially founded practical digital circuit design.

In November of 1937, George Stibitz, then working at Bell Labs, completed a relay-based computer he dubbed the "Model K" (for "kitchen", where he had assembled it), which calculated using binary addition. Bell Labs authorized a full research programme in late 1938 with Stibitz at the helm. Their Complex Number Calculator, completed January 8, 1940, was able to calculate complex numbers. In a demonstration to the American Mathematical Society conference at Dartmouth College on September 11, 1940, Stibitz was able to send the Complex Number Calculator remote commands over telephone lines by a teletype. It was the first computing machine ever used remotely, in this case over a phone line. Some participants in the conference who witnessed the demonstration were John Von Neumann, John Mauchly, and Norbert Wiener, who wrote about it in his memoirs.

In 1939, John Vincent Atanasoff and Clifford E. Berry of Iowa State University developed the Atanasoff–Berry Computer (ABC), a special purpose digital electronic calculator for solving systems of linear equations. (The original goal was to solve 29 simultaneous equations of 29 unknowns each, but due to errors in the card puncher mechanism the completed machine could only solve a few equations.) The design used over 300 vacuum tubes for high speed and employed capacitors fixed in a mechanically rotating drum for memory. Though the ABC machine was not programmable, it was the first to use electronic circuits. ENIAC co-inventor John Mauchly examined the ABC in June 1941, and its influence on the design of the later ENIAC machine is a matter of contention among computer historians. The ABC was largely forgotten until it became the focus of the lawsuit *Honeywell v. Sperry Rand*, the ruling of which invalidated the ENIAC patent (and several others) as, among many reasons, having been anticipated by Atanasoff's work.

In 1939, development began at IBM's Endicott laboratories on the Harvard Mark I. Known officially as the Automatic Sequence Controlled Calculator, the Mark I was a general purpose electro-mechanical computer built with IBM financing and with assistance from IBM personnel, under the direction of Harvard mathematician Howard Aiken. Its design was influenced by Babbage's Analytical Engine, using decimal arithmetic and storage wheels and rotary switches in addition to electromagnetic relays. It was programmable via punched paper tape, and contained several calculation units working in parallel. Later versions contained several paper tape readers and the machine could switch between readers based on a condition. Nevertheless, the machine was not quite Turing-complete. The Mark I was moved to Harvard University and began operation in May 1944.

Colossus

During World War II, the British at Bletchley Park achieved a number of successes at breaking encrypted German military communications. The German encryption machine, Enigma, was attacked with the help of electro-mechanical machines called *bombes*. The bombe, designed by Alan Turing and Gordon Welchman, after the Polish cryptographic *bomba* (1938), ruled out possible Enigma settings by performing chains of logical deductions implemented electrically. Most possibilities led to a contradiction, and the few remaining could be tested by hand.

The Germans also developed a series of teleprinter encryption systems, quite different from Enigma. The Lorenz SZ 40/42 machine was used for high-level Army communications, termed "Tunny" by the British. The first intercepts of Lorenz messages began in 1941. As part of an attack on Tunny, Professor Max Newman and his colleagues helped specify the Colossus. The Mk I Colossus was built between March and December 1943 by Tommy Flowers and his colleagues at the Post Office Research Station at Dollis Hill in London and then shipped to Bletchley Park.

Colossus was the first totally *electronic* computing device. The Colossus used a large number of valves (vacuum tubes). It had paper-tape input and was capable of being configured to perform a variety of boolean logical operations on its data, but it was not Turing-complete. Nine Mk II Colossi were built (The Mk I was converted to a Mk II making ten machines in total). Details of their existence, design, and use were kept secret well into the 1970s. Winston Churchill personally issued an order for their destruction into pieces no larger than a man's hand. Due to this secrecy the Colossi were not included in many histories of computing. A reconstructed copy of one of the Colossus machines is now on display at Bletchley Park.

ENIAC

The US-built ENIAC (Electronic Numerical Integrator and Computer) was the first electronic general-purpose computer. Built under the direction of John Mauchly and J. Presper Eckert, it was 1,000 times faster than its contemporaries. ENIAC's development and construction lasted from 1943 to full operation at the end of 1945.

When its design was proposed, many researchers believed that the thousands of delicate valves (*i.e.* vacuum tubes) would burn out often enough that the ENIAC would be so frequently down for repairs as to be useless. It was, however, capable of up to thousands of operations per second for hours at a time between valve failures. It publicly validated the use of electronics for large-scale computing. This was crucial for the development of modern computing. ENIAC was unambiguously a Turing-complete device. A "programme" on the ENIAC, however, was defined by the states of its patch cables and switches, a far cry from the stored programme electronic machines that evolved from it. To programme it meant to rewire it. (Improvements completed in 1948 made it possible to execute stored programmes set in function table memory, which made programming less a "one-off" effort, and more systematic.)

FIRST-GENERATION VON NEUMANN MACHINE AND THE OTHER WORKS

Even before the ENIAC was finished, Eckert and Mauchly recognized its limitations and started the design of a new computer, EDVAC, which was to have stored-programme. John von Neumann wrote a widely-circulated report describing the EDVAC design in which both the programmes and working data were stored in a single, unified store. This basic design, which became known as the von Neumann architecture, would serve as the basis for the development of the first really flexible, general-purpose digital computers.

In this generation, temporary or working storage was provided by acoustic delay lines, which used the propagation time of sound through a medium such as liquid mercury (or through a wire) to briefly store data. As series of acoustic pulses is sent along a tube; after a time, as the pulse reached the end of the tube, the circuitry detected whether the pulse represented a 1 or 0 and caused the oscillator to re-send the pulse. Others used Williams tubes, which use the ability of a television picture tube to store and retrieve data. By 1954, magnetic core memory was rapidly displacing most other forms of temporary storage, and dominated the field through the mid-1970s.

The first working von Neumann machine was the Manchester "Baby" or Small-Scale Experimental Machine, built at the University of Manchester in 1948; it was followed in 1949 by the Manchester Mark I computer which functioned as a complete system using the Williams tube and magnetic drum for memory, and also introduced index registers. The other contender for the title "first digital stored programme computer" had been EDSAC, designed and constructed at the University of Cambridge. Operational less than one year after the Manchester "Baby", it was also capable of tackling real problems. EDSAC was actually inspired by plans for EDVAC (Electronic Discrete Variable Automatic Computer), the successor to ENIAC; these plans were already in place by the time ENIAC was successfully operational. Unlike ENIAC, which used parallel processing, EDVAC used a single processing unit. This design was simpler and was the first to be implemented in each succeeding wave of miniaturization, and increased reliability. Some view Manchester Mark I/EDSAC/EDVAC as the "Eves" from which nearly all current computers derive their architecture. The first universal programmable computer in the Soviet Union was created by a team of scientists under direction of Sergei Alekseyevich Lebedev from Kiev Institute of Electrotechnology, Soviet Union (now Ukraine). The computer MESM (*"-!", Small Electronic Calculating Machine*) became operational in 1950. It had about 6,000 vacuum tubes and consumed 25 kW of power. It could perform approximately 3,000 operations per second. Another early machine was CSIRAC, an Australian design that ran its first test programme in 1949.

In October 1947, the directors of J. Lyons & Company, a British catering company famous for its teashops but with strong interests in new office management techniques, decided to take an active role in promoting the commercial development of computers. By 1951 the LEO I computer was operational and ran the world's first regular routine office computer job.

Manchester University's machine became the prototype for the Ferranti Mark I. The first Ferranti Mark I machine was delivered to the University in February, 1951 and at least nine others were sold between 1951 and 1957.

In June 1951, the UNIVAC I (Universal Automatic Computer) was delivered to the U.S. Census Bureau. Although manufactured by Remington Rand, the machine often was mistakenly referred to as the "IBM UNIVAC". Remington Rand eventually sold 46 machines at more than $1 million each. UNIVAC was the first 'mass produced' computer; all predecessors had been 'one-off' units. It used 5,200 vacuum tubes and consumed 125 kW of power. It used a mercury delay line capable of storing 1,000 words of 11 decimal digits plus sign (72-bit words) for memory. Unlike IBM machines it was not equipped with a punch card reader but 1930s style metal magnetic tape input, making it incompatible with some existing commercial data stores. High speed punched paper tape and modern-style magnetic tapes were used for input/output by other computers of the era.

In November 1951, the J. Lyons company began weekly operation of a bakery valuations job on the LEO (Lyons Electronic Office). This was the first business application to go live on a stored programme computer.

In 1952, IBM publicly announced the IBM 701 Electronic Data Processing Machine, the first in its successful 700/7000 series and its first IBM mainframe computer. The IBM 704, introduced in 1954, used magnetic core memory, which became the standard for large machines. The first implemented high-level general purpose programming language, Fortran, was also being developed at IBM for the 704 during 1955 and 1956 and released in early 1957. (Konrad Zuse's 1945 design of the high-level language Plankalkül was not implemented at that time.)

IBM introduced a smaller, more affordable computer in 1954 that proved very popular. The IBM 650 weighed over 900 kg, the attached power supply weighed around 1350 kg and both were held in separate cabinets of roughly 1.5 meters by 0.9 meters by 1.8 meters. It cost $500,000 or could be leased for $3,500 a month. Its drum memory was originally only 2000 ten-digit words, and required arcane programming for efficient computing. Memory limitations such as this were to dominate programming for decades afterward, until the evolution of hardware capabilities and a programming model that were more sympathetic to software development.

In 1955, Maurice Wilkes invented microprogramming, which was later widely used in the CPUs and floating-point units of mainframe and other computers, such as the IBM 360 series. *Microprogramming* allows the base instruction set to be defined or extended by built-in programmes (now sometimes called *firmware*, *microcode*, or *millicode*).

In 1956, IBM sold its first magnetic disk system, RAMAC (Random Access Method of Accounting and Control). It used 50 24-inch metal disks, with 100 tracks per side. It could store 5 megabytes of data and cost $10,000 per megabyte. (As of 2006, magnetic storage, in the form of hard disks, costs less than one tenth of a cent per megabyte).

SECOND GENERATION: TRANSISTORS

Post-1960: Third Generation and Beyond

The explosion in the use of computers began with 'Third Generation' computers. These relied on Jack St. Clair Kilby's and Robert Noyce's independent invention of the integrated circuit (or microchip), which later led to the invention of the microprocessor, by Ted Hoff and Federico Faggin at Intel.

During the 1960s there was considerable overlap between second and third generation technologies. As late as 1975, Sperry Univac continued the manufacture of second-generation machines such as the UNIVAC 494.

The microprocessor led to the development of the microcomputer, small, low-cost computers that could be owned by individuals and small businesses. Microcomputers, the first of which appeared in the 1970s, became ubiquitous in the 1980s and beyond.

Steve Wozniak, co-founder of Apple Computer, is credited with developing the first mass-market home computers. However, his first computer, the Apple I, came out some time after the KIM-1 and Altair 8800, and the first Apple computer with graphic and sound capabilities came out well after the Commodore PET. Computing has evolved with microcomputer architectures, with features added from their larger brethren, now dominant in most market segments.

An indication of the rapidity of development of this field can be inferred by the Burks, Goldstein, von Neuman, seminal article, documented in the *Datamation* September-October 1962 issue, which was written, as a preliminary version 15 years earlier. By the time that anyone had time to write anything down, it was obsolete.

8

Metadata for Digital Libraries : a Research Agenda

Introduction

"Metadata" is the Internet-age term for structured data about data. Typical examples are library catalogue records, bibliographic headers in Web pages, "terms of use" statements, and ratings. Different user communities—from librarians and computer scientists to government agencies, cultural heritage organizations, publishers, businesses, and the legal community—scope and purpose metadata differently. International communities in areas such as biodiversity, the space sciences, and museums seek to refine the semantics of specialized metadata for the rapidly evolving needs of their fields. Likewise, publishers and other content providers are seeking agreements on standards to enable new forms of electronic commerce.

The creation and management of metadata is a sizeable and rapidly expanding industry. In the scholarly communities, libraries and abstracting and indexing services invest heavily in the creation of metadata to manage the published literature. Scholars are increasingly publishing their work in electronic journals or in less formal Web forums, and scientific datasets are proliferating. Metadata will be needed for these materials. As libraries and museums digitize cultural heritage information, they must create metadata to organize and manage it; indeed, the cost of creating this metadata is often comparable to the cost of digitization itself. In the consumer world, metadata in the form of ratings and reviews has long been important. Now it is becoming clear that good metadata is needed to allow consumers to find products for sale on the Web as well. As we look towards worldwide commerce in intellectual property over the Internet, metadata to support rights management will be an essential part of this new marketplace.

In all such contexts, metadata helps people find what they need, verify its authenticity, process it in an appropriate format, and perhaps to order or pay for it online. Some types of metadata will be used by humans; others will be processed automatically by new types of software tools and systems. No single type of metadata can suit every such application, every type of resource, and every community of users. How the diverse forms of metadata will co-exist and interoperate is a complex issue for research.

The EU-NSF Working Group on Metadata focused on the architectures, tools, and models needed for managing metadata in a distributed, networked environment and on aspects very broadly related to the problem of resource discovery. We did not cover specialized uses of metadata *within* information services, such as using thesauri to reformulate queries. Also outside our scope was metadata for knowledge representation in the broader sense of natural-language ontologies, classification schemes, domain-specific terminologies, and controlled vocabularies of element values.

Architectural Issues for Metadata

A number of high-level issues concern the management of metadata and the relation of metadata to the overall design of networked information systems.

Models for Metadata-Resource Association

There are several models for associating resources and metadata. For simple text documents on the Web, descriptive information is most commonly embedded in documents using the META tag of the Hypertext Markup Language (HTML). No additional infrastructure is needed for this other than the Web itself. The metadata can be created by authors and others who build networked resources, and it can be harvested automatically by indexing robots. Alternatively, metadata can be tightly coupled with a resource and transported together with that resource's contents in Web transactions using the Hypertext Transport Protocol (HTTP). This allows metadata and resources to be maintained separately, but at the cost of a somewhat more complex infrastructure. A third model finds metadata located physically apart from a resource in a separate database, managed in some cases by the owners of the information described, in other cases by third parties. Research is needed to understand the implications of these models for performance, cost, scalability, interoperability, implementation, maintenance, and systems design.

Trusted third-party resource description has long been provided by libraries, archives, and indexing services in a well-established metadata industry that predates the Internet, with well-established standards such as the MAchine-Readable Cataloguing format (MARC). Since the rise of the Web, new entrepreneurial metadata services have emerged, including ratings bureaus, which may operate in conjunction with filtering systems in browsers, and full-text search engines. Search engines typically derive their metadata algorithmically, rather than intellectually, from a statistical and semantic analysis of full-text documents on the Web. This metadata is used only to resolve queries and is not made available directly to users.

As work advances on metadata in areas as diverse as resource discovery, electronic commerce, and rights management, it is becoming clear that interoperability will depend on a clearer understanding of data models for information objects. Efforts are underway to explore the relationships among the data models underlying the so-called Digital Object Identifier (DOI), the Dublin Core Element Set for resource description, and INDECS (INteroperability of Data in E-Commerce Systems), a metadata initiative for supporting global commerce in intellectual property. One common reference point for these various communities is the Functional Requirements for Bibliographic Records of the International Federation of Library Associations and Institutions (IFLA), which describes a range of possible "states" for information resources from the abstract *work* through the physical *item*. Defining a logical framework that subsumes or reconciles a variety of data models is a major research challenge with implications for the exchange and reuse of different types of metadata for a broad range of applications.

Metadata Creation and Management

Producing metadata has long been the task of professionals such as librarians and indexers. Today, metadata is also being produced by non-specialists (*e.g.*, ordinary users), publishers, for-profit commercial agents, and even software systems. Creating metadata is often labour-intensive, though automated procedures and new types of tools for creating and managing metadata are evolving and will continue to become more sophisticated. Some word processors, editors, and format filters generate embedded metadata tags when a document is first created. Other tools automatically extract metadata values from the documents themselves.

Metadata may be generated or updated at various times in the life cycle of a resource, so workflows must be designed accordingly. Declarative rules or prescriptions can be used to explicitly describe how, when, and by whom a metadata element will be produced or updated. Research on metadata creation and management will enable systems to use document analysis to automate metadata capture, automatically extract subject classifications, trigger the update of metadata when a resource is modified, support the capture of temporal metadata, certify metadata at the time of publication, and remove metadata when a resource is obsolete. Such tools must become integrated into a variety of environments from Web site management utilities to databases, data warehouses, and legacy resources. If used on a wide scale, they could significantly improve the quality and cost-effectiveness of metadata in the networked environment.

Metadata for Repositories and Services

Proprietary digital resources will increasingly be stored in data repositories and may not be accessible to external Web harvesters. Publishers may want to use metadata to advertise their materials, which would then be available for a fee. Metadata will play a crucial role as a surrogate which makes the contents of such restricted resources and services visible to searchers. Some services, such as weather forecasts, may make their contents accessible only through dynamic interfaces that cannot be harvested. Metadata will not just serve as advertising for content; some kinds of metadata, such as reviews, will have markets in their own right.

Designing effective mechanisms for such repositories will enable large-scale commercial publishing on the Web. One repository model, the Kahn-Wilenski Digital Object Repository, supports formal specification of the services, policies, and transaction methods associated with a collection of resources. Research on repository architectures and their metadata will need to balance market forces and organizational needs to ensure that the technological options enable rather than constrain the expression of policy.

Simplicity, Complexity, and Interoperability

Current approaches to metadata, such as the Warwick Framework, assume that complex metadata needs are best met by a multiplicity of separate but functionally focused metadata schemes, relatively orthogonal and independently maintained by communities of expertise and practice, which can be mixed and matched as needed, rather than by just one comprehensive but monolithic set of elements. The metadata associated with a given object would be separated into a series of "packages" that would be marked as using these various metadata schemes.

The foundations for such modularity are already in place. Further research is needed now to scope and elaborate new schemes and to specify the interrelations among packages.

There are also research issues involved in the management of multiple packages for an object under the Warwick Framework within various distributed computing environments, including questions of consistency, overlap, relationships among packages, and the linkage of packages to nested or complex objects.

Core Metadata Sets

Metadata schemes that meet fundamental functional needs of users in a wide range of fields and applications are called "core element sets." The most important work in this area to date has been in resource description, where the Dublin Core forms a central reference point of fifteen broad categories onto which more complex or specialized descriptive schemas can map. Such core element sets are needed now for functions complementary to description, such as structure and navigation, administration of digital objects, authentication, certification and provenance, terms and conditions, trust and quality, privacy, and longevity.

Particular communities will develop discrete (but possibly overlapping) packages of metadata for various purposes. For example, structural metadata for display and navigation is needed for specifying the range of file formats a library can deliver, the size of particular documents, or the parts of documents that are accessible individually, such as tables of contents and chapters.

Administrative metadata can cover the creation of an object (such as date of capture or digitization technology used), identify an instantiation (version or edition), or specify the technology needed to view or use an object (*e.g.*, storage or delivery file format, compression scheme, or location). Metadata on trust might include certifications or ratings of the quality of services or content offered by information providers. It is probably impossible, at this stage of development, to establish a comprehensive enumeration of core element sets; however, the need for a number of such sets is clear, and managing their evolution and scoping will be a challenge.

Metadata Pidgins and Complexification

In all forms of human communication there is a tension between the virtue of simplicity and the need for complexity. Historically, attempts to create simplified common languages such as Esperanto have often splintered between those who wanted to keep it simple to promote mass usage versus those who called for larger vocabularies and grammatical nuance.

Pidgins--simple languages improvised by speakers of different languages who need to work together or conduct trade—also start with small vocabularies and simple grammars. When adopted by entire communities, however, pidgins typically evolve into more complex and expressive "creoles."

Such dynamics have been evident in efforts to define global standards in metadata. The effort to simplify and hybridize the resource description conventions of various communities has led to the pidgin-like (unqualified) Dublin Core Element Set. Such core schemas are extensible via additional elements or local refinements, but complexified adaptations can compromise or at least reduce interoperability. As users seek greater nuance of semantics and syntax, the natural follow-on to this pidginization is a re-complexification, or creolization, resulting in metadata that may be more precise and expressive, yet less compatible with the global standard.

This tension between simplicity (hence interoperability) and greater semantic richness is a natural feature of evolving metadata conventions. A search for balance has been evident in the evolution of the Dublin Core, particularly in the differences between qualified and unqualified approaches. Each new core metadata set will pose the same problem of balance as it is extended and specialized beyond its original core use.

Metadata for Complex Digital Resources

There are well-established conceptual models and practices for describing the contents and structure of traditional resources. For example, the consensus understanding of component parts of texts (titles, chapters, paragraphs) is so strong that it is often implied by layout and typography. This understanding can be formalized, along with higher-level structures, through constructs such as the Document Type Definitions (DTDs) of the Standard Generalized Markup Language (SGML) or word processor style templates. Other practices surrounding the use of text (*e.g.* citation and quotation) are also relatively well established, as are means of associating metadata with texts (*e.g.*, independent MARC records, HTML META tags, and DTDs of the Text Encoding Initiative). A relatively limited number of encodings are in popular use for text documents—ASCII, word processor formats, PDF, HTML, SGML, and perhaps soon XML—and viewing software often allows users to convert among these formats.

For non-textual data the variety of encodings in use is much wider, and the problem of conversion is accordingly more complex. Many of these conversions will need to be controlled and automated by new types of metadata. Time-based media such as audio and video will need "mechanical" metadata for controlling processes such as synchronization (*e.g.*, sampling rates and frame sizes), which will need to be linked to higher-level descriptive metadata through abstractions that are still very much at the research stage. For describing the intellectual contents and structure of resources that are more complex and less well understood than normal text documents—such as collections of documents, time-based media, and dynamically generated objects—there are few conventions in general use.

A "Multimedia Content Description Interface" (MPEG-7) is currently under development within the Moving Pictures Experts Group (MPEG), a committee of the International Organisation for Standardisation that focuses on the encoding and processing of motion pictures, audio, and related multimedia formats. MPEG-7 is intended to include not just basic description, but metadata on terms and conditions, ratings, encoding formats, and "scenarios" of how multimedia components are combined in presentations.

More broadly, we have a relatively good understanding of traditional publication genres such as printed newspapers, magazines, journals, books, music CDs, and movie videos. Each of these genres is associated with a relatively clear, often long-standing analytical, intellectual, economic, and legal framework. However, we do not yet have such an understanding or consensus about evolving genres of digital publication. We may need to define new genres as the sum of multiple dimensions relevant for their management and handling, such as their encoding format, publication type, access controls, description, and terms and conditions of use. For all genres, including text, we need metadata conventions that support versioning.

Metadata is also needed for describing groups of resources as collections. Collections may be purely administrative entities, or they may be characterized by attributes such as medium, subject, or provenance. Collections may exist within other collections, such as a reference collection within a library. Distinctions between "whole" and "component" collections could facilitate navigation by helping users discover specific databases.

Collection description could also provide at least some access where no item-level descriptions exist, such as in certain image databases and manuscript archives.

Metadata Diversity and Resource Discovery

While we have much experience with homogeneous descriptive metadata (*i.e.*, the library catalogue), very little is known about how to effectively repurpose and integrate the much broader range of metadata now being associated with digital objects into the discovery process. Moreover, the availability of various types of metadata will be highly variable in practice, and it is unclear how best to use types of metadata that may be only sparsely or spottily available. We face the challenge of breaking a vicious circle: without enough metadata of a given type, people will not build harvesters, but if that type of metadata is not widely used, there will be no motivation to create it in the first place. Solutions to this problem will advance metadata deployment, discovery systems, and networked services in general.

Infrastructure

Interoperability among applications benefits from common conventions on semantics and syntax. Semantic interoperability may be achieved either by agreeing on shared meanings or by using mediating software to create coherence across applications. Syntactic interoperability requires standard formats and protocols for expressing metadata structures.

Metadata and Information Architecture Standards

A number of standards that are emerging for the Internet and the Web will provide much of the basic architecture and context for digital libraries. For example, a working group of the World Wide Web Consortium (W3C) is developing the Resource Description Framework (RDF), a set of standards for supporting the exchange of metadata on the Web. This group has recently published the public specification of a general model for metadata. Its underlying encoding syntax is the eXtensible Markup Language (XML), which is expected to become a primary format for document encoding on the Web. RDF has been designed to support the encoding of metadata semantics in discrete functional packages that can be used by applications in the modular, plug-and-play manner called for by the Warwick Framework. The use of Dublin Core metadata in RDF will provide early deployment experience that should expose some of the strengths and weaknesses of this evolving infrastructure.

RDF uses metadata schemas to specify the structure and semantics of formal metadata standards in a way that is usable both by humans and by machines. Schemas will be extensible, either by referencing other schemas or by adding local refinements or specialized elements. Sharing a common set of elements across multiple metadata schemas will promote semantic interoperability by allowing the creation of new schemas that inherit and preserve (while perhaps specializing) the semantics of a parent schema. Languages, techniques, and systems for expressing such schemas will remain an important area for research. The refinement of a generalized metadata architecture based on RDF will require several iterations as it is deployed for digital libraries and in commercial applications.

Generalized formal models of metadata, such as RDF, provide a common language for defining the structure of the many types of metadata used in digital libraries. Within such overarching frameworks, more specific models may be needed to define specialized domains or facets of resources, such as intellectual property restrictions or geospatial coordinates. These formal models may exist in a hierarchy of description, with general models such as RDF pointing to more specific models. For example, the Federal Geographic Data Committee Content Standard might describe specialized aspects of geospatial data, while a more general model is used to associate that data with related non-geospatial resources. The combination of general and specific models is more practical and flexible than monolithic approaches and supports the integration of heterogeneous resources into coherent collections.

The metadata activity of W3C also includes work on standards for privacy and rating services. PICS (Platform for Internet Content Selection) and P3P (Platform for Privacy Preferences) are intended to provide a foundation for this work. Metadata for both will be expressible in RDF. These standards, however, have not yet been widely deployed. Research is needed both on technical and social aspects of their use and on their interaction with other metadata sets.

Other evolving standards involving substantial use of metadata will require continued refinement through deployment experience. In many cases, metadata-using standards have developed somewhat independently of the efforts of the metadata research community, and considerable work may be needed to understand how the conceptual models in these standards relate to work such as RDF and the Warwick Framework. Examples include the Common Object Request Broker Architecture (CORBA) under development by the Object Management Group, which enables applications to manipulate distributed computing objects; the various proposals for electronic rights management and digital identifier systems (such as the DOI); and the Z39.50 protocol for information retrieval, which includes methods of providing metadata to characterize databases and servers. The standard ISO/IEC 11179 (Specification and Standardization of Data Elements) will need to address the varied requirements of metadata for digital libraries and electronic commerce. ISO's Basic Semantic Register will be relevant to the future standardization of metadata vocabularies and to the development of ontologies across schemas.

Crosswalks and Registries

A variety of constructs allow users to search and retrieve across different metadata schemas by translating the elements of one system or subject organization into the terms of a second. Mappings, whether based on tables or on formal definitions, represent relationships that are unambiguous; they support transparent searching across domains. Crosswalks are more complex frameworks that establish the relationship between schemas that have significantly different syntaxes or semantics. They can be based on thesauri or on more elaborate semantic frameworks, such as ontologies, which describe the metadata elements for each domain and map their internal relations. Crosswalk tools could use ontologies to help users understand semantic complexities across systems, but further work is needed on formalisms for expressing such linkages.

The metadata schemas available on the Web will form a global collection of namespaces that will effectively function as a distributed registry. These registries will need to be managed, coordinated, and ultimately connected. Registries will define the elements of metadata schemas in a machine-readable syntax (*e.g.*, RDF) and offer authoritative listings of legal values, local extensions, mappings to other schemas, and guidelines for good usage. They will serve both humans, with readable text, and programmes, with structured content that can automatically be parsed. Their role will be both to promote and to inform, thereby encouraging the use of standard formats.

Like good dictionaries, registries will need to describe actual usage while prescribing good practice. They will help providers of content in languages other than English both in keeping their translations of global standards up-to-date and in constructing specialized local schemas that are as compatible as possible with global standards. They will also assist in aligning element definitions among diverse existing and proposed schemas, thus reducing duplication of effort. At a more complex level, registries could offer knowledge bases that support the automatic translation of metadata into other languages and schemas, automatic validation, and the automatic updating of remote metadata to new versions.

The interaction between metadata registries and particular user communities will never be simply a technical problem. Like natural languages, metadata languages will evolve with use. Interoperability over time can be ensured only if registries are supported by a public forum with formal processes that allow user communities both to negotiate meanings collectively and to adapt these rules to local needs. Since the shared semantics of communities differ in complex ways, the definition and maintenance of crosswalks and registries imply support for complex social processes. Building such systems must draw on our understanding of how ontologies, whether of specialized vocabularies or of natural languages, can formally be related or linked among themselves. Constructions used in federations of thesauri, such as "interlinguas," could be adapted for linking ontologies of metadata. Metadata element sets will be managed by agencies that are responsible for their development and maintenance. An ecology of registries will emerge that reflects a diversity of organizational motives, market forces, and user requirements. A distributed model for registries will reflect this diversity by supporting cooperation at multiple levels—global, regional, domain (by subject or resource type), and sector. The development of such infrastructures will provide an important focal point for international collaboration.

Policy and Management

The Web has substantially reduced barriers to information flow and access around the world and we now see increased interaction across sectors and disciplines on an international basis. Content and metadata are both moving rather casually between communities and across national boundaries. This radical change in accessibility has major implications for creating and managing both content and metadata.

Trans-Border Information Policy

Legislators and policy-makers are paying increased attention to the Internet environment and to harmonizing both intellectual property law and a wide range of information policies (*e.g.*, privacy, content rating, commerce, and censorship) on a global basis. However, national differences in policies and legislation on such issues will inevitably become more prominent. The semantics of metadata, the operational characteristics of applications that use metadata, and the interaction of diverse forms of metadata will receive substantial scrutiny. Libraries, archives, museums, government agencies, and publishers—as well as their constituents—will need to take account of international implications as they establish metadata standards and infrastructures in support of their goals and interests.

Various classes of assertions embodied in metadata may well have legal status, at least in some usage contexts and legal regimes. We need to understand the implications of this within a complex diversity of national and international law and practice, especially when metadata crosses borders and jurisdictions. In some situations, it may be necessary to translate metadata values between languages to another or to map metadata packages from one legal regime to another. The assertions embodied in metadata and the sources of metadata will raise issues of liability and accountability; in order to cross borders, for example, some metadata may have to be digitally signed.

Metadata Research and the International Standards Process

Much of the value of metadata comes from its character as a shared community understanding. This means that progress in metadata rapidly moves into the arena of standardization. Work on metadata standards—and particularly the sort of cross-community standards discussed in much of this paper—is particularly challenging because it demands collaboration from historically autonomous and specialized communities of practice and their standards development organizations. This is creating significant difficulties as the various standards organizations struggle to define their roles and establish processes for coordination and collaboration with other groups.

It is becoming clear to many communities of practice that as their activities and information resources move into a highly distributed network-based environment they will need to evolve community metadata standards. Research is needed to develop faster, more effective and efficient ways for these communities to develop, achieve consensus upon, and document community practices, processes, and data models. Streamlining such efforts could have a high impact on a range of fields, from scientific disciplines to the cultural heritage community.

The development of standards for digital libraries and networked information is a very important process for establishing consensus about intellectual models and for translating research into practice.

Standards development, particularly at the international level, is a slow and costly process that has in the recent past been dominated by commercial interests and government representatives with the resources to participate. It is essential that resources be made available to permit the metadata and digital library research communities to participate fully in these ongoing efforts.

Integrity, Accuracy, and Authenticity of Metadata

As metadata becomes more important both for discovering information and for expressing assertions about networked content, it will become increasingly necessary to verify its accuracy, integrity, and trustworthiness. One can already see situations in which content providers attempt to mislead Web indexing services with irrelevant index terms in order to make their content more visible to searchers. In the present environment, Web indexers can inspect the actual source content of Web pages to check for such subterfuge, and the major commercial services have developed proprietary algorithms that attempt to filter out indexing misinformation. As metadata use expands to capture more abstract assertions about objects (*e.g.*, ratings or subject analysis), the design of such validation algorithms and heuristics becomes an extremely challenging and largely unexplored problem for research.

An alternative to verifying metadata is to consider the source of each metadata assertion associated with an object. This suggests research in at least two areas. The first is the design of systems to verify the source of metadata assertions, presumably in conjunction with digital signatures and a public key infrastructure, in a highly distributed international environment. The second is how to factor user-provided (and third-party-provided) constraints about the relative trustworthiness of metadata providers into processes such as resource discovery.

Evaluation and Metrics

The deployment of metadata through standard mechanisms such as RDF provides an opportunity to explore the evolving use of metadata within various communities. The sampling and analysis of metadata will provide a valuable window onto the Web as a medium for distributing the cultural, scientific, and technical products of a society and onto the practices used to describe them. Knowledge gained from tracking the diffusion of metadata use can be applied to the further development of metadata schemes and to the creation of dictionaries that track the transition from pidgin to creole. Usage patterns can serve as a guide for developers of schemas and feed back into the design of core metadata sets and functional packages. A fundamental question about the use of metadata, particularly in areas such as resource discovery, is cost-effectiveness. Is intellectually derived descriptive metadata sufficiently better than algorithmically computed metadata to justify the cost of its creation? Benchmarks and experimental evaluation frameworks similar to the Text Retrieval Conference (TREC) for full-text databases will be needed. Tracking deployment will also help identify which data elements users consider to be important in processes such as resource discovery and show how these elements are being used. Such data will guide the further evolution of core metadata sets.

Conclusion

This paper identifies numerous topics for research on issues that will be central to fostering the growth of networked information resources, digital libraries, electronic commerce, and network-based publishing. In the near term, a commitment to work on registry infrastructures could provide an important focal point and source of cohesion for research and development in many of these areas, as well as being an important research project in its own right. The Dublin Core seems poised to provide a metadata system for resource discovery that is consistent across a wide range of applications and domains, usable by both experts and non-experts, interoperable with existing library catalogs and legacy databases, and coherent across many languages (over twenty to date). RDF is a deployment vehicle not only for Dublin Core but also for a wide range of new core and discipline-specific metadata sets that will be developed.

Effective research progress on metadata will need to involve intense collaboration between metadata specialists and communities trying to solve functional problems, such as rights management, resource discovery, archiving and preservation, or the organization and management of data specific to various disciplines. The definition and maintenance of metadata standards over time is a complex social process requiring negotiation, consensus-building, and iteration. Learning to manage such processes effectively and to coordinate the ever-growing activities of many disparate communities of interest is clearly a long-term research undertaking involving complex economic, technical, and social questions.

The world has never had information systems of this scale, nor has it ever tried to provide consistent organization and access to sets of resources and services as large and diverse as those appearing on the Internet today. We must seek not just to serve specific disciplines or communities of practice, nor must we focus just on facilitating the use of information across communities. Rather, we must seek to provide the emerging global information infrastructure with coherent methods of organization and access that transcend the historical boundaries of nations, languages, and cultures. Addressing these challenges will require a two-pronged research approach: engagement in near-term, applied questions involving specific metadata sets and architectural issues raised by developments such as RDF, and a continued investment in theoretical and foundational work that can abstract out broad principles and model the effects of scaling.

LANGUAGES FOR DUBLIN CORE

Over the past three years, the Dublin Core Metadata Initiative has achieved a broad international consensus on the semantics of a simple element set for describing electronic resources. Since the first workshop in March 1995, which was reported in the very first issue of *D-Lib Magazine* [Weibel 1995], Dublin Core has been the topic of perhaps a dozen articles here. Originally intended to be simple and intuitive enough for authors to tag Web pages without special training, Dublin Core is being adapted now for more specialized uses, from government information and legal deposit to museum informatics and electronic commerce.

To meet such specialized requirements, Dublin Core can be customized with additional elements or qualifiers. However, these refinements can compromise interoperability across applications. There are tradeoffs between using specific terms that precisely meet local needs versus general terms that are understood more widely. We can better understand this inevitable tension between simplicity and complexity if we recognize that metadata is a form of human language. With Dublin Core, as with a natural language, people are inclined to stretch definitions, make general terms more specific, specific terms more general, misunderstand intended meanings, and coin new terms. One goal of this paper, therefore, will be to examine the experience of some related ways to seek semantic interoperability through simplicity: planned languages, interlingua constructs, and pidgins [Baker 1997b].

The problem of semantic interoperability is compounded when we consider Dublin Core in translation. All of the workshops, documents, mailing lists, user guides, and working group outputs of the Dublin Core Initiative have been in English [Dublin Core Metadata Initiative]. But in many countries and for many applications, people need a metadata standard in their own language. In principle, the broad elements of Dublin Core can be defined equally well in Bulgarian or Hindi. Since Dublin Core is a controlled standard, however, any parallel definitions need to be kept in sync as the standard evolves. Another goal of the paper, then, will be to define the conceptual and organizational problem of maintaining a metadata standard in multiple languages.

In addition to a name and definition, which are meant for human consumption, each Dublin Core element has a label, or indexing token, meant for harvesting by search engines. For practical reasons, these machine-readable tokens are English-looking strings such as *Creator* and *Subject* (just as HTML tags are called *HEAD*, *BODY*, or *TITLE*). These tokens, which are shared by Dublin Cores in every language, ensure that metadata fields created in any particular language are indexed together across repositories. As symbols of underlying universal semantics, these tokens form the basis of semantic interoperability among the multiple Dublin Cores.

As long as we limit ourselves to sharing these indexing tokens among exact translations of a simple set of fifteen broad elements, the definitions of which fit easily onto two pages, the problem of Dublin Core in multiple languages is straightforward. But nothing having to do with human language is ever so simple. Just as speakers of various languages must learn the language of Dublin Core in their own tongues, we must find the right words to talk about a metadata language that is expressable in many discipline-specific jargons and natural languages and that inevitably will evolve and change over time.

DC-Multilingual

Translating the two-page, fifteen-element standard known as Unqualified Dublin Core [RFC 2413] has proven to be relatively easy. Typical in this regard is the experience of the cataloguing experts who created DC-Indonesian (in Bahasa Indonesia, which uses the Latin alphabet). Some elements had obvious translations: *format* is identical in English and Indonesian. Some elements were translated uncontroversially with English loanwords: *subject* as *subjek*; *contributor* as *kontributor* (the giver of an idea, as opposed to *penyumbang*, a charitable donor); and *description* with *deskripsi* (which is more general than *ringkasan isi* for summaries of text or *menggambarkan* for images). The term *creator* is usually rendered in Indonesian as *pencipta*, but to many people this evokes a deity, analogously to *Schöpfer* in German, *skapare* in Swedish, and arguably even *creator* in English. After rejecting some overly specific alternatives, the committee opted for a loanword that covered the proper scope with none of the distracting cultural baggage—*kreator* [Prabawa 1998].

Problems such as these must be resolved in the element definitions. This is especially crucial in cases where local concepts divide along lines much different from those of DC-English. To date, the translators of Dublin Core have reported few such conflicts, but one problem with legal implications deserves mention. For historical reasons, the Romance languages use equivalents of the French term *éditeur* to refer both to "editors" (in Dublin Core a type of *contributor*) and "publishers" (an element of the Core). Although I am told this has created some difficulties with the wording of legal deposit laws, it has not been raised as a serious problem with regard to Dublin Core.

Discussions of such issues have taken place over the past year or two in many languages. The creation of a DC-Arabic was coordinated by Hachim Haddouti, a researcher of the Bavarian Research Centre for Knowledge-Based Systems (FORWISS), with the involvement of colleagues in Germany,

Canada, Tunisia, USA, Morocco, United Arab Emirates, and Jordan [DC-Arabic]. In his view, "DC-Arabic constitutes a milestone in promoting metadata in the Arabic language and Arabic-language computing. Reactions from my colleagues at research libraries, documentation centres, software firms, and publishers in the Arabic-speaking world confirm that this standard is addressing a recognized need."

In Japan, the University of Library and Information Science in Tsukuba has begun a large-scale digital library project based on Dublin Core [DC-Japanese]. A DC-Chinese in "Big5" encoding (traditional characters) has been posted at the Department of Library and Information Science at Fu-Jen University in Hsin-Chunag, Taiwan [DC-Chinese (Big5)]. Another DC-Chinese, in "GB" encoding (simplified characters), has been proposed by a masters student at the Asian Institute of Technology [Wu 1998].

Several Asian initiatives to translate Dublin Core have involved centres for scientific information. DC-Korean was undertaken by researchers at the Korea Research Information Centre together with colleagues from Yonse University, Ehwa Women's University, and Chung Ang University [DC-Korean]. In Thailand, a translation was prepared at the Technical Information Access Centre of the National Science and Technology Development Agency in consultation with colleagues from the Library Association of Thailand and the Asian Institute of Technology [DC-Thai]. DC-Indonesian was discussed and approved by members of the National Library of Indonesia, the University of Indonesia, the Centre for Scientific Documentation and Information of the Indonesian Institute of Sciences, and the Library Development Coordination Unit of the Directorate General of Higher Education [Prabawa 1998].

In Southern Europe, work on Dublin Core has often begun on the initiative of government research institutions. DC-Italian was created at the Istituto di Elaborazione dell'Informazione [Institute for Information Processing] of the Italian National Research Council in collaboration with the Istituto Centrale per il Catalogo Unico (ICCU), which maintains a union catalogue of Italian libraries. A DC-Spanish has been posted by RedIRIS, an academic network under Spain's Scientific Research Council [DC-Spanish]. DC-French was created at the National Institute for Research in Computer Science and Control (INRIA) [DC-French]. The Greek Dublin Core has been an initiative of the Foundation for Research and Technology—Hellas (FORTH) in Heraklion, Crete [DC-Greek].

In several countries, Dublin Core has been adopted for use in national repositories or directories of online resources. The National Library of Portugal may adopt Dublin Core for the deposit and preservation of Portuguese digital publications and is promoting the standardization of Dublin Core sub-elements for Portuguese materials [DC-Portuguese]. Having mandated that all public documents be published online, the government of Denmark is teaching thousands of administrators how to create and manage metadata as an integral part of their workflow. A national metadata standard based on Unqualified Dublin Core (with four added sub-elements under *Title* and *Relation*) forms a common template for the Danish Library Centre, Danish National Library Authority, legal deposit libraries, and the Danish State Information Service. This template is used by online publishers to register their documents for inclusion in the national bibliography and for storage on a legal deposit server in the Royal Library.

Following the Danish example, the government of Finland has begun projects to implement legal deposit, archive online publications, and add Dublin Core metadata to public documents [DC-Finnish]. In the Nordic Metadata Projects, researchers from these countries have collaborated extensively with colleagues to promote regional metadata strategies. There is a DC-Norwegian, and work is underway on DC-Icelandic and DC-Swedish [DC-Norwegian, DC-Swedish]. As a practical matter, all of the tools and documents of the Nordic Metadata Project are published in English [Nordic Metadata Projects]. Koninklijke Bibliotheek, the national library of the Netherlands, has created a DC-Dutch for a project to compile a Directory of Netherlands Online Resources [DC-Dutch].

There are over thirty projects using Dublin Core in Germany. The biggest of these involve Germany's learned societies, Humboldt University, the Lower Saxony State and University Library in Göttingen, Die Deutsche Bibliothek, the Bavarian State Library, the Library of the Max Planck Institute for Human Development, the German Library Institute in Berlin, and the Southwest Consortium of University Libraries [Information and Communication Commission of the Learned Societies, Metadata Projects at German Libraries, German Metadata Registry, Meta-Lib Project]. Die Deutsche Bibliothek will host the next full Dublin Core workshop in October 1999. A German translation of Dublin Core has been posted at the Max Planck Institute for Human Development and Education [DC-German]. In practice, however, many projects have created their own local versions, which are partly in English, partly in German, and partly mixed. These local variants of Dublin Core are being tracked in a comparative database at the Lower Saxony State and University Library [MetaForm].

Work has started on a DC-Burmese. Its first users will be the academics, research librarians, and independent scholars of the Burma Archives Project, which aims at encouraging the collection, preservation, and indexing of materials related to contemporary Burma. Of particular interest are materials related to the Burmese democratic movement of the 1980s and 1990s, from posters, photographs, pamphlets, diaries, correspondence, and memoirs to records from political parties, labour unions, student organizations, and ethnic associations. Having a Dublin Core in Burmese will help the project train Burmese in the techniques of preservation while making these materials available for wider usage.

Shortly before publication deadline, we received news that the Software Research and Development Centre of the Middle East Technical University in Ankara is planning to prepare a DC-Turkish. A team of researchers at the School of Information, Library, and Archive Studies at the University of New South Wales plans to work with documentalists from Cambodia on a DC-Khmer.

Expressions, Versions or Translations?

It seems natural to talk about DC-Arabic as the Arabic-language *version* of Dublin Core, and this is what many of us have been doing. But this term has become the object of debate since the Dublin Core workshop of 2-4 November at the Library of Congress. At that workshop, it became clear that part of the

Dublin Core community wants to focus on clarifying the semantics of a simple element set that has been relatively stable since December 1996 and already forms the basis of numerous implementation projects. Others, however, wish to redesign parts of that element set in order to address weaknesses that have emerged from implementation experience and to make the elements more useful for potential new users in the publishing and entertainment industries. As a result, the existing element set has been dubbed Dublin Core Version 1.0; a refined version of the same will be called Version 1.1; and work is beginning on a more fundamentally revised Dublin Core Version 2.0. If the current DC-Japanese is now the Japanese-language *version* of DC-English Version 1.0, does this make it a *version of a version*?

One obvious alternative is *translation*. The current DC-Japanese is in fact a translation of DC-English Version 1.0. None of them change the scope of definitions or add new "Dublin Core" elements beyond the canonical fifteen. Everyone involved in this process to date has recognized that the Dublin Core in English is the canonical result of an international process. Everyone also recognizes the need to have one version from which all others derive; a DC-Ukrainian should be prepared directly from DC-English and not from DC-Russian. Moreover, everyone recognizes that translations which exactly render an original wording may not be as effective as translations which use some poetic license to convey the intended meanings to a particular audience. Nevertheless, the term has drawbacks. As one participant points out, "*translation* transmits the idea that DC is an English thing, which can be negative for its acceptance and probably even for its understanding". In an age of automatic translators, available even as pocket gadgets, the word *translation* evokes a process that is largely mechanical and one-way. What national library, some ask, will want to define its role primarily as custodian of a translation?

Yet none of the alternatives are clearly better. It is natural to talk about Dublin Core *expressed in Estonian*, though it seems awkward to speak of Dublin Core in its *Estonian expression*. Nor does it seem entirely satisfactory to talk about the *Malay manifestation*, *Finnish format*, *Armenian edition*,

Arabic adaptation, *Danish description*, *Romanian release*, *Vietnamese variant*, or *Russian rendering*. Many of these terms have points of theory in their favour, or even precedents in library science. But unfortunately they are all a bit unusual and would require some explanation. Further complicating matters is the question of what to call manifestations of Dublin Cores in multiple *software formats* such as XML, GIF, PostScript, LaTeX, MSWord, and HTML. Final agreement on standard names for these phenomena—in English, of course—will bring us full circle to the problem of how to translate these terms and explain their distinctions in other languages.

Many discussants do agree that *version* becomes appropriate when the line is crossed between *translation* and *adaptation*. For example, if a DC-French were to modify Dublin Core with unique qualifiers or definitions for specific local uses, then one might no longer have just a French *translation* of Dublin Core Version 1.0, but a new French *version* that is "based on" Dublin Core Version 1.0 for the purposes of software interoperability. This distinction may apply to Site Preview Format (SPF), an adaptation of DC-English for use on Netscape's Netcenter [Miller 1998]. SPF uses the indexing tokens shared by all Dublin Cores but substitutes four of the official labels—*Description*, *Relation*, *Subject*, and *Publisher*—with four nearly equivalent labels of its own—*Content Summary*, *Related Items*, *Category*, and *Provider*. Such changes may have little practical effect on the resulting resource descriptions, but SPF is clearly not simply a translation of Dublin Core.

In Germany, Ralf Schimmer of the MetaForm Project has noticed that similar *adaptations* of Dublin Core (he calls them *manifestations*) have been created locally for specific projects. These typically deviate somewhat from the standard: "One definitely sees that they belong to the same language, but a closer examination reveals certain unique and idiosyncratic characteristics of the kind one sees in *dialects*. Despite the common language they invoke and from which (in this case) they claim legitimacy, subtle semantic shifts creep in. In the end, these could make understanding between Dublin Core applications as difficult as between different dialect regions. The Dublin Core label and brand name do not guarantee uniformity of contents and semantics." Such differences of dialect or usage are an inevitable feature of natural languages. Even within one language, differences can be great between the jargons of scientific and cultural fields.

There were moments during the first Dublin Core workshops when people realized they had debated at length on the basis of widely different understandings of fundamental terms such as *type*, which evokes different things to librarians and computer programmers. Even experienced bibliographers can find themselves at a loss about how to apply traditional concepts such as *author* and *publisher* to the description of new electronic genres, such as Web pages.

Indeed, Dublin Core itself could prove to be a new type of genre within the electronic environment. John Kunze suggests that Dublin Core could cease to be "versionable" in the sense of controlled software releases (*e.g.*, 1.0, 1.1, 2.0) if it were to evolve into a larger, dynamically evolving set of elements in common use. Such a system would more closely resemble controlled vocabularies and natural languages, which do not in practice need version numbers to fulfil their functions. The evolution of such a metadata language would need to be marked in only a rough sense (*e.g.*, by year) for the benefit of specialists, which could free the term *version* for variants of the element set in multiple languages.

Dublin Core as a Planned Language

The Dublin Core Metadata Initiative began as a hall conversation at the Second International World Wide Web Conference in October 1994—the year when the Internet first made the cover of popular magazines. The number of Web pages was doubling every few weeks, and it was becoming harder to find anything, even with new full-text indexing services such as Lycos. Many people agreed that the Web needed a catalogue, that there would never be enough librarians to handle it all, and that existing library standards were generally too complex for ordinary people to learn. To promote semantic interoperability between specialized communities on the Web, then, the first Dublin Core workshop drew up a short list of metadata elements that would efficiently yield "simple descriptions of data in a wide range of subject areas" [Weibel 1995].

It is tempting to compare those early 1990s with the 1870s, when the expansion of international trade and colonial empires and the explosion of literature in print posed similar problems of information management and semantic interoperability. It was a decade that saw the creation of library associations, international librarianship, and Dewey Decimal Classification. It also saw the first of several dozen proposals for *artificial* or *planned languages*.

At the time, the diversity of national languages seemed an obstacle to progress, but returning to Latin was not an option, and agreement on English or French seemed politically unlikely. Many scholars and practitioners of that time believed that the interests of international understanding and of science would be served by devising a universal auxiliary language that was easy enough for everyone to learn. The first of these to achieve much success was was Volapük or "World Speak" (1879), a morphologically complex synthesis of German, English, and Latin. Its decline coincided with the rise of Esperanto (1887), a simpler language with a Slavic flavour. Most such languages were syntheses of existing natural languages, using Western European word roots and simplified grammars.

Typically, these planned languages were created by a single author, working in isolation, then adopted by a small circle of followers. As in the Dublin Core movement, however, early users of planned languages disagreed about whether to accommodate new words or constructions. Debates often reflected the conflicting requirements of everyday needs versus the demands of specialists. The Volapük movement split over a conflict between its inventor, who wanted it to be as subtle and expressive as a natural language, and followers who wanted to improve its chances of adoption by making it simpler. The Esperanto movement likewise argued over issues such as its use of the circumflex, and factions broke off to promote alternative versions, such as Ido (1907) and Novial (1928).

The Dublin Core movement has experienced an analogous tension between Minimalists, who value the intuitive simplicity of its fifteen broadly-defined elements, and Structuralists, who see the elements as a complexifiable set of primitives for richer and more specialized resource description. It is useful, therefore, to consider how a planned language of the sort proposed in the late nineteenth century might actually have succeeded. Theorists speculate that it would need a critical mass of speakers, official endorsement by governments, and widespread use in mass media. Ideally, it would have an international board to maintain standards, review proposals, and control the language's continued evolution. This institutional control from above would need to be loose enough to allow speakers to coin new terms and constructions for expressing their everyday experiences [Eco 1995]. Other scholars point out that planned languages are by their nature closed in design, rather strictly governed by rules, linguistically unnatural, and ill-suited to change. Natural languages, in contrast, are versatile and open-ended. To achieve success, they suggest, language designers need to provide for peoples' propensity to change or create rules, adapt systems, and negotiate meanings. And to understand such processes, the designers would do well to examine how communities of users interact spontaneously to create pidgins [Laycock and Mühlhäusler 1994].

Pidgin Metadata and its Creolization

Pidgins are makeshift, hybrid languages that arise when speakers of different languages in regular but superficial contact must work together or conduct trade. They usually have small vocabularies (borrowed largely from a socially dominant group), little inflection, and loose word order. Emphasis is achieved with reduplication and gestures. In the absence of grammatical precision, speakers must sometimes resort to elaborate circumlocutions, and usage is inconsistent between speakers. Interpretation can depend heavily on context; the sentence *Sista fo hospitu bin luk wom* (from Cameroonian pidgin) can mean either "The nurse at the hospital saw worms" or "The nurse saw worms at the hospital" [Schneider 1966]. Historically, pidgins have arisen among hired or slave workers on ethnically mixed plantations, though "pidginization" constantly occurs today in vacation resorts, port cities, and immigrant communities.

As a pidgin becomes more valuable to its users, for example to conduct business, it stabilizes, its vocabulary expands, and it becomes flexible enough to be used as a speaker's primary language. Researchers have found that when children are raised using a pidgin as their mother tongue during the critical period before adolescence, they use their instinctive language skills to improvise grammatical subtleties, transforming their parents' crude pidgins into grammatically richer, more expressive *creoles*. Creoles are bona fide languages, with subtle grammatical markers and consistent word orders. Creoles acquire prepositions, extensive vocabularies, and a syntax less dependent on context [Pinker 1994].

By analogy, the Dublin Core Element Set arose when natives of different resource description communities—from librarians, archivists, scientists, humanities scholars, and geographers to the makers of Internet standards—suddenly needed to interoperate on the Web and so created a process to negotiate a metadata hybrid. The metaphor of the "virtual tourist" who uses Dublin Core as a phrase book for browsing collections in unfamiliar fields over the Web is especially fitting because real-life tourists are naturally inclined to pidginize (*e.g.*, "Nix spreken Deutsch. Zwei beer, okay?"). This melding of diverse resource description conventions yielded Dublin Core in its unqualified, minimalist form.

A creolized Dublin Core, in contrast, would draw a richer vocabulary from controlled lists of semantically refined sub-elements and qualifiers. Its grammar would be provided by the Resource Description Framework (RDF), a new and more sophisticated conceptual model and encoding syntax for expressing metadata on the Web. RDF allows resource descriptions to reference multiple schemas and externally maintained vocabularies, further broadening its expressive scope. Its grammatical repertoire of *subjects*, *predicates*, and *objects*, along with capabilities such as *reification* (*i.e.*, referencing statements as wholes) significantly expand its expressive capabilities.

RDF syntax can support a wide range of metadata applications beyond resource description, such as push channel definitions, ratings, site maps, and digital signatures, so it is seen by many content and service providers—from Netscape and CNN to New York Times and Amazon.com—as a crucial enabling technology for electronic commerce [Netscape 1997]. Dublin Core can provide key descriptive elements for many such applications, such as news feeds from wire services. In particular, the entertainment industry is interested in using Dublin Core elements and RDF grammar to construct statements that express business deals about the use of entertainment content and trade publications. For example, RDF can be used to express the following (hypothetical) agreement:

ASCAP declares that Joan Quincy composed the song "Rising Tide" and registered it for copyright in the USA in 1995, and that ASCAP has exclusively acquired the right to administer on behalf of Joan Quincy and her publisher Diva Songs, Inc the right for worldwide public performance from the time of composition until further notice.

Suppose the Harry Fox Agency were to act as the worldwide agent for Diva Songs for the right to record the song; Joan Quincy were to make a recording of her own song; and Nakamura Records were to acquire a license to use this song in a compact disk. One might then formulate a statement like the following:

Nakamura Records says that it has acquired from JASRAC [the Japanese copyright society] acting as agent for the Harry Fox Agency acting as agent for Diva Songs Inc, the mechanical reproduction right in respect of the song "Rising Tide" by Joan Quincy for inclusion in the CD "Californian Sunsets" for distribution only in Japan.

Statements could become even more elaborate if they were to factor in complications such as the rights of individual band members or ownership rights for any pre-existing samples used in a recording. Changes in ownership or representation anywhere in a chain of such statements could affect thousands of related agreements and licenses. Such complex dependencies have hitherto been tracked by hand, so the entertainment and publishing industries are highly motivated to perfect a language for expressing such metadata statements in ways that are automatically parsable, legally binding, and that ensure efficient flows of royalties and payments.

Interlinguas, Switching Languages, Registries and Dictionaries

Some members of the Dublin Core community see the value of its fifteen broad elements less as a native pidgin or creole for direct use in creating catalogue records than as a standardized *switching language* between richer, domain-specific descriptive languages such as MARC (for library catalogs), GILS (for government information), and Z39.50 (for distributed databases). Nobody seems to know the origin of this term, but everyone understands that it has to do with establishing a common reference point of widely understood semantics to which a variety of other schemas can map many-to-one, thus achieving semantic interoperability over multiple systems at little cost and effort [Koch, Hakala, and Husby 1996]. Nobody questions that in practice, the semantics of this focal point must be expressed in English.

Such a construct has analogs in the area of natural language processing. The EuroWordNet project aims at supporting cross-language retrieval by linking comprehensive ontologies of Spanish, English, Dutch, and Italian words to a central *InterLanguage* or *interlingua* that holds a superset of all concepts found in the component languages [EuroWordNet]. Similarly, a ten-year project coordinated by the United Nations University in Tokyo aims at mapping the more than one hundred languages of the United Nations to a common *Universal Networking Language*—an intermediate encoding of grammar and semantics from which, in theory, it will be possible to generate equivalent sentences in any of the other languages [Universal Networking Language]. Like the switching language, both of these constructs involve central reference points that in theory are language-neutral but in practice express their universal semantics in English.

The notions of switching language and interlingua are compatible with the need for *metadata registries* to express schemas in both human-and machine-readable formats and offer authoritative usage guidelines, local extensions, crosswalks to related schemas, and lists of legal values. There is a convergence of interest in such registries not just from the digital library community, for resource discovery, but from other service providers in government, business, and education and for a wide range of applications. An ecology of registries could emerge that reflects a diversity of organizational motives, market forces, and user communities [Baker and Lynch 1998].

Metadata registries could use constructs such as interlinguas to link diverse ontologies of elements among themselves. In addition to prescribing certified elements and promoting standards of good practice, registries could also function as metadata dictionaries by monitoring patterns of usage, whether "correct" or not, and describing alternative definitions in actual use [Kunze 1996]. Mediating between these functions could be something like the Usage Panel of the American Heritage Dictionary, whose 173 writers, critics, and scholars help the dictionary editors find a balance between descriptions of actual usage and prescriptions of preferred forms, while evaluating potential entries against "the fundamental linguistic virtues—order, clarity, and conciseness" [Nunberg 1992].

Focal points such as switching constructs, interlinguas, registries, and dictionaries can provide metadata languages with the public forum that any language needs in order to grow and evolve. But interoperability over time can be ensured only if such constructs are supported by social processes that allow user communities to negotiate global meanings while adapting them to local needs. Ideally, such a process would allow a user of DC-Korean to propose a local extension, defined in English, for addition to the global standard. The process would then see this proposal through a formal review, vote of approval, and incorporation into the canon.

The Working Group on Dublin Core in Multiple Languages

The Working Group on Dublin Core in Multiple Languages grew out of a break-out group at the Canberra workshop of March 1997 at which we agreed that versions of the Dublin Core in multiple languages could interoperate by sharing a set of globally valid, machine-readable tokens [Baker 1997a]. The mission of the working group today is to coordinate the development of Dublin Core as a multilingual metadata standard by addressing the related issues of policy and application [Dublin Core in Multiple Languages].

For starters, we need to develop a common vocabulary and shared understanding of the status of these various Dublin Cores. The discussion of *translation* versus *version* summarized above is not entirely closed. Until now, we have been calling them *versions*, but since the current DC-English has been declared to be Version 1.0 and work has begun both on Version 1.1 and on Version 2.0, this term will no longer serve. Clearly, we will need to approach these issues in a modular fashion. Translations of the two-page document that define the fifteen elements of Version 1.0 are unambiguously *translations*. Henceforth, local Dublin Cores should specify the version of DC-English on which they are based (*e.g.*, DC-Finnish Version 1.0 would be a translation of DC-English Version 1.0).

In practice, however, many local schemas contain additional elements outside the scope of Dublin Core itself. For example Netscape's Site Preview Format includes *Title of Channel, Text of Content*, and *Image*. Rather than shoehorning such extended semantics into the "catch-all" element of Dublin Core, *Description*—as some implementors have done—Netscape follows the good practice of deriving its SPF schema from multiple namespaces. Dublin Core elements within the schema point to the Dublin Core namespace, while the local extensions point to a local namespace for SPF.

The principle of modularity, however, poses challenges for multilinguality. The Dublin Core Data Model Working Group has quite sensibly proposed that the Dublin Core community avoid reinventing wheels. Where reasonable, it should "beg and borrow" sets of terms, controlled vocabularies, and metadata schemas from communities that already maintain them. For example, an organization called the Internet Mail Consortium promotes "vCard", a core set of metadata elements covering email and Web addresses, identification photos, telephone numbers, and company logos—a "Dublin Core", as it were, for business cards [vCard]. Rather than repropose identical sub-elements for Dublin Core itself, Dublin Core should officially point to the external namespace where this schema is held. How one in practice would maintain local versions of these external vocabularies and schemas for use in non-English-speaking environments is a question we have done no more than pose.

From the standpoint of implementors in other languages, of course, the translation of a two-page schema is just a beginning. As Shigeo Sugimoto has pointed out, it is significantly more expensive for non-English-speaking countries to follow the evolution of the standard because supporting materials must also be produced in the local language. User guides must be translated—or written from scratch. Crosswalks must be maintained to legacy schemas such as the many variants of the MARC format for libraries. Metadata creation tools must be localized with links to local classification schemes and subject headings.

So far, we have freely invited metadata-using institutions in many countries to translate Dublin Core into their own languages. More than once, a translation begun by a single person has been adopted by a national institution, so we see no need to discourage initiatives by individuals as well. All such efforts spread awareness of the standard, thereby increasing the number of potential users and hence the value of Dublin Core for cross-language interoperability. Regional linguistic differences or institutional rivalries could eventually result in the creation of more than one Dublin Core for any given language, but we see no need to discourage this either; the creators and users of metadata in each country or language area will eventually vote with their templates.

In the medium term, however, we may need a process for evaluating these versions, with peer review for translation quality and verification of an institution's commitment to maintaining the standard on an ongoing basis. Dublin Cores that meet certain criteria could perhaps obtain official endorsement or certification. Peer review could also help maintain the modular distinction between pure Dublin Core and local extensions or adaptations. Through the mechanism of a distributed registry, certified Dublin Core elements in various languages could be offered for automatic loading into browser templates or metadata editors. As a first step in this direction, we have implemented at the Asian Institute of

Technology a simple registry of Dublin Core in about twelve languages [Xu 1998]. Users who request to see Dublin Core in Thai can choose to view the schema directly in HTML, if their browser supports the proper font; to receive the schema as a bitmap image; or, if their browser supports Java, to view the schema using the "Multilingual HTML" system developed at the University of Library and Information Science in Tsukuba, Japan, which wraps files in Thai, Korean, and other languages with the glyphs and applets necessary for properly displaying their fonts [Multilingual HTML].

Starting Simple

One engineering maxim holds that "Large successful systems start as small successful systems" [Kelly and Reiss 1998]. As Freeman Dyson has pointed out, computers only really took off when they built them small and fast, shortening the iteration of design. In part this is because the underlying problem is not one of theory, but of practice. There was a theory of flight, but it did not help the Wright brothers build an airplane. Nor were bicycles designed by theory, but by trial and error; indeed, theory still cannot really explain why they work as they do. Projects that start big are doomed to fail, he believes, because you never have time to fix all the bugs [Brand 1998].

If there is any truth to this, then Dublin Core offers a useful starting point for building a metadata infrastructure that covers multiple languages. That starting point is a two-page set of definitions that can quickly and easily be translated into any modern language. Since these translations are, for all practical purposes, semantically identical, linking them into a distributed registry is straightforward. We can proceed with the complexification of this model—adding sub-elements and qualifiers as they are approved by the Dublin Core community, or making links to semantically related schemas such as GILS or MARC—incrementally and as the needs arise.

To encourage participation worldwide, we must focus on promoting and adapting open standards such as RDF for expressing schemas, formatting records, and eventually for managing more complex semantic relations within a diverse ecology of metadata registries and ontologies. The open source software movement, which has achieved such visible success with products such as the Linux operating system and the Apache Web server, provides an inspiring model of implementor communities dedicated to the free propagation of tools. Each effort to localize Dublin Core for a particular community or language stands to benefit from the free availability of metadata templates and editors, Java utilities, user guides, and crosswalks to common element sets.

In its simpler form (versions 1.0 and 1.1), Dublin Core could stabilize as a metadata pidgin. A natural-language precedent for this is Tok Pisin, which has stabilized in an extended form, short of full creolization, as the lingua franca of 1.5 million people and the language of government in Papua New Guinea. At the same time, an emerging infrastructure of metadata registries, more sophisticated metadata grammars and data models, and a broadening consensus on the use of controlled vocabularies, qualifiers, and multiple namespaces could lead to the development of a more complex metadata language based on Dublin Core. This process of creolization is likely to be driven in part by the needs of new user communities, such as news agencies, Internet portals, online retailers, and the entertainment industry.

The design of Web-based processes to support these developments could address some of the reasons why universalist language projects have failed in the past. In contrast to Esperanto, Dublin Core stands to acquire a critical mass of users. It already has the official endorsement of some governments. Its use on the Web will give it wide exposure in a mass media. And the formalization of a maintenance agency for Dublin Core will provide a forum for controlling its evolution. To remain relevant and useful, Dublin Core will need to evolve and grow like any other language. This will require processes that strike a balance between institutional control from above and natural change in usage from below. The challenge will be to design these processes so that speakers of all languages can participate in the definition of global semantics. The reward for this effort will be better access to resources across disciplines and languages worldwide.

Bibliography

Alfred Aho, John Hopcroft, and Jeffrey Ullman: *Data Structures and Algorithms*, Addison-Wesley, 1983.

Bazirjian, Rosann: *The Acquisitions Librarian,* New York: Haworth, 1995.

Cargill, Jennifer: *Technical Services Today and Tomorrow of Library and Mass Communicatioin,* Michael Gorman. Englewood, Colo.: Libraries Unlimited, 1990.

Dennis S. Arnon. Scrimshaw: *Electronic Publishing: Origination, Dissemination and Library,* 1993.

Magrill, Rose Mary, and John Corbin: *Acquisitions Management and Collection Development in Libraries,* Chicago: ALA, 1989.

Mark S. Ackerman and Roy T. Fielding: *Proceedings of the Second Annual Conference on the Theory and Practice of Digital Libraries,* 1995.

Paul S. Adler and Terry Winograd: *Usability : turning technologies into tools and Library,* Oxford University Press, 1992.

Ricardo Baeza-Yates and Berthier Ribeiro-Neto: *Modern Information Retrieval of Library Science,* Addison-Wesley-Longman, 1999.

Strauch, Katina, and Bruce Strauch: *The Acquisitions Librarian,* New York: Haworth, 1990.

Schmidt, Karen A.: *Understanding the Business of Library Acquisitions,* Ann Arbor: Books on Demand, 1990.

Index

□□□